From Motherhood to Mothering

FROM MOTHERHOOD TO MOTHERING

The Legacy of Adrienne Rich's
Of Woman Born

edited by

ANDREA O'REILLY

STATE UNIVERSITY OF NEW YORK PRESS

Published by
STATE UNIVERSITY OF NEW YORK PRESS
ALBANY

© 2004 State University of New York

For information, address
State University of New York Press
90 State Street, Suite 700, Albany, NY 12207

Production by Marilyn P. Semerad
Marketing by Fran Keneston

Library of Congress Cataloging-in-Publication Data

From motherhood to mothering : the legacy of Adrienne Rich's Of woman born / edited by
Andrea O'Reilly.
    p. cm.
  Includes bibliographical references and index.
  ISBN 0-7914-6287-0 (alk. paper) — ISBN 0-7914-6288-9 (pbk. : alk. paper)
    1. Rich, Adrienne Cecile. Of woman born. 2. Motherhood. 3. Feminist theory. 4.
Motherhood in literature. I. O'Reilly, Andrea, 1961–

HQ759.F748 2004
306.874'3—dc22

                                                                            2004041741

10   9   8   7   6   5   4   3   2   1

To Jesse, Erin, and Casey

For our journey from motherhood to mothering

Contents

PART THREE
Narrating Maternity: Writing as a Mother

Acknowledgments

I would like to express my deepest appreciation to the following people who helped me bring this book to life. Special thanks are due to my research assistant Roni Hoffman who, once again, created order from chaos in the preparation of this manuscript and to Randy Chase who, as always, proofed the text and prepared the index with care and skill. I am grateful to Jane Bunker for her sustaining belief in this manuscript and to Marilyn Semerad for her skill (and patience) in turning it into a book. Thank you also to the members of the Association for Research on Mothering; my thinking on mothering, as always, was enriched and sustained by this splendid community of scholars. My deepest gratitude to the contributors of this volume for conveying with eloquence, passion, and wisdom the importance of *Of Woman Born* in their own lives and that of the larger feminist community. Special thanks, as always, are due to Cheryl Dobinson: my sister-comrade at ARM who commiserates and comforts when I need it the most. Finally, I would like to thank Jennifer Conner, dear friend and former coordinator of ARM; the idea for this book was born during one of our frenzied lunch meetings. Thank you, Jenn, for believing in the importance of a book on the *Legacy of* Of Woman Born.

Last, but not least, I would like to thank my family. As always I am grateful to my children Jesse, Erin, and Casey O'Reilly-Conlin. Once again, they have graciously and generously shared their childhood with one of my books. And finally, thank you to my life partner of twenty-two years, Terry Conlin, who made possible my move from motherhood to mothering.

Introduction

ANDREA O'REILLY

Adrienne Rich opened *Of Woman Born: Motherhood as Experience and Institution* with the observation, "We know more about the air we breath, the seas we travel, than about the nature and meaning of motherhood" (11). In the twenty-eight plus years since the publication of *Of Woman Born*, the topic of motherhood has emerged as a central issue in feminist scholarship. "American feminism," as Lauri Umansky observes in *Motherhood Reconceived*, "has subjected the institution of motherhood and the practice of mothering to their most complex, nuanced and multifocused analysis" (2). While the increasing centrality of motherhood in feminist scholarship has been studied by Umansky among others, what has been less recognized is how this new field of feminist inquiry has developed in reference to one theoretical work, namely Rich's *Of Woman Born*, recognized as the first and arguably still the best feminist book on mothering and motherhood. Rich's book—a wide ranging, far reaching meditation on the meaning and experience of motherhood that draws from the disciplines of anthropology, feminist theory, psychology, literature, as well as narratives of Rich's personal reflections on her experiences of mothering—has had a broad and enduring impact on feminist thought on motherhood. Described by Penelope Dixon, in her 1991 annotated bibliography on mothers and mothering, as "one of the major feminist studies on mothering," *Of Woman Born* has indeed influenced the way a whole generation of scholars thinks about motherhood (11).

The purpose of this volume is to examine how Rich's ovarian work has informed and influenced the way feminist scholarship "thinks and talks" motherhood in disciplines as diverse as Literature, Women's Studies, Law, Sociology, Anthropology, Creative Writing, and Critical Theory. In particular, the collection will explore how two key theoretical insights made by Rich in *Of Woman Born* provided the analytical tools to fully study and report upon the meaning and experience of motherhood. The first of these is the distinction Rich made "between two meanings of motherhood, one superimposed on the other: the *potential* relationship of any woman to her powers of reproduction—and to children; and the *institution*—which aims at ensuring that that potential—and all women—shall remain under male control" (13, emphasis in original). "This book," Rich writes, "is not an attack on the family or on mothering *except as defined and restricted under patriarchy*" (14, emphasis in original). The term "motherhood" refers to the patriarchal institution of motherhood that is male-defined and controlled and is deeply oppressive to women, while the word "mothering" refers to women's experiences of mothering that are female-defined and centered and potentially empowering to women. The reality of patriarchal motherhood thus must be distinguished from the possibility or potentiality of gynocentric or feminist mothering. In other words, while motherhood, as an institution, is a male-defined site of oppression, women's own experiences of mothering can nonetheless be a source of power.

The oppressive and the empowering dimensions of maternity, as well as the complex relationship between the two, first identified by Rich in *Of Woman Born* have been the focus of feminist research on motherhood over the last two and a half decades. Umansky, in her study of feminism between 1968 and 1982, ascertained two competing feminist views on motherhood: the "negative" discourse that "focus[ses] on motherhood as a social mandate, an oppressive institution, a compromise of woman's independence," and the "positive" discourse that argues that "motherhood minus 'patriarchy' [...] holds the truly spectacular potential to bond women to each other and to nature, to foster a liberating knowledge of self, to release the very creativity and generativity that the institution of motherhood denies to women" (2–3). Umansky's classification is drawn from the distinction Rich made between the patriarchal institution of motherhood and a nonpatriarchal experience of mothering. Chapters in parts 1 and 2 of this volume draw upon this first theoretical insight of Rich to explore, in part 1, motherhood as institution and, in part 2, mothering as experience.

The third part is developed from the second central theme of *Of Woman Born,* the relationship between mothering and writing. As parts 1 and 2 consider how Rich's book came to define mothering versus motherhood as a central concern in feminist theory on motherhood over the last twenty-eight years, part 3 examines how this book made visible the tensions between mothering and writing, in particular how mothering both inhibits and fosters creativity. Furthermore, *Of Woman Born* influenced the *way* feminist scholars theorize mothering-motherhood. "It seemed impossible from the first," explains Rich, "to write a book of this kind without being often biographical, without often saying I" (15). The "heart" of this landmark book, as Rich herself acknowledges, is the "painful and problematic plunges into [her] own life" (16). In privileging subjective knowledge and by blending, blurring, and bending the conventional oppositions of theory and experience, *Of Woman Born* cleared the way for a feminist narration of maternity in both literature and theory.

"I told myself," Rich comments in *Of Woman Born,* "that I wanted to write a book on motherhood because it was a crucial, still relatively unexplored, area for feminist theory. But I did not choose this subject, it had long ago chosen me" (15). Rich's reflections on her book capture well my reasons for doing this volume on the legacy of *Of Woman Born.* I first read *Of Woman Born,* the tenth anniversary edition, in the summer of 1987 when my first two children were three years and six months of age. I had just completed the first year of my PhD and was staying for a few weeks at my mother's cottage with my two young children. I had heard of Rich's book and, planning to do my graduate work in the area of Mothering and Women's Writing, had promised myself that I would read the book at the cottage that summer. I did not read *Of Woman Born* when it was first published in 1976; in that year I was fifteen and motherhood was the farthest thing from my mind. Eleven years later, at the age of twenty-six and the mother of two young children and a feminist scholar of motherhood, I was academically and personally well-suited to now read this book in its tenth anniversary edition. While with most books I am able to remember reading them, with just a few am I able to recall—vividly, almost viscerally—how I felt when reading them. *Of Woman Born* was one such book. One memory stands out in particular. I had managed to steal an hour of reading time while my baby daughter and toddler son napped, and I was reading the book in the front room when I experienced what only can be described as a torrent of anger rushing through me. On that hot afternoon in July reading *Of Woman Born,* I saw my life for the first time as it was and not as I wished or imagined it to be. I was an overwhelmed and exhausted mother, young and poor, struggling to do a graduate degree with no mother friends and in a relationship that was, in its early years, quite rocky and in which I was the one mainly responsible for the kids and the housework. I pretended otherwise and had convinced myself and the world at-large that I was a modern, feminist mom who was content with, and in control of, her life. Reading Rich I was forced to see and name my oppression as a mother; as well, it gave me permission to be angry. I also remember feeling a huge sense of relief—I was not the only woman who raged against motherhood, and at times, her children. At the age of twenty-six though, I was not able to fully live with or act upon this realization. It would take a few years more, and the birth of a third child, before I put into practice the insights of that July afternoon and challenge and change the way I lived motherhood. Seventeen years have passed since I first read Rich, and, while I have read *Of Woman Born* more than a dozen times since, I can still vividly recall that first time on the cottage couch when my identity as a feminist mother was conceived.

I tell this story to illuminate how fully and deeply my interest in, indeed passion for, Rich is linked to my own lived life as a mother and how central and crucial *Of Woman Born* was/is to the development of my feminist-maternal consciousness, both professionally and personally. In preparing this collection I learned that I was not alone in this. When I distributed the call for chapters for this volume I did not expect to receive the fifty plus submissions that I did, nor was I prepared for the deeply personal notes from prospective authors that accompanied the submissions. Most of the writers spoke passionately about how reading Rich "changed their lives" and recounted stories similar to mine. While I recognized along with most feminist scholars that Rich pioneered the field of maternal scholarship and that *Of Woman Born* continues to influence the themes and concerns of motherhood research, and believed consequentially that a volume on the legacy of Rich was needed and long overdue, I had not realized how fully and deeply Rich had touched the lives of so many women. This volume, as it considers how *Of Woman Born* defined the content and style of maternal inquiry over the last twenty-eight years, will seek to make apparent the profound impact this book has had on our minds *and* hearts as mothers and scholars of motherhood.

MOTHERHOOD AS INSTITUTION: PATRIARCHAL POWER AND MATERNAL OUTRAGE

Building upon Rich's theoretical concept of the institution of motherhood, the contributors in part 1 examine how motherhood operates as a patriarchal institution to constrain, regulate, and dominate women and their mothering. "[F]or most of what we know as the 'mainstream' of recorded history," Rich writes, "motherhood as institution has ghettoized and degraded female potentialities" (13). However, as Rich argues, and her book seeks to demonstrate, this meaning of motherhood is neither natural nor inevitable. "The patriarchal institution of motherhood," Rich explains, "is not the 'human condition' any more than rape, prostitution, and slavery are" (33). Rather motherhood, in Rich's words, "has a history, it has an ideology" (33). The first five chapters of *Of Woman Born* narrate this history of motherhood, tracing the development of motherhood from neolithic Gathering and Hunting Goddess cultures in which maternity was a site of power for women, through the early agricultural period in which women's powers of maternity began to be contained and controlled, to the domestication of motherhood post-industrialization. While recent scholars have clarified and corrected some of the details of this narrative, its overall plot and themes continue to inform contemporary feminist historical readings of motherhood. Feminist historians agree that motherhood is primarily *not* a natural or biological function; rather, it is specifically and fundamentally a cultural practice that is continuously redesigned in response to changing economic and societal factors. As a cultural construction, its meaning varies with time and place; there is no essential or universal experience of motherhood. Works such as Ann Dally's *Inventing Motherhood: The Consequences of an Ideal,* Elizabeth Badinter's *Mother Love: Myth and Reality,* and Shari Thurer's *The Myths of Motherhood: How Culture Reinvents the Good Mother,* detail how the modern image of the good mother—the full-time, stay-at-home mother, isolated in the private sphere and financially dependent on her husband—came about as a result of industrialization that took work out of the home and repositioned the domestic space, at least among the middle class, as an exclusively nonproductive and private realm, separate from the public sphere of work. In the Victorian period that followed industrialization, the ideology of moral motherhood that saw mothers as naturally pure, pious, and chaste emerged as the dominant discourse of motherhood. This ideology, however, was race- and class-specific; only white, middle-class women could wear the halo of the Madonna and transform the world through their moral influence and social housekeeping. After World War II, the time when Rich became a mother, the discourse of the "happy homemaker" made the "stay-at-home mom and apple pie" mode of mothering the normal and natural motherhood experience. But again, only white, middle-class women could, in fact, experience what discursively was inscribed as natural and universal. In each of its manifestations, motherhood remains, at its core, a patriarchal institution deeply oppressive to women.

In *Of Woman Born* Rich highlights two features of modern patriarchal motherhood that are particularly harmful to mothers. First is the assumption that mothering is natural to women and that child rearing is the sole responsibility of the biological mother and that as such it should be performed as what feminist writer Sharon Hayes has coined "intensive mothering." Second is the practice that assigns mothers sole responsibility for motherwork, but gives them no power to determine the conditions under which they mother. Mothering, in its current ideological manifestation, regards maternity as natural to women and essential to their beings conveyed in the belief, as Pamela Courtenay Hall notes, that women are *naturally* mothers—"they are born with a built-in set of capacities, dispositions, and desires to nurture children [. . . and that this] engagement of love and instinct is utterly distant from the world of paid work [. . .]" (337). This assumption over the last fifty years gave rise to and resulted in the modern ideological construction of "intensive" mothering. Intensive mothering, as Hayes explains, is defined by three themes: "first, the mother is the central caregiver"; second, such mothering requires "lavishing copious amounts of time, energy, and material resources on the child"; and finally, "the mother regards mothering as more important than her paid work" (8). "The methods of appropriate child rearing according to the ideology of intensive motherhood," Hayes concludes, "are constructed as child-centred, expert-guided, emotionally absorbing, labor-intensive and financially expensive" (8). For Rich, and more recent theorists, this discourse becomes oppressive to mothers not because children have these needs, but because we, as a culture, dictate that only the biological mother is capable of fulfilling them. Petra Buskens explains: "Infancy and early childhood *are* periods of high emotional and physical dependency and, moreover this is not a pure invention of patriarchal science. [. . .] *The problem is not the fact of this requirement but rather that meeting this need has come to rest exclusively, and in isolation, on the shoulders of biological mothers*" (81, emphasis in original).

In *Of Woman Born* Rich writes of how she was "haunted by the stereotype of the mother whose love is 'unconditional' and by the visual and literary images of motherhood as single-minded identity" (23). But she also recognized that "this circle, this magnetic field [of selfless mothers and needy children] in which [she] lived, was not a natural phenomenon" (23). Children need love and care, but it is culture, not children, that demands that the mother be the one to provide such love and care. As Rich's eldest son, at age twenty-one, commented when he read his mother's journals of early motherhood: "You seemed to feel you ought to love us all the time. But there *is* no human relationship where you love the other person at every moment." "Yes I tried to explain to him, but women—above all, mothers—have been supposed to love that way" (23). That is the defining belief of the ideology of natural-intensive mothering.

Most women mother in the patriarchal institution of motherhood and, in contemporary times, according to the patriarchal ideology of natural-intensive mothering. Women's mothering, in other words, is defined and controlled by the larger patriarchal society in which they live. Mothers do not make the rules, as Rich reminds us, they simply enforce them. Motherhood, in Rich's words, is an experience of "powerless responsibility." Whether it is in the form of parenting books, a physician's advice, or the father's rules, a mother raises her children in accordance with the values and expectations of the dominant culture. Mothers are policed by what Sara Ruddick calls the "gaze of others." Under the gaze of others, mothers "relinquish authority to others, [and] lose confidence in their own values" (111). "Teachers, grandparents, mates, friends, employers, even an anonymous passerby," continues Ruddick, "can judge a mother and find her wanting" (111–112). "Fear of the gaze of others," she continues, "can be expressed intellectually as inauthenticity, a repudiation of one's own perceptions and values"(112). In *Of Woman Born* Rich remembers her mother locking her in the closest at the age of four for childish behavior— "[her] father's order, but [her] mother carried them out" and being kept too long at piano lessons when she was six, "again, at [her father's] insistence, but is was [her mother] who gave the lessons" (224). Ruddick calls this an abdication of maternal authority. Patriarchal motherhood is predicated upon such abdication of maternal authority and inauthentic mothering.

The ideology of natural-intensive mothering enacted in the patriarchal institution of motherhood has become the official and only meaning of motherhood, marginalizing and rendering illegitimate alternative practices of mothering. In so doing, this normative discourse of mothering polices *all* women's mothering and results in the pathologizing of those women who do not or can not practice intensive mothering. Coupled with this is the fact that in the patriarchal institution of motherhood women have little or no power to challenge this ideology or any other aspect of their motherhood experience. These two features of the modern ideology of motherhood make mothering deeply oppressive to women because the first belief—natural-intensive motherhood—requires the repression or denial of the mother's own selfhood, while the second—powerless responsibility—denies the mother the authority and agency to determine her own experiences of mothering. Women's mothering, as Rich asserts, is fully controlled and arbitrated by the patriarchal institution of motherhood. "The institution of motherhood," Rich writes, "is not identical with bearing and caring for children, any more than the institution of heterosexuality is identical with intimacy and sexual love. Both create the prescriptions and the conditions in which choices are made or blocked; they are not 'reality' but they have shaped the circumstances of our lives" (42).

The first two chapters in part 1 use Rich's concept of the patriarchal institution of motherhood to explore how women's motherhood, in particular reproduction, becomes regulated by the law and the state. In her chapter "The Supreme Court of Canada and What It Means to Be 'Of Woman Born,'" Diana Ginn explores connections between Rich's reflections on motherhood and recent jurisprudence on intervention in pregnancy. Her article focuses upon "two decisions of the Supreme Court of Canada: *Winnipeg Child and Family Services v. G* (1997), which held that a pregnant woman could not be confined to an addiction treatment centre 'for the good of her fetus,' and *Dobson (litigation Guardian of) v. Dobson* (1999), which refused to allow a child to sue his mother for harms allegedly caused by her negligence during pregnancy." Ginn explores how four themes central to *Of Woman Born* are manifest in these two cases; they include: Motherhood is a form of social control exercised over women as they bear and rear children; Mothers are made almost solely responsible for the well-being of their children; Women are either idolized or despised; and, finally, there is a need for new ways to describe the nature of pregnancy. "The fact that there is significant congruence between Rich's critique of social control of mothers, and the concerns regarding state intervention in pregnancy expressed by the majority [decision], is indicative," Ginn concludes, "of the impact that Rich [. . .] has had on thinking about motherhood, and by extrapolation, pregnancy" (28). Moreover, the cases in showing how actual mothers, in their everyday experiences of motherhood, are coerced to conform to an unnatural and unattainable idea of motherhood and chastised when they do not, confirm the truth of Rich's insights on the patriarchal institution of motherhood and their continuing relevance twenty-eight years after their publication.

Sarah Stevens's chapter illustrates the cross-cultural relevance of Rich's *Of Woman Born* by examining the institution of motherhood and reproductive politics in the People's Republic of China. The paper traces the evolution of political control over women's bodies in China, including an analysis of Cultural Revolution Propaganda about reproduction and the implementation of the one-child policy in the early 1980s. Rich's investigation of motherhood as an institution and her identification of motherhood as locus of female power provides, according to Stevens, a useful lens through which to see these developments. The one-child policy, while representing the pinnacle of political power over reproduction, is nonetheless merely one link in a long chain of patriarchal control over motherhood. Stevens argues that the Chinese nationalist rhetoric functioned to make formerly private spaces (the womb, the home) into public spaces where the interests of the nation-state are preeminent. Using Rich's reflections upon the public and private dichotomy, Stevens examines the ways in which a blurring of the public/private boundary can lead to an increase in patriarchal control over motherhood. The Chinese case illustrates both the dangers of a strict public/private divide and the dangers inherent in a complete conflation of the private and public, individual and nation-state. Both of these theoretical extremes, as Stevens concludes and as Rich observed in *Of Woman Born*, reinforce patriarchal control over reproduction and undermine motherhood as a site of power.

As the first two chapters in part 1 explore the various ways the patriarchal institution of motherhood is enacted in and reinforced by public policy and jurisprudence, the final chapter examines the impact of the institution on the daily lives of women and their children. The final chapter of *Of Woman Born*, entitled "Violence: The Heart of Maternal Darkness," opens with the story of Joanne Michulski, thirty-eight, mother of eight children, who killed and mutilated her two youngest in June 1974. Responding to the media's attempt to "explain, exonerate, psychologize," the event, Rich commented in a letter to a local newspaper, "the expectations laid on her and on millions of women with children are 'insane expectations.' Instead of recognizing the institutional violence of patriarchal motherhood, society labels those women who finally erupt in violence as psychopathological" (263). The institution of motherhood, to use Emily Jeremiah's words, is "violently oppressive [. . .] and give[s] rise to violent behavior on the part of mothers." "Motherhood without autonomy, without choice," Rich explains, "is one of the quickest roads to a sense of having lost control" (264). The powerless responsibility of patriarchal motherhood discussed earlier is what gives rise to mothers' suffering and often results in violence against children. Violence, whether it be manifested in child neglect and abuse, the murder of children or a mother's suicide, is caused by the patriarchal institution of motherhood, not the demands of mothering per se. "We have, in our long history," Rich continues, "accepted the stresses of the institution as if they were a law of nature" (276). These stresses, however, created as they are by a constructed—hence changeable—institution are, Rich insists, preventable. Only in the institution of motherhood does such suffering and violence become natural *and* inevitable. This is the focus of the final chapter of part 1.

Emily Jeremiah's chapter begins with a consideration of Rich's conception of mothers as victims of violence, and themselves as capable of violence. She links this view to more recent feminist perspectives on the issues of maternal violence and murder in a variety of disciplines; history (Elizabeth Badinter), philosophy (Sara Ruddick), and psychoanalysis (Estela V. Welldon). Such perspectives challenge the traditional view of mothers as naturally passive and loving, and they point up the ambivalent character of maternity. They also raise the issues of choice and autonomy. Jeremiah deploys such ideas to probe and illuminate Toni Morrison's 1987 novel *Beloved*, which she argues both confirms and extends Rich's thesis, in particular by positing a postmodern maternal subjectivity that is relational and in process. Jeremiah, in her intertextual reading of Rich and Morrison, highlights the contingent nature not only of the mother but also of conceptions of maternity. She concludes with an assessment of Rich's importance. While Jeremiah identifies problems with Rich's account, in particular the notion of motherhood as a monolithic institution, these problems, Jeremiah concludes, can be explained in terms of the context in which Rich was writing. As well, Rich's awareness of the constructed nature of maternity allows for the possibility of change.

MOTHERING AS EXPERIENCE: EMPOWERMENT AND RESISTANCE

"To destroy the institution is not to abolish motherhood," Rich writes, "It is to release the creation and sustenance of life into the same realm of decision, struggle, surprise, imagination and conscious intelligence, as any difficult, but freely chosen work" (280). Rich, as noted above, distinguished "between two meanings of motherhood, one superimposed on the other: the *potential* relationship of any woman to her powers of reproduction—and to children; and the *institution*—which aims at ensuring that that potential—and all women—shall remain under male control" (13, emphasis in original). Patriarchal motherhood is thus to be differentiated from the possibility or potentiality of mothering. In *Of Woman Born*, however, there is little discussion of mothering or how its potentiality may be realized. The notable exception is the brief reference Rich made to her summer holiday in Vermont when her husband was away and she and her sons lived "as conspirators, outlaws from the institution of motherhood" (195). However, while mothering is not described or theorized in *Of Woman Born*, the text, in distinguishing mothering from motherhood and in identifying the potential empowerment of mothering, made possible later feminist work on mothering, particularly those that analyzed mothering as a site of power and resistance for women. As well, in interrupting and deconstructing the patriarchal narrative of motherhood, Rich destabilized the hold this discourse has on the meaning and practice of mothering and cleared the space for the articulation of counternarratives of mothering, in particular woman-centered and feminist meanings and experiences of mothering.

A feminist counternarrative of motherhood is concerned with imagining and implementing a view of mothering that is *empowering* to women as opposed to oppressive, as it is within the patriarchal institution of motherhood. Alternatively called authentic, radical, feminist, or gynocentric mothering, this mode of mothering positions mothers, in Rich's words, as "outlaws from the institution of motherhood." This new perspective, in emphasizing maternal power and ascribing agency to mothers and value to motherwork, gave rise to the view of mothering as a socially engaged enterprise that seeks to effect cultural change in the home through feminist child rearing and the world at-large through political/social activism. The first two chapters of part 2 consider why and how the mother role is a site of power and resistance in non-Western cultures. Here the emphasis is upon the woman's experiences of mothering and the meanings she and her culture attach to it. Specifically, the chapters look at the economic, political, and cultural centrality and importance of the mother and the mother role in these societies and how this, in turn, makes motherhood a site of power in and for these cultures. The final five chapters consider mothering as a site of power *in* the home. They explore how motherwork is, or may be, a socially engaged practice that seeks to effect cultural change through new feminist modes of socialization and interactions with daughters and sons. These woman-centered and feminist counternarratives of mothering resulted from and give rise to the destabilization of the patriarchal institution of motherhood. In all seven chapters we encounter a challenge to patriarchal motherhood through the formation of feminist mothering; or to use Rich's words, a mothering against motherhood. Rich writes: "We do not think of the power stolen from us and the power withheld from us in the name of the institution of motherhood" (275). The chapters in this part analyze the mother power that already exists in non-Western cultures and consider how mother power becomes possible in Western culture through the abolition of the patriarchal institution of motherhood.

In the preface to the 1986 edition Rich revisited the claim she made in the first edition "that in the mainstream of recorded history, motherhood as institution has ghettoized and degraded female potentialities" to argue that woman-centered experiences of mothering and acts of mother power can be found throughout history if we look at cultures other than the dominant Western one. "Relying on ready-to-hand Greek mythology," Rich writes, "I was lead to generalize that 'the cathexis between mother and daughter' was endangered always and everywhere. A consideration of American Indian, African and Afro-American myth and philosophy might have suggested other patterns" (xxv). In the 1986 preface she corrects the cultural blindspot of the 1976 edition to consider, albeit briefly, hitherto marginalized and neglected traditions of mothering, in particular that of African American mothering, wherein mothering is a site of power.

Rich identified, and later research shows, that two interrelated themes distinguish the African American tradition of motherhood from the Western patriarchal institution of motherhood and define it as a counternarrative wherein mothering is a site of power for black women. First, mothers and motherhood are valued by, and central to, African American culture, and secondly, black culture recognizes that mothers and mothering are what make possible the physical and psychological well-being and empowerment of African American people and the larger African American culture. The focus of black motherhood, in both practice and thought, is how to preserve, protect, and more generally empower black children so that they may resist racist practices that seek to harm them and grow into adulthood whole and complete. To fulfill the task of empowering children, mothers must hold power in African American culture and mothering likewise must be valued and supported. There are three traditions in African American culture that are distinct from the Eurocentric or Western view of motherhood analyzed by Rich and which serve to empower black mothers and make black motherhood a site of power; they are: "Other-Mothering/Community Mothering," "Motherhood as Social Activism," and "Nurturance as Resistance."[1]

Stanlie James defines othermothering as "acceptance of responsibility for a child not one's own, in an arrangement that may or may not be formal" (45) while community mothers, as Njoki Nathani Wane explains, "take care of the community. These women are typically past their childbearing years" (112). "The role of community mothers," as Arlene Edwards notes, "often evolved from that of being othermothers" (88). Both othermothering and community mothering are strategies of survival in that they ensure that all children, regardless of whether the biological mother was present or available, would receive the mothering that delivers psychological and physical well-being and makes empowerment possible. "Biological mothers," as Patricia Hill Collins notes, "are expected to care for their children. But African and African-American communities have also recognized that vesting one person with full responsibility for mothering a child may not be wise or possible. As a result, 'othermothers,' women who assist bloodmothers by sharing mothering responsibilities, traditionally have been central to the institution of Black motherhood" (1993, 47). Community mothering and othermothering emerged in response to black mothers' needs and serves to empower black women and enrich their lives.

Black women's role of community mothers, as Patricia Hill Collins explains, redefines motherhood as social activism and hence a site of power: "Black women's feelings of responsibility for nurturing the children in their extended family networks have stimulated a more generalized ethic of care where Black women feel accountable to all the Black community's children" (1993, 49). This construction of mothering as social activism empowers black women because motherhood operates, in Collins's words, as "a symbol of power." "More than a personal act," write Bernard and Bernard, "Black motherhood is very political. Black mothers and grandmothers are considered the 'guardians of the generations.'" (47). Black motherhood, as Jenkins concluded, "is a site where [black women] can develop a belief in their own empowerment. Black women can see motherhood as providing a base for self-actualization, for acquiring status in the Black community and as a catalyst for social activism" (206).

A third way that African American mothering differs from the dominant mode and defines motherhood as a site of power for black women is the way nurturance of children is understood to be an act of resistance. In African American culture, as theorist bell hooks has observed, the black family, or what she terms homeplace, is a site of resistance. She explains:

> Historically, African-American people believed that the construction of a homeplace, however fragile and tenuous (the slave hut, the wooden shack), had a radical political dimension. Despite the brutal reality of racial apartheid, of domination, one's homeplace was one site where one could freely confront the issue of humanization, where one could resist. Black women resisted by making homes where all black people could strive to be subjects, not objects, where one could be affirmed in our minds and hearts despite poverty, hardship, and deprivation, where we could restore to ourselves the dignity denied to us on the outside in the public world. (42)

In a racist culture that deems black children inferior, unworthy, and unlovable, maternal love of black children is an act of resistance; in loving her children, the mother instills in them a loved sense of self and high self-esteem, enabling them to defy and subvert racist discourses that naturalize racial inferiority and commodify blacks as other and object. Racial ethnic women's motherwork is concerned with, as Collins explains, "foster[ing] a meaningful racial identity in children within a society that denigrates people of color" (1994, 57). This perspective of nurturance as resistance along with the African American traditions of othermothering and mothering as social activism, position mothering as an identity and role of power and empowerment. Specifically they challenge the two defining tenets of patriarchal motherhood discussed earlier and that make motherhood deeply oppressive to women, namely that the biological mother is the one who should raise the children and that intensive mothering is the manner in which children should be raised.

The first two chapters in part 2 examine these themes in cross-cultural, matrilineal communities and in Native American culture. While their subjects are not African American, they share themes similar to those described previously as marginalized cultures; likewise they position maternity as a site of agency and authority for women, or more specifically a site of resistance from which mothers may challenge racial oppression. As well, the final five chapters investigate how the power exemplified in African and African American mothering may be obtained in the dominant Eurocentric culture of North America. As Doreen Fumia observed: "In order to begin to think about alternative family structures, or households headed by the mother-lesbians, it is necessary to find an entry point into motherhood outside the North American ideal of womanhood" (91).

Maria-Barbara Watson-Franke in "'We Have a Mama but No Papa': Motherhood in Women Centered Societies" builds upon Rich's discussion of matrilineal and gynocentric cultures in prepatriarchal history to examine contemporary matrilineal, woman-centered cultures around the world. She explores the various ways mothers secure power and prestige in these cultures through their roles as "builders of generations" and as economic providers. Watson-Franke also considers the family arrangements in these cultures to argue that "motherhood in matrilineal systems is not as strongly defined by heterosexuality, if at all, as it is in the sexual family [of the Western tradition]." She concludes her chapter by considering how the matrilineal model "can provide an alternative to the heterosexual family" and allow us to envision in Rich's words "a wholly different way for women to exist in the world" (1986, 85).

Building upon Rich's observation that history is one of the most problematic areas with which women have had to deal, Dannabang Kuwabong in the second chapter of part 2 argues that, for Native women, this problem is exacerbated by cultural dislocation and disarticulation, which originate from the history of European colonization of the Americas. Kuwabong reads Monique Mojica's play *Princess Pocahontas and the Blue Spots* as a drama of Native women's self-representation within the rubrics of the mother figure in prepatriarchal societies, as theorized by anthropologists such as Erich Neuman, Karen Sacks, and Robert Briffault, among others, and reviewed by Rich in chapter 4 on "The Primacy of the Mother." Kuwabong explores how Mojica's play successfully blends gynocentric motherhood discourse and Native American cosmogony to create a rhetoric of recovery for Native American women through the historical foremother Pocahontas. In *Princess*, Mojica reestablishes Pocahontas and other key Native American historical women as mothers worth venerating. Her re-visionary writing, Kuwabong concludes, "provides a framework for the development of an ongoing discourse of recovery of Native American matrilineage. The play legitimates the centrality of the Native American mother/woman in the project of recuperation of Native American personhoods and traditions."

The third chapter of this part, "Of Woman (but Not Man or the Nuclear Family) Born: Motherhood Outside Institutionalized Heterosexuality," considers the extent to which Rich's analysis, now commonplace in academic circles, entered the realm of popular or material culture in the United States. Examining popular books as diverse as Arlene Eisenberg et al.'s *What to Expect When You're Expecting,* Rachel Pepper's *The Ultimate Guide to Pregnancy for Lesbians,* Ariel Gore's *The Hip Mama's Survival Guide,* Anne Lamott's *Operating Instructions: A Journal of My Son's First Year,* and Cherrie Moraga's *Waiting in the Wings: Portrait of a Queer Motherhood,* Kate McCullough examines the degree to which Rich's feminist critique has translated into popular culture and considers whether we see in texts by "marginalized" mothers such as Gore, Pepper, Moraga, and Lamott a challenge to the patriarchal institution of motherhood. McCullough explores how these four authors denaturalize the nuclear family and celebrate non-normative versions of motherhood; as well they interrogate the relationship of motherhood to patriarchy. McCullough finds that while these books continue and amplify Rich's challenge to the patriarchal institution of motherhood, Rich's critique has not yet had, in McCullough words, "a socially significant impact." While the conditions of class-privileged, privatized maternal isolation faced by Rich have in some degree shifted due to labor demands of global economy, working-class women continue to be demonized for both their poverty and their employment and middle-class women are now required to be successful as both professionals and mothers under the new "supermom" model. "The structures of motherhood, the nation-state, and even contemporary icons (like the soccer mom)," McCullough concludes, "work jointly to reinforce a narrative of motherhood that remains deeply destructive for women."

In chapter 7 Fiona Joy Green argues that still missing from scholarship on motherhood is an examination of Rich's monumental contention that motherhood can successfully be a site of empowerment and potential political activism. Green's chapter, developed from interviews with self-identified feminist mothers, considers how mothers successfully negotiate the tension between the "institution" and the "experience" of motherhood. This study shows, Green contends, that mothers can, and do, find opportunities within motherhood to explore and cultivate their own agency and to develop their relationships with children and others to foster social change. Some openly resist the pressures to live by the patriarchal script of "good" motherhood, while others consciously use their socially sanctified role of motherhood in a subversive way to raise their children to be critically conscious of, and challenge, various forms of oppression. "Regardless of the strategies invented and utilized by these feminist mothers," Green concludes, "they successfully challenge and bring about social change as Rich suggested a quarter century ago."

In the following chapter, Voth Harman explores how the Demeter/Persephone myth utilized and celebrated by Rich functions in contemporary women's fiction. Reading authors as diverse as Jenny Joseph, Rita Dove, Maggie Gee, and Barbara Kingsolver, she explores how mother-daughter separation serves to empower both mother and daughter. These texts, Voth Harman emphasizes, search for a vision of maternity in which the mother is not solely responsible for the daughter. In these contemporary renditions of the myth, temporary loss of the daughter actually strengthens the mother. And for the daughter in the text and the reader of the text there is, Voth Harman contends, "a growing awareness that the mother cannot serve as Ground of Being." In this, the stories describe a mother-daughter separation that does not sever that "first love" of the mother-daughter bond as required under patriarchy, rather separation in these female authored and centered texts seek to promote the autonomy of mother and daughter alike while still preserving the connection between the two.

Chapter 9, written by myself, focuses upon the formulation of a female-defined and centered experience of mothering and the development of a feminist practice of gender socialization. While the two aims seem similar, the first is concerned with mothering in terms of the mother herself—her experiences of mothering, the meanings she attaches to it—while the second theme focuses upon the mother's relationship with her children and in particular the manner in which she raises them. It has been long recognized that Rich was one of the first feminist writers to call for nonsexist child rearing and women-centered practices of mothering. What has been less acknowledged, and what will be the focus of this chapter, is how the two, in Rich's view, are intrinsically linked in so far as the goal of nonsexist child rearing depends upon the abolition of patriarchal motherhood and the achievement of feminist mothering. Rich argues that nonsexist child rearing—a challenge to traditional practices of gender socialization for both daughters and sons—depends upon motherhood itself being changed; it must become, to use Rich's terminology, mothering. In other words, only in mothering becoming a site, role, and identity of power for women is feminist child rearing made possible.

Chapter 10 develops in response to Rich's observation that: "Motherhood is one part of the female process; it is not an identity for all time. The process of 'letting go'—though we are charged with blame if we do not—is an act of revolt against the grain of patriarchal culture." Margaret Gullette argues that, while feminists have developed many other ideas of this landmark book, they have not developed the concepts that underlie these sentences; they have not theorized postmaternity. Gullette's chapter develops the term postmaternal to counter "empty nester." The first section of the chapter considers some of the worst of these cultural images of the empty nester and their effects. In the second, she develops new concepts and more positive views of postmaternity, based on the questionnaire she developed with adult students to encourage postmaternal women to discuss their experiences of mothering adult children.

In conclusion, she considers possible reasons for the feminist avoidance of the postmaternal figure to argue that an affirmation of postmaternity is a crucial and essential dimension of the feminist challenge to patriarchal motherhood.

NARRATING MATERNITY: WRITING AS A MOTHER

The well-known science fiction writer, Ursula K. Le Guin once commented:

> There is less censure now, and more support, for a woman who wants both to bring up a family and work as an artist. But it's a small degree of improvement. The difficulty of trying to be responsible, hour after hour, day after day, for maybe twenty *years*, for the well-being of children and the excellence of books, is immense: it involves an endless expense of energy and impossible weighing of competing priorities. And we don't know much about the process, because writers who are mothers haven't talked much about their motherhood—for fear of boasting? For fear of being trapped in the Mom trap, discounted? Nor have they talked much about their writing as in any way connected with their parenting, since the heroic myth demands that the two jobs be considered utterly opposed and mutually destructive. (174)

"The idea of maternal writing," Emily Jeremiah notes in her recent article "Troublesome Practices: Mothering, Literature and Ethics," "undermines one of the oppositions upon which motherhood in Western culture has traditionally rested, namely that between maternity and creativity, or 'the binary system that conceives woman and writer, motherhood and authorhood, babies and books, as mutually exclusive' (Freidman 1987, 65–66)" (7). In so doing, Jeremiah continues, maternal writing "upsets other [. . .] oppositions, such as public/private and mind/body [; . . . as well it] entails a publicizing of maternal experience, [. . .] subverts the traditional notion of the mother as an instinctual, purely corporeal being [and] challenge[s] dominant ideals of individuality and autonomy" (7). Maternal writing therefore, as it interrupts and deconstructs the normative script of maternity as private and silent, also disturbs and counters the received narrative of creativity, specifically the liberal humanist view of subjectivity and authorship. Jeremiah contends that, contrary to the liberal humanist view of creativity, writing, much like mothering, is based on relationality, reciprocity, and mutuality: "Reading and writing involve an imaginative engagement with others, a process which might strategically be linked to the idea of maternal thinking [; . . .] that is they constitute activities which produce and encourage a relational mode of subjectivity which might [. . .] help challenge and overcome Western capitalist models of individualism" (12–13). Jeremiah insists that this idea of relationality may be understood as subversive: "To posit reciprocity as an ideal is to challenge the notion of the rational autonomous subject dominant in modern capitalist societies—a fiction which fosters the marginalization of those who do make the grade, the denial to these 'failures' any kind of state support, and the continuing fragmentation of community" (12). "The advantage of motherhood for a woman artist," Alicia Ostriker writes:

> is that it puts her in immediate and inescapable contact with the courses of life, death, beauty, growth, corruption. If the woman artist has been trained to believe that the activities of motherhood are trivial, tangential to the main issues of life, irrelevant to the great themes of literature, she should untrain herself. The training is misogynist, it protects and perpetuates systems of thought and feeling which prefer violence and death to love and birth, and it is a lie. (as quoted in Le Guin, 176)

Mothering, therefore, as Jeremiah concludes, may be understood as not only "compatible" with art but more significantly as *conducive* to it; and this perspective, in turn, constitutes a "strategy of subversion," an undoing of the hegemonic constructions of both mothering and writing (10–11).

However, as Jeremiah asserts that mothering is advantageous to writing, mother writers have been marginalized and silenced. "Until recently," as Tillie Olsen has observed, "almost all distinguished literary achievement has come from childless women" (50). "The reasons for the widespread absence of creative achievement on the part of mothers," Jeremiah argues, "are in part practical and financial" (3). Indeed, as early as 1929 Virginia Woolf wrote in *A Room of One's Own*, "a woman must have money and a room of her own if she is to write fiction" (6). Likewise, writing has traditionally been viewed as an exclusive, if not biologically determined, male activity and achievement in so far as artistic creativity has been equated with paternity, and the pen regarded as a metaphorical penis. "In patriarchal Western culture," as Gilbert and Gubar note, "the text's author is a father, a progenitor, a procreator and aesthetic patriarch whose pen is an instrument of generative power like his penis" (6).

Motherhood in a Western context, as Rich and numerous feminist theorists on motherhood have pointed out, is organized as a patriarchal institution that is deeply oppressive to women. "The predominant image of the mother in white Western society," as Donna Bassin, Margaret Honey, and Meryle Mahrer Kaplan write, "[assumes mothers are] ever-bountiful, ever-giving, self-sacrificing . . . not destroyed or overwhelmed by the demands of [their] child[ren]" (2–3). When white middle-class mothers write about motherhood, as Elizabeth Johnson explains, "they write about their own struggles for identity in the institution of motherhood" (33). Adrienne Rich wrote, in "When We Dead Awaken: Writing as Re-Vision":

[T]o be maternally with small children all day . . . requires a holding back, a putting-aside of that imaginative activity, and demands instead a kind of conservatism. . . . [T]o be a female human being trying to fulfill traditional female functions in a traditional way is in direct conflict with the subversive function of the imagination. (43)

And in *Of Woman Born* Rich wrote: "Once in a while someone used to ask me, 'Don't you ever write poems about your children?' The male poets of my generation did write poems about their children—especially their daughters. For me, poetry was where I lived as no-one's mother, where I existed as myself" (1986, 31). Women in the dominant Anglo-American culture often experience the demands of work, in this instance writing or art more generally, in conflict with those of mothering because of the way this culture defines and positions the public sphere of work in opposition to the private/reproductive sphere of the home/family. Women, according to this maternal ideology, are categorized and regulated by what has been termed the "either-or dichotomy": women must choose between work and motherhood. "The price for the middle-class mother who would be an artist," Gerber argues in *Portrait of the Mother-Artist*, "is high—she must forsake either her child or her creative work" (12–13). Thus while mothering may be conducive to writing as Jeremiah speculates, sexist ideologies and practices have kept mothers *from* writing.

Jeremiah's argument on the paradoxical standpoint on mothering and writing serves as a useful introduction to the theme "Writing as a Mother" explored by Rich and examined in this section. Chapters in part 3 consider how mothering, particularly in the relationality of maternal subjectivity, may foster or inspire creative expression; likewise they explore how the work of mothering may simultaneously frustrate or inhibit the expression of this creativity.

Responding to Rich's observation, "For me, poetry was where I lived as no-one's mother, where I existed as myself" (31), D'Arcy Randall considers how *Of Woman Born* may be read as a meditation on the writing and reading of maternal literature. "Whatever Rich's reasons may have been for avoiding the maternal in her poetry," Randall writes, "*Of Woman Born* contributes substantially to the field if we read it as literary criticism." The book functions as literary criticism that elucidates not poems themselves but the cultural and social expectations that Western readers commonly bring to them. Identifying the various societal and psychological factors that keep mothers from writing and keep readers from seeing mothers as writers and writers as mothers, Rich, Randall argues, makes maternal writing imaginable. Elsewhere, as Randall notes, Rich commented that "[t]he critic's task is not to try to deflate, shrink, and contain poetry, but rather, as John Haines has written, to provide 'a space in which creation can take place, a clearing in the imagination.'" Randall's chapter explores how the creation and appreciation of maternal writing is made possible through the clearing of the imagination that *Of Woman Born* provides.

Jeannette E. Riley's chapter, "'A Sense of Drift': Adrienne Rich's Emergence from Mother to Poet" addresses Rich's conflicting emotions caused by her motherhood and writing in order to explain the emergence of poems that appear in *Snapshots of a Daughter-in Law*. The conflict between Rich's role as mother and wife versus her desire to write described in *Of Woman Born* is analyzed in this chapter. Riley explores how these conflicting emotions resulted in Rich being unable to write for eight years until the publication of *Snapshots*. Riley argues that Rich's efforts to understand what was happening to her and to find "clues" that would illuminate her position and identity—all explored in *Of Woman Born*—led Rich finally after years of "reading in fierce snatches, scribbling in notebooks, writing poetry in fragments" to an emotional and literary breakthrough in *Snapshots*. That eight year period, Riley concludes, created a new vision in Rich's work as she approached subject matter previously avoided, resulting in a collection with new material that handles, albeit cautiously, experiences of "real" life as a wife-mother.

Ann Keniston's chapter begins with the author's reflections on the significance of *Of Woman Born* in her own life as a mother-scholar. She writes: "I first read Rich's *Of Woman Born* as a beginning doctoral student on the verge of dropping out of graduate school because I could not find a way to make my own experiences relevant to my scholarly work." Her essay, in homage to what she considers to be the central elements of Rich's work, begins with the author's often conflicted experiences as woman-scholar-poet-mother. In integrating academic with personal discourse, Keniston honors Rich's mix of memoir and social critique while illustrating the paradoxes in this fusion. Keniston foregrounds these difficulties in Rich's work, arguing that its personal narrative ultimately resists being joined with its historical/political account. The chapter examines in detail Rich's adoption of inconsistent and mutually exclusive "I"s while arguing that Rich's split narrative mimics a split within feminist theory of the past ten years. Keniston concludes by looking at several recent feminists who have adopted Rich's method of inquiry while refining and re-visioning it.

CONCLUSION

I wrote most of this introduction in the week before Christmas when the end of the teaching term freed up a block of time for intensive writing. However, the week of tranquility I imagined and longed for in order to reflect upon and compose this introduction never quite materialized. Instead, my thirteen-year-old daughter was home for the week ill with a cold. My computer broke, which required me to write the introduction on an old laptop and, with no access to email, I had to conduct my university administrative duties the old-fashioned and, I may add, more time-consuming way over the telephone. Our lizard's heating light burnt out, which necessitated a drive to the city for a replacement. Our home experienced a major electrical "brown out," which caused our meter box to catch on fire, more or less implode, and cut off our electricity. For two days we had an electrician and various Hydro technicians in and out of our home and went without electricity—that is, heat and light on one of the coldest days this year—for close to ten hours. During that time, when the power was suddenly turned off for the repair, I lost over a page of writing on the laptop. Furthermore, the other children had to be driven to school, the boyfriend's house, and driving lessons; and Christmas shopping of course had to be done. In the midst of this domestic chaos I thought and wrote about motherhood, about how Adrienne Rich has influenced, indeed inspired, the work I and others do as mothers and as scholars. Concluding this introduction and reflecting upon my week of writing and mothering in the context of Rich's *Of Woman Born*, I am drawn to the words that end the final chapter. Rich writes:

> What is astonishing, what can give us enormous hope and belief in a future in which the lives of women and children shall be mended and rewoven by women's hands, is that we have managed to salvage, of ourselves, for our children, even within the destructiveness of the institution: the tenderness, the passion, the trust in our instincts, the evocation of a courage we did not know we owned, the detailed apprehension of another human existence, the full realization of the cost and precariousness of life. (280)

I want to suggest, as I conclude this introduction, that *Of Woman Born* and the feminist writing on motherhood it inspired, has enlightened and empowered countless mothers to survive, resist, dismantle, and abolish the institution of patriarchal motherhood in their own lives and in the lives of others. While the patriarchal institution of motherhood can never be destroyed as Rich wished and believed, it is being ambushed on all sides by mothers who have imagined and put into place feminist mothering, informed and inspired by Rich and other feminist maternal scholars' radical vision of an empowering and empowered maternity. They are purposely and courageously mothering against motherhood. In so doing, to cite Rich again, these feminist mothers have "released the creation and sustenance of life into the same realm of decision, struggle, surprise, imagination and conscious intelligence as any other difficult, but freely chosen work" (280). Looking back on this busy week, I see my days of writing and mothering as a lived example of such "difficult but freely chosen work" and understand that this was possible only from my position as an "outlaw from the institution of motherhood"; in other words, a feminist mother who demands and expects the same feminist living from her partner, her children, and the world around her.

NOTES

1. Two other themes characterize African American mothering: "Matrifocality" and "The Motherline: Mothers as Cultural Bearers." The five themes are discussed at length in my article "'I come from a long line of Uppity Irate Black Women': African-American Feminist Thought on Motherhood, the Motherline and the Mother-Daughter Relationship," in *Mothers and Daughters: Connection, Empowerment, Transformation*, Eds. Andrea O'Reilly and Sharon Abbey (New York: Rowman and Littlefield, 2000).

WORKS CITED

Badinter, Elizabeth. *Mother Love: Myth and Reality*. New York: MacMillan, 1980.

Bassin, Donna, Margaret Honey, and Meryle Mahrer Kaplan, Eds. *Representations of Motherhood*. New Haven: Yale UP, 1994.

Bernard, Wanda Thomas and Candace Bernard. "Passing the Torch: A Mother and Daughter Reflect on Their Experiences Across Generations." *Canadian Woman Studies Journal* 18.2, 3 (Summer/Fall 1998):46–50.

Buskens, Petra. "The Impossibility of 'Natural Parenting' for Modern Mothers: On Social Structure and the Formation of Habit." *Journal of the Association for Research on Mothering* 3.1 (Spring/Summer 2001):75–86.

Collins, Patricia Hill. "Shifting the Center: Race, Class, and Feminist Theorizing About Motherhood." *Mothering: Ideology, Experience, and Agency*. Eds. Evelyn Nakano Glenn, Grace Chang, and Linda Rennie Forcey. New York: Routledge, 1994:45–65.

———. "The Meaning of Motherhood in Black Culture and Black Mother-Daughter Relationships." *Double Stitch: Black Women Write About Mothers and Daughters*. Eds. Patricia Bell-Scott, et al. New York: HarperPerennial, 1993:42–60.

Dally, Ann. *Inventing Motherhood: The Consequences of an Ideal*. London: Burnett, 1982.

Debold, Elizabeth, Marie Wilson, and Idelisse Malave. *Mother Daughter Revolution: From Good Girls to Great Women*. New York: Addison-Wesley, 1993.

Dixon, Penelope. *Mothers and Mothering: An Annotated Feminist Bibliography*. New York: Garland, 1991.

Edwards, Arlene. "Community Mothering: The Relationship Between Mothering and the Community Work of Black Women." *Journal of the Association for Research on Mothering* 2.2 (Fall/Winter 2000):87–100.

Fumia, Doreen. "Marginalized Motherhood and the Mother-Lesbian Subtext." *Journal of the Association for Research on Mothering* 1.1 (Spring/Summer 1999):88–95.

Gerber, Nancy. *Portrait of the Mother-Artist: Class and Creativity in Contemporary American Fiction*. New York: Lexington, 2003.

Gilbert, Sandra M. and Susan Gubar. *The Madwoman in the Attic: The Woman Writer and the Nineteenth-Century Literary Imagination*. New Haven and London: Yale UP, 1979.

Hall, Pamela Courtenay. "Mothering Mythology in the Late Twentieth Century: Science, Gender Lore, and Celebratory Narrative." *Canadian Woman Studies Reader: An Introductory Reader*. Eds. Nuzhat Amin et al. Toronto: Inanna, 1999:337–345.

Hayes, Sharon. *The Cultural Contradictions of Motherhood*. New Haven: Yale UP, 1996.

hooks, bell. "Homeplace: A Site of Resistance." *Yearning: Race, Gender, and Cultural Politics*. Boston: South End, 1990:41–49.

Huf, Linda. *A Portrait of the Artist as a Young Woman: The Writer as Heroine in American Literature*. New York: Frederick Ungar, 1983.

James, Stanlie M. "Mothering: A Possible Black Feminist Link to Social Transformation." *Theorizing Black Feminism: The Visionary Pragmatism of Black Women*. Eds. Stanlie James and A. P. Busia. Routledge, 1999:44–54.

Jenkins, Nina. "Black Women and the Meaning of Motherhood." *Redefining Motherhood: Changing Patterns and Identities*. Eds. Sharon Abbey and Andrea O'Reilly. Toronto: Second Story, 1998:201–213.

Jeremiah, Emily. "Troublesome Practices: Mothering, Literature and Ethics." *Journal of the Association for Research on Mothering* 4.2 (Fall/Winter 2003):7–16.

Johnson, Elizabeth Bourque. "Mothers at Work: Representations of Maternal Practice in Literature." *Mothers and Daughters: Connection, Empowerment, Transformation*. Eds. Andrea O'Reilly and Sharon Abbey. New York: Rowman and Littelfield, 2000:21–35.

Le Guin, Ursula K. "The Fisherman's Daughter." *The Mother Reader: Essential Writings on Motherhood*. Ed. Moyra Davey. New York: Seven Stories, 2001.

Olsen, Tillie. *Silences*. New York: Laurel, 1983.

O'Reilly, Andrea. "'Ain't That Love?': Anti-Racism and Racial Constructions of Mothering." *Everyday Acts Against Racism*. Ed. Maureen Reddy. Seattle: Seal, 1996:88–98.

———. "Across the Divide: Contemporary Anglo-American Feminist Theory on the Mother-Daughter Relationship." *Redefining Motherhood: Changing Identities and Patterns*. Eds. Sharon Abbey and Andrea O'Reilly. Toronto: Second Story Press, 1998:69–91.

———. "Mothers, Daughters and Feminism Today: Empowerment, Agency, Narrative." *Canadian Woman Studies* 18:2 & 3 (Summer/Fall 1998):16–21.

———. "'I come from a long line of Uppity Irate Black Women': African-American Feminist Thought on Motherhood, the Motherline and the Mother-Daughter Relationship." *Mothers and Daughters: Connection, Empowerment, Transformation*. Eds. Andrea O'Reilly and Sharon Abbey. New York: Rowman and Littlefield, 2000:143–159.

———. Introduction. *Mothers and Daughters: Connection, Empowerment, Transformation*. O'Reilly and Abbey, 1–18.

————. Introduction. *Mothers and Sons: Feminism, Masculinity and the Struggle to Raise Our Sons*. Ed. Andrea O'Reilly. New York: Routledge, 2001:1–21.

————. "In Black and White: Anglo-American and African-American Perspectives on Mothers and Sons." *Mothers and Sons: Feminism, Masculinity and the Struggle to Raise Our Sons*, 91–118.

Rich, Adrienne. *Of Woman Born: Motherhood as Experience and Institution*. New York: Norton, 1986.

————. "When We Dead Awaken: Writing as Re-Vision." *On Lies, Secrets, and Silence*. New York: Norton, 1979.

Ruddick, Sara. *Maternal Thinking: Toward a Politics of Peace*. Boston: Beacon, 1989.

Thurer, Shari. *The Myths of Motherhood: How Culture Reinvents the Good Mother*. New York: Penguin, 1994.

Umansky, Lauri. *Motherhood Reconceived: Feminism and the Legacies of the Sixties*. New York: New York UP, 1996.

Wane, Njoki Nathani. "Reflections on the Mutuality of Mothering: Women, Children and Othermothering." *Journal of the Association for Research on Mothering* 2.2 (Fall/Winter 2000):105–116.

Woolf, Virginia. *A Room of One's Own*. New York: Granada, 1978.

PART ONE

Motherhood as Institution

Patriarchal Power and Maternal Outrage

ONE

The Supreme Court of Canada and What It Means to Be "Of Woman Born"

DIANA GINN

INTRODUCTION

IN HER LITERARY CRITICISM, Adrienne Rich speaks of the need to "re-vision" literature, a term that she defines as "the act of looking back, of seeing with fresh eyes, of entering an old text from a new critical direction" ("When We Dead," 167). In *Of Woman Born*, Rich attempts to see motherhood with new eyes, distinguishing between the "potential relationship" (13) that she envisions existing between mother and child, free of oppressive social constraints, and the socially created institution of motherhood that, in Rich's view, allows a patriarchal society to control women as they bear and raise children.

In this chapter, I look for connections between Adrienne Rich's reflections on motherhood and recent jurisprudence on intervention in pregnancy. Given that "[w]e place law in a very privileged position" (Smart 111), in order to fully understand the ways in which *Of Woman Born* has influenced thinking about motherhood and pregnancy, it is necessary to consider the extent to which Rich's perceptions are reflected within current legal thinking. For the purposes of this discussion, I focus on two decisions of the Supreme Court of Canada: *Winnipeg Child and Family Services v. G.* (1997) and *Dobson (Litigation Guardian of) v. Dobson* (1999). In *Winnipeg Child and Family Services*, the majority of the court held that it did not have the authority to confine a pregnant woman to an addiction treatment center, while in *Dobson* the majority refused to allow a child to sue his mother for harms allegedly caused by her negligence during pregnancy.

While not all the issues canvassed in *Of Woman Born* are relevant to my topic, certain aspects of Rich's commentary on motherhood provide a useful perspective on both the majority and dissenting opinions in *Winnipeg Child and Family Services* and *Dobson*. In particular, the following themes from *Of Woman Born* reverberate, in one way or another, in these judgments: Rich's analysis of the control that a patriarchal society exerts over women as they bear and rear children; her observation that society makes mothers almost entirely responsible for meeting the needs of children; her critique of society's tendency either to idolize or despise women; and her attempts to find new ways of describing the nature of pregnancy. The connections that can be drawn between themes from *Of Woman Born* and jurisprudence of the Supreme Court of Canada are a testament to the impact that the writings of Rich and other feminists have had on the way in which motherhood and pregnancy are conceptualized.

I begin my discussion with a brief description of the majority and dissenting judgments in *Winnipeg Child and Family Services* and *Dobson*. I then attempt to relate aspects of these judgments to each of the themes just identified.

WINNIPEG CHILD AND FAMILY SERVICES V. G.

This case involved a young aboriginal woman, Ms. G., who was pregnant for the fourth time. Ms. G. had been addicted to glue sniffing for years and on occasion she supported this addiction through prostitution. Her three previous children had been removed by Children and Family Services (C.F.S.), and two of the three exhibited symptoms that were attributed to Ms. G.'s solvent abuse during pregnancy. Ms. G. had sought treatment for her addiction several years earlier, as well as during the current pregnancy, but was unable to find a counseling program with an opening for her. When C.F.S. became aware that Ms. G. was pregnant again, it was able, with Ms. G.'s consent, to arrange for addiction treatment. On the day that Ms. G. was to enter the treatment program, however, she was intoxicated and refused to accompany the C.F.S. worker to the treatment center. C.F.S. immediately applied, on behalf of the fetus, for a court order detaining Ms. G. in a treatment center, and requiring her to undergo treatment for her addiction. The order was granted by the Manitoba Court of Queen's Bench, and Ms. G. entered the treatment program. Although the court order was set aside two days later by the Manitoba Court of Appeal, Ms. G. remained in the treatment center voluntarily. C.F.S. was unsuccessful in its appeal to the Supreme Court of Canada to have the original order upheld. By the time the appeal was heard by the Supreme Court, Ms. G. had already given birth to an apparently healthy child; however, the court agreed to hear the case because of the seriousness of the legal issues involved.

Justice McLachlin, writing for seven judges of the Supreme Court, stated the issue on appeal as follows: "assuming evidence that a mother is acting in a way which may harm her unborn child, does a judge, at the behest of the state, have the power to order the mother to be taken into custody for the purposes of rectifying her conduct?" (paragraph 5). McLachlin J. held that the order sought could not be justified on current legal principles and that the court could not expand the law so as to provide a basis for the order. McLachlin J. pointed out that, at present, a person could be lawfully confined against his or her will only through the criminal law, or under mental health legislation, neither of which were applicable in this case. Justice Major, writing the dissenting opinion for himself and Justice Sopinka, held that the common law was intended to evolve to meet new situations where a remedy was required: "Society does not simply sit by and allow a mother to abuse her child after birth. How then should serious abuse be allowed to occur before the child is born?" (paragraph 103).

DOBSON (LITIGATION GUARDIAN OF) V. DOBSON

In *Dobson*, the Supreme Court of Canada addressed the issue of whether a woman could be sued by her child on the grounds that her negligence during pregnancy caused the child to be born with disabilities. Shortly after his mother was involved in a car accident, Ryan Dobson was born prematurely, with "permanent mental and physical impairment, including cerebral palsy" (760). Ryan's maternal grandfather then sued his mother on Ryan's behalf, alleging that the accident was caused by Ms. Dobson's negligent driving. With the consent of the parties, the issue of liability was severed, so that the court did not consider whether Ms. Dobson had actually been careless in her driving, or if so, whether that negligence had caused Ryan's disabilities. Instead, the decision focused entirely on "whether Ryan Dobson has the legal capacity to bring a tort action against his mother for her allegedly negligent act which occurred while he was in utero" (760). Although Ms. Dobson was named as defendant, the action was actually defended by the insurance company that had issued motor vehicle insurance to Ms. Dobson.

Seven judges of the Supreme Court of Canada held that public policy concerns regarding "(1) the privacy and autonomy rights of women and (2) the difficulties inherent in articulating a judicial standard of conduct for pregnant women" (768) indicated that "a legal duty of care should not be imposed upon a pregnant woman towards the foetus or subsequently born child" (767–68).[1] The dissent weighed the interests of the pregnant woman against the interests of the fetus and concluded that public policy required that such a legal duty be imposed.

OF WOMAN BORN AND THE SUPREME COURT
OF CANADA: A CRITIQUE OF MOTHERHOOD

Of Woman Born combines personal reminiscences of motherhood as experienced by Rich in the 1950s and 1960s with historical and sociological commentary. Marie Ashe describes Rich as "the most well-known American precursor" to postmodern feminist explorations of "the construction of mothers by law and other cultural forces" (148). Rich writes that when she first considered writing a book on motherhood,

> I could remember little except anxiety, physical weariness, anger, self-blame, boredom, and division within myself: a division made more acute by the moments of passionate love, delight in my children's spirited bodies and minds, amazement at how they went on loving me in spite of my failures to love them wholly and selflessly. (15)

While much of Rich's text is critical, she notes in her foreword that she is attacking motherhood only *"as defined and restricted under patriarchy"* (14, emphasis in original), not mothering itself. Ashe suggests that "[b]y faithfulness to a first-person narrative form, Rich expresses what she is able to say about her experience without claiming that her account includes the experiences of *all* women or of *all mothers*. This voice and method assure an avoidance of the grand narrative eschewed by postmodernism" (148, emphasis in original).

Rich moves from a recounting of her own experience to a broader consideration of motherhood, and in these portions of the book, I would suggest that Rich does seem to universalize her conclusions, and therefore is closer to postulating a "grand narrative" applicable to all mothering. *Of Woman Born* reflects Rich's conviction that motherhood as experienced by women over the centuries in no way represents the "natural" order of things. Arguing that "for most of what we know as the 'mainstream' of recorded history, motherhood as institution has ghettoized and degraded female potentialities" (13), Rich explores the possibility that there existed a prehistorical, prepatriarchal "golden age ruled by women" (73). While acknowledging at one point that we cannot know whether such an age existed (73), Rich paints a glowing picture of "ancient motherhood" as "filled with a *mana* (supernatural force)" (67):

> [t]hroughout most of the world, there is archeological evidence of a period when Woman was venerated in several aspects, the primal one being maternal; when Goddess-worship prevailed, and when myths depicted strong and revered female figures. In the earliest artifacts we know, we encounter the female as primal power. (93)

Rich suggests that this power was then "domesticated" and forced to serve the interests of a patriarchy. In her view, "the patriarchal institution of mother-hood is not the 'human condition' any more than rape, prostitution, and slav-ery are" (34). According to Rich, motherhood, as socially constructed, elevates the bearing and raising of children to the one true destiny for all women, devalues women who do not have children, and controls those who do, by placing unrealistic demands on mothers and leaving little or no room for other aspects of their personalities and experience. She sees "[t]he physical and psy-chic weight of responsibility on the woman with children [as] by far the heav-iest of social burdens" (52).

Because of the sweeping nature of certain of Rich's statements about motherhood, as it existed in the (perhaps mythical) past or in more recent times, some aspects of her analysis now appear dated. Many feminists today would, I think, tend to give a more nuanced and varied accounting of the fac-tors that have led at least some women to experience motherhood as oppres-sive. Feminism has evolved in the last twenty-eight years into a multiplicity of overlapping feminisms that go farther toward recognizing the differences as well as the commonalities among women, and thus acknowledge the impact of race, culture, class, and sexual orientation on women's experiences.[2] In *Win-nipeg Child and Family Services*, Justice McLachlin recognized that the vul-nerability of women to state intervention in pregnancy would depend on a variety of factors. She pointed out that if the law were to place a pregnant woman in a legal duty-of-care relationship with her fetus, "[m]inority women, illiterate women, and women of limited education will be the most likely to fall afoul of the law and the new duty it imposes and to suffer the conse-quences of injunctive relief and potential damage awards" (paragraph 40).

While I would question the statement that, for all women, motherhood is "by far the heaviest of social burdens," I do, however, acknowledge the importance of Rich's legacy to feminist thinking. Her willingness to challenge accepted norms and to attempt to "re-vision" societal relations has allowed for a rethinking of old paradigms and continues to have relevance today. It is Rich's impact on the ways in which we think about pregnant women and pregnancy itself that I explore in the next section.

RELEVANCE TO JURISPRUDENCE

Neither the majority nor the dissenting judges in *Winnipeg Child and Family Services* or *Dobson* referred to Adrienne Rich's writings, yet I would suggest that one can find clear echos of her analysis of motherhood in these cases. A number of Rich's themes can be related to the way in which the court responded to the arguments for and against authorizing intervention in preg-nancy, or allowing tort liability arising out of pregnancy. Four such themes are discussed below.

1. Motherhood is a form of social control exercised over women as they bear and rear children. Rich sees the institution of motherhood as having "withheld over one-half of the human species from decisions affecting their lives" (13). She argues that "[t]here always has been, and there remains, intense fear of the suggestion that women should have the final say as to how our bodies are to be used" (30).

Clearly, control is a central issue in *Winnipeg Child and Family Services* and *Dobson*. To what extent can the state or individuals use the law to exert control over the behavior of a woman during pregnancy? Julia E. Hanigsberg argues, in an article cited by Justice McLachlin in *Winnipeg Child and Family Services,* that "[w]hile state 'protection' of fetuses appears benevolent, when it is coercive it can have no effect but to disempower women and further subject them to arbitrary control by patriarchal power" (paragraph 41). In *Winnipeg Child and Family Services,* the attempt at state coercion is obvious, since it is C.F.S. that makes the application (although supposedly on behalf of the fetus). In *Dobson,* although the tort action was brought on Ryan's behalf by his grandfather, had the court found that a cause of action could exist, the state would still be involved in controlling women during pregnancy. If the majority had held in *Dobson* that a child can sue his or her mother for harms caused by the mother's negligence during pregnancy, the state, via the courts, would have to set the standard of behavior for "reasonable" pregnant women. Women could then be held legally responsible for any deviance from this standard, if the child was born with harm caused by the behavior and the harm was forseeable. According to the Royal Commission on New Reproductive Technologies,

> [i]f we impose a legal obligation upon a woman to care for her fetus . . . the potential for curtailing women's choices and behaviour becomes staggering. The kinds of substances and activities that could pose a danger to the fetus are many, varied, and increasing. . . . As scientific knowledge develops, the list is becoming longer. Many women's management of pregnancy could be subject to challenge and scrutiny, and pregnancy could become the source of potential liability suits against women who failed to comply with certain standards of behaviour. (Canada 958)

The majority decisions in both *Winnipeg Child and Family Services* and *Dobson* recognized that finding for the plaintiff would have seriously undermined women's autonomy rights. In *Winnipeg Child and Family Services,* McLachlin J. stated,

> [l]eaving the special relationship between mother and unborn child aside for the moment, there is little precedent for suing any defendant in tort for damages one has suffered as a consequence of his or her lifestyle. . . . The diffi-

culties multiply when the lifestyle in question is that of a pregnant woman whose liberty is intimately and inescapably bound to her unborn child. (paragraph 34).

In *Dobson*, Cory J. concluded that because "[e]verything the pregnant woman eats or drinks, and every physical action she takes, may affect the foetus" (770), "[t]here is no rational or principled limit to the types of claims which may be brought if . . . a tortious duty of care were imposed upon pregnant women" (771). Thus, placing a legal duty of care on a pregnant women with regard to her fetus would be far more onerous that any other legal duty-of-care relationship.

The dissenting judges in *Winnipeg Child and Family Services* were much less worried about the dangers of increased surveillance and control of pregnant women. It is true that, before making an order such as that sought in *Winnipeg Child and Family Services*, Justice Major would require that it be shown on a balance of probabilities that "abusive activity" by a pregnant woman was likely to lead to "serious and irreparable harm to the foetus," that the remedy sought was "the least intrusive option," and that the legal process was fair (paragraph 96). If those tests were met, however, intervention was justified in Justice Major's view, since "[o]nce the mother decides to bear the child the state has an interest in trying to ensure the child's health" (paragraph 95). In response to arguments in *Winnipeg Child and Family Services* that allowing any intervention could lead to significant curtailment of liberty and autonomy interests, Major J. stated that the appropriate level of intervention could be decided on a case-by-case basis, and that "slippery slope" arguments should not cause "the state to stand idly by while a reckless and/or addicted mother inflicts serious and permanent harm on a child she had decided to bring into the world" (paragraph 95). Justice Major not only minimized the degree of state interference to which pregnant women would be subject, but also portrayed the pregnant woman as ultimately in control of the situation:

> [w]hen confinement is determined to be the only solution that will work in the circumstances, this type of imposition on the mother is fairly modest when balanced against the devastating harm substance abuse will potentially inflict on her child. . . . The mother's *continuing ability to elect an abortion and end her confinement* makes the intrusion of her liberty relatively modest when weighed against the child from birth being seriously and permanently impaired. (paragraph 132, emphasis mine)[3]

The suggestion that a woman could simply regain control of her life by choosing to have an abortion is not only dismissive of the difficult nature of such a decision, but also fails to reflect reality. Abortion services are not uniformly available across Canada, and even if they were, a majority of abortions occur early in the pregnancy.[4] Ms. G. was five months pregnant when C.F.S. obtained the original order, and such an order, if upheld, could have required Ms. G. to stay in the detention center until she gave birth. Surely Justice Major was not suggesting that a pregnant woman has the option of an abortion right up until the time of birth—or that even if such an option were available, that this satisfactorily answers concerns about state coercion?

In *Dobson*, Justice Major did not accept that allowing a woman to be sued, after her child was born, on the grounds that the child had been harmed by her negligence during pregnancy, would represent a significant change in the law, and would increase the potential for pregnancies to become sites of "challenge and scrutiny" (Canada 958). Justice Major stated that because the action was brought on behalf of a child, not a fetus, the policy concerns raised in *Winnipeg Child and Family Services* did not apply in *Dobson*. Justice Major concluded that tort liability would not restrict a pregnant woman's freedom of action, or affect the liberty and equality interests of women (809–810).

Anne Woollett and Ann Phoenix write of the "dual, and hence often conflicting, nature of motherhood as an experience and development which is mainly lived out in a private, domestic sphere, but which is evaluated within the public domain" (217). This evaluation is carried out both informally by relatives, neighbors, teachers, and others, and formally when a social worker or child welfare agency becomes involved with a child. The dissenting opinions in *Winnipeg Child and Family Services* and *Dobson* would have increased the opportunities for judging pregnant women, by allowing the legal scrutiny of women during pregnancy. The majority decisions in these cases drew the line at authorizing increased surveillance of pregnant women.

2. Mothers are made almost solely responsible for the well-being of their children. Rich expands her analysis of the coercive elements of institutionalized motherhood by arguing that motherhood not only removes autonomy from mothers, but also makes mothers almost completely responsible for meeting all their children's needs: "My singularity, my uniqueness in the world as *his mother* evoked a need vaster than any single human being could satisfy, except by loving continuously, unconditionally, from dawn to dark, and often in the middle of the night" (24, emphasis in original). If Rich's critique holds true even for some women, then those mothers are in a double bind, lacking control over their own lives, yet responsible for the lives of others. Rich suggests that the almost complete dependence of children on mothers is a burden created by a patriarchal society:

> I was haunted by the stereotype of the mother whose love is "unconditional"; and by the visual and literary images of motherhood as a single-minded identity. . . . I did not understand that this circle, this magnetic field in which we lived, was not a natural phenomenon. (23)

A recent feminist analysis of childcare manuals concluded, with regard to the manuals' construction of "the nature of motherhood":

> [t]he responsibility falls on to mothers for the "normal development" of a well-adjusted individual. To mother adequately a woman needs to be present with her child 24 hours each day and to be continually and actively engaged, providing stimulating and attentive company. If her child's development is not normal, the blame falls on the mother. (Marshall 83)

The discussion of dependency, and what kind of responsibility that dependency should call forth, is particularly complex when one tries to disentangle moral obligations from legal ones, and when one shifts from mothering to pregnancy. As Isabel Grant notes,

> [t]he issue is not whether a pregnant woman has a moral obligation to conduct her life in a manner consistent with the best interests of her fetus. For most of us that is beyond question. Rather, the issue is whether the law should be used to enforce this moral responsibility. There are many areas where moral duties are not enforced legally, a general duty to rescue being an obvious example. (220)

Similarly, a group that made a presentation before the Supreme Court of Canada in *Winnipeg Child and Family Services* stated, "[f]undamentally, the case at bar is about the limits of the law. Legal process is not an appropriate response to every social problem" (Women's Health Clinic Incorporated, paragraph 3).

In *Winnipeg Child and Family Services* and *Dobson,* the majority of the Supreme Court of Canada refused to translate moral responsibility into legal obligations such that the state could confine and control women whose behavior during pregnancy is thought likely to harm the fetus, or allow a pregnant woman who does cause such harm to her fetus to be sued in tort.[5]

If, as Rich argues, the dependency of children on their mothers is largely socially constructed, presumably much of the mother's responsibility could be shifted to others, since there is nothing innate about mothering, other than breastfeeding, that could not be done by the father or someone else. However, pregnancy cannot be shared in the same way, and as Justice Cory noted in *Dobson,* "the very existence of the foetus depends upon the pregnant woman" (767). Justice Major concluded from this that

> [w]here a woman has chosen to carry a foetus to term . . . that woman must accept some responsibility for its well-being. In my view, that responsibility entails, at the least, the requirement that the pregnant woman refrain from the abuse of substances that have . . . a reasonable probability of causing serious and irreparable damage to the foetus. (984)

Thus, Major J. did not differentiate in any way between moral and legal responsibility, seeming to suggest that moral responsibilities are always, and automatically, enforceable in law.

While a fetus is directly dependent on the woman carrying it, the woman's ability to nurture the fetus does not lie with her alone. Although Justice McLachlin used the language of "lifestyle choices" in *Winnipeg Child and Family Services,* she was careful to point out that "'choices' like alcohol consumption, drug abuse, and poor nutrition may be the products of circumstance and illness rather than free choice" (paragraph 41). This suggests that another way of protecting fetuses would be to try to ensure the well-being of pregnant women. Whether a woman is able to live free from physical violence, whether she has adequate housing, whether she is able to nourish herself and the fetus, and whether she has access to adequate prenatal care (including treatment for addictions) involve societal as well as individual responsibility. Harriette Marshall points out that one implicit corollary of characterizing mothers as solely responsible for the development of their children is "to locate any social problems in faulty mothering. . . . [S]ociety and structural influences are omitted from the equation" (83). Allowing a woman to be detained during pregnancy, or requiring her to pay tort damages to her child once born, releases society from its obligations for the well-being of pregnant women, mothers, and children. A brief presented to the Supreme Court in *Winnipeg Child and Family Services* by the Women's Health Clinic Incorporated and others quoted Michelle Harrison, who suggests that

> [i]n a country in which many [children] still do without homes or food, it is clear that it is the "idea" of children which holds our concerns, if not the children themselves. It is easier to punish one pregnant woman than to alleviate the lethal conditions of many. (quoted in Women's Health Clinic, paragraph 2)

I would argue that rather than placing legally enforceable obligations on pregnant women that are not placed on others, we should be trying to ensure that there are sufficient social and economic supports in place such that a pregnant woman will be better able to make choices that enhance her own and the fetus's well-being.

3. Women are either idolized or despised. In *Of Woman Born,* Rich writes that patriarchy has viewed the female body as "impure [and] corrupt," yet as mothers, women are idolized as "beneficent, sacred, pure, asexual, nourishing." Rich suggests that, "[i]n order to maintain two such notions . . . the masculine imagination has had to divide women . . . as polarized into good or evil" (34). Some feminists[6] have suggested that society also tends to create two extreme images of motherhood: the nurturing, selfless, "good" mother, and the self-centered, irresponsible "bad" mother, and that "what is widely accepted as 'good mothering' by 'good mothers' is socially constructed and has political implications and consequences" (Phoenix and Woollette, 25). This idealizing or devaluing of mothers has been criticized on a number of grounds: that the ideal of the good mother is almost unattainable; that focusing solely on the mother ignores relevant factors in her life, such as violence or poverty;[7] and that the label of "bad mother" can be applied to women from particular cultural or class backgrounds,[8] or women who simply do not conform to social stereotypes (Fineman, 217).

Proponents of fetal rights would seem to apply the same dichotomy to pregnant women. Justice Major's description of Ms. G. in *Winnipeg Child and Family Services* is clearly that of a "bad" pregnant woman who knew that her behavior could harm the fetus: "it is clear that D.F.G. has had ample knowledge of the effects of substance abuse on her foetus. She was sadly aware of giving birth to two permanently handicapped children" (paragraph 128) and yet chose to continue her irresponsible "lifestyle." Nowhere in his opinion does he address the issue of whether an addiction can be construed as a choice. It is easy to forget, in reading the dissent, that by the age of sixteen, Ms. G. was living in poverty, addicted to glue-sniffing, and pregnant with her first child; that she sought treatment for herself several times, including during the first trimester of her fourth pregnancy, but on her most recent attempt had been turned down because of lack of space at the treatment center (Women's Legal Education Action Fund, paragraph 2); that she agreed, at least initially, to C.F.S. arranging treatment for her; and that she remained voluntarily in the treatment center once she was there. There is far less focus on the pregnant woman in *Dobson*, and I have suggested elsewhere that Ms. Dobson may have come much closer to Major J.'s image of a "good" mother.

The majority decisions in both *Winnipeg Child and Family Services* and *Dobson* were far more careful to avoid labeling pregnant women as good or evil. In *Winnipeg Child and Family Services*, Justice McLachlin appeared sensitive to the dangers of portraying Ms. G. as uncaring, stating "[t]his is not a story of heroes and villains. It is the more prosaic but all too common story of people struggling to do their best in the face of inadequate facilities and the ravages of addiction" (paragraph 5). In *Dobson*, Justice Cory suggested that the focus should not be on maternal liability for alleged negligence during pregnancy, but on what resources society is willing to commit to the care of disabled persons.

I would suggest that most pregnant women do the best they can, and where their behavior endangers the fetus, this is usually not because of selfish choices, but because of the lack of any real choice. That said, even if full social and economic supports were in place for pregnant women, it is possible that a few women would still act irresponsibly. It seems naive to suggest otherwise—yet I would argue that this still would not justify state intervention, for at least three reasons. First, the law does not always demand that we place the interests of others first. For instance, the law cannot be used to force me to donate blood, even though another person might die unless I donate. Unless we truly want to move to a society that uses the law to coerce altruism in all situations, it is inconsistent to advocate invention in pregnancy. Second, there is little certainty that intervention, if permitted, would be limited to those pregnant women who, with the luxury of real choice (i.e., not circumscribed by poverty, addictions, or other factors), still choose to act in ways that are harmful to their fetus. In fact, such women would, almost by definition, be less vulnerable to state intervention. It seems more likely that the trend already documented in the United States and Canada would continue: most intervention orders or compensation awards would be directed against women who are already marginalized.[9] Finally, it seems likely that the harm done to fetuses by threatening pregnant women with coercive interventions or tort liability would outweigh any good that would be done by authorizing the state to "rescue" fetuses from irresponsible women. As the Royal Commission on New Reproductive Technologies points out, if pregnant women fear "that they could be confined against their will, forced to submit to medical treatment, or charged with criminal offences, they might well avoid seeking medical care" or might even choose to have an abortion (Canada 958).

4. We need to find new ways of describing the nature of pregnancy. In my discussion of the previous three themes, I extrapolated from Rich's critique of motherhood to apply her insights to pregnancy. This final theme draws directly on Rich's commentary about pregnancy.

One of the most difficult aspects of pregnancy discourse is finding ways of appropriately characterizing the connection between the pregnant woman and the fetus. As Justice Cory stated in *Dobson:* "There is no other relationship in the realm of human existence which can serve as a basis for comparison" (769). The complexity of this issue is further compounded when we go beyond a consideration of how various women experience pregnancy and respond to the fetus they carry, to a consideration of how pregnancy is most appropriately to be characterized in law.

Legal writing has tended either to view the pregnant woman and fetus as "one organic unit" or as a "conflicting dyad" (Cosslett 119); the majority analysis in *Winnipeg Child and Family Services* and Dobson tends toward the former characterization, and the dissenting opinions tend toward the latter.

Thus, Justice McLachlin stated in *Winnipeg Child and Family Services* that "for practical purposes, the unborn child and its mother-to-be are bonded in a union separable only by birth" (paragraph 29), while Justice Major spoke in that case of weighing the competing interests of the pregnant woman and the fetus. In *Dobson*, Justice Cory referred to the "inseparable unity between an expectant woman and her foetus" (769), while Justice Major stated that "[i]t is no answer to the plaintiff in this case that unilateral concerns about a pregnant woman's competing rights are sufficient to 'negative' a negligent violation of his physical integrity. His rights, too, are at stake" (813).

In her description of her own pregnancies, Rich reminds us that both images of organic unit and conflicting dyad may be overly simplistic: "[n]or in pregnancy did I experience the fetus as decisively internal . . . but rather, as something inside and of me, yet becoming hourly and daily more separate, on the way to becoming separate from me, and of-itself" (64).

Legal questions about the nature of pregnancy have tended to be couched in terms of whether a fetus is, or should be, recognized as a legal person, and whether a fetus does, or should have, legally enforceable rights. As Justice McLachlin stated in *Winnipeg Child and Family Services,* it is an established principle in Canadian law that a fetus is "not a legal person and possess[es] no legal rights" (939); therefore, "the law has always treated the mother and unborn child as one" (945). It is only after birth that a child is recognized as having a legal personality separate from that of its mother (945).[10] The corollary of this is that no third party can initiate a legal action on behalf of the fetus.

Hanigsberg speaks of "the inadequacy of rights discourse in describing the mother/fetus relationship" (43) and T. Brettel Dawson suggests that

> [i]t is . . . timely to seek ways to move beyond the paradigm of personhood, individuation, and rights-based analysis in the area of women's reproduction. This situation is inherently relational; to disconnect woman and fetus is to create, rather than solve, problems. An ethic of care, interconnection, and responsibility provide the basis for beginning to imagine new legal frameworks. (228)

I would suggest that feminist thinking on how to characterize pregnancy is still a work in progress, and in this work, we should remind ourselves of Rich's perception that the fetus she carried was both "of" and "not of" her. Thus, we need to find ways to "re-vision," and then reflect accurately in our law, the connections between a pregnant woman and her fetus. I would not, however, want to see this revisioning abandon the concept of rights entirely, for a pregnant woman may still need to rely on legal rights, not as a sword to be used against her fetus, but as a shield against coercive state intervention in pregnancy.

CONCLUSION

It is interesting to try to map aspects of Supreme Court of Canada jurisprudence onto the writing of Adrienne Rich. Taken together, the first three themes that I have identified from *Of Woman Born* speak of the pressure exerted on women to conform to an unnatural and unattainable idea of motherhood—an ideal which, even if it were achieved, would, Rich suggests, not be particularly beneficial to either mother or child. The fourth theme reminds us of the difficulty of finding language and legal concepts that are appropriate to the unique nature of pregnancy. There is significant congruence between Rich's critique of societal control of mothers and the concerns regarding state intervention in pregnancy expressed by the majority in *Winnipeg Child and Family Services* and in *Dobson,* reflecting the impact that Rich, and those later feminists whom she has influenced, have had on thinking about motherhood, and by extrapolation, pregnancy.

NOTES

I would like to thank Barbara Darby for her assistance with this chapter. Her research, editing, and thoughtful insights were extremely helpful.

1. Tort law apportions civil liability for injuries that one person inflicts on another, frequently through negligence. Where it is forseeable that a particular negligent act by one person could harm another, then these individuals are said to be in a legal duty-of-care relationship, and if that duty of care is breached such that the negligent act takes place and the forseeable harm is inflicted, then the injured person may sue the one who was negligent. If negligence and harm are proven, then the defendant will be ordered to pay damages to compensate the plaintiff for the harm done.

2. For instance, see the introduction in *The State of Women in the World Atlas,*

[t]he world of women is defined both by commonality and difference. The commonalities are many: women everywhere share primary responsibility for having and rearing children, for forming and maintaining families, for contraception; women everywhere confront conflicting demands of multiple roles. We share too the lead in fighting for women's rights and other civil rights. Rich and poor, we share distinctive health concerns, a vulnerability to violence, to the degradation of pornography, to the exploitation of our sexuality by the media and the economy. Nevertheless, if we have learned anything from the feminist movement of the past two decades, it is that global generalizations must not be used to make the very real differences that exist among women country by country, region by region. There are significant inequalities in wealth and in access to opportunities from place to place; these are then refracted and magnified through social prisms such as race, ethnicity, age, or religious affiliation. (Seager 9)

3. Martin and Coleman write that in the view of "proponents of intervention . . . the woman's consent to the continued pregnancy translates any moral obligation she may have towards her fetus into an irrevocable conferral of legally enforceable fetal rights. These rights may then be used against the pregnant woman to mandate her conduct. The woman's decision not to abort is interpreted as a waiver of her rights" (987).

4. Statistics Canada reports for 1995 that "[an] increasing proportion of abortions are being performed in the early stages of pregnancy. Those in which the pregnancy was less than 13 weeks accounted for 9 out of every 10 hospital abortions in 1995. . . . Over 39% of abortions performed in clinics occurred when the women had been pregnant less than nine weeks, compared with 29% of abortions at the same stage in hospitals. In addition, 17% of abortions performed in clinics involved pregnancies of 13 to 20 weeks' duration, compared with only about 10% at the same stage in hospitals." In 1994, between 42% (hospital) and 57.4% (clinic) of abortions occurred before 20 weeks of pregnancy. In 1993, the percentage of abortions performed on women pregnant less than 13 weeks was 91.7%. ProChoice Connection notes that "[a]bortions after 16 weeks are rare." Planned Parenthood Federation of America's 1990 statistics indicate that "[m]ost women have abortions in the first trimester," or 91% of women having abortions. All statistics are from the websites listed in the works cited.

5. The Supreme Court of Canada did make it clear, however, that, subject to the *Canadian Charter of Rights and Freedoms,* Parliament or provincial legislatures could pass legislation allowing for greater direct state intervention in pregnancy, or allowing a child to sue his or her mother for harm negligently inflicted during pregnancy.

6. For instance, see Fineman and Ashe.

7. See, for instance, MacIntosh.

8. In its intervener factum to the Supreme Court of Canada in *Winnipeg Child and Family Services,* Women's Legal Education Action Fund stated that "[a]boriginal women have been stereotyped as 'bad mothers' according to Western social constructions and norms. This has led to their punishment, including the loss of their children to welfare agencies" (paragraph 11). Phoenix and Woollett write that "current social constructions of normal motherhood do not reflect the realities of working class mothers' and children's lives, and this results in any differences between them and middle class mothers and children being seen as pathological or deviant. In a similar way black mothers and those from minority ethnic groups are socially constructed as 'other' and hence are viewed as deviating from 'good/normal' mothering" (18).

9. In a 1989 article published in the American Bar Association Journal, Kenneth Jost speaks of

> an increasing trend of judicial intervention in the lives of pregnant women. In the past decade, doctors and hospital administrators have asked judges at least 20 times for authority to perform caesarian sections on unconsenting women, and have been turned down just three times. Under the rubric of fetal rights, judges have also put pregnant women in jail to take better care of the fetuses or to prevent the women from abusing drugs. And in some jurisdictions, judges routinely remove newborns from their mothers' custody if they are born with drugs in their system. (84)

According to Martin and Coleman, pregnant women in the United States have also been "subjected to criminal sanctions or civil liability for their conduct during pregnancy" (949). Although there are fewer cases of this nature in Canada, there does seem to be a similar trend: see Canada Royal Commission on New Reproductive Technologies and Martha Jackman's article.

10. This explains why, even in the cases that allow a child to sue a third party for injuries caused in utero, the action cannot be brought on behalf of a fetus. The child must be born alive in order to be seen as having a cause of action arising from harms suffered before birth.

WORKS CITED

Ashe, Marie. "Postmodernism, Legal Ethics, and Representation of 'Bad Mothers.'" Fineman and Karpin. New York: Columbia UP, 1995:142–166.

Canada. *Proceed With Care: Final Report of the Royal Commission on New Reproductive Technologies.* Vol. 2. Ottawa: The Commission, 1993.

Cosslett, Tess. *Women Writing Childbirth: Modern Discourses of Motherhood.* Manchester: Manchester UP, 1994.

Dawson, T. Brettel. "First Person Familiar: Judicial Intervention in Pregnancy, Again: G. (D.F.)." *Canadian Journal of Women and Law* 10 (1998):213–228.

Dobson (Litigation Guardian of) v. Dobson, [1999] 2 S.C.R. 753.

Fineman, Martha Albertson. "Images of Mothers in Poverty Discourse." Fineman and Karpin. New York: Columbia UP, 1995:205–223.

Fineman, Martha Albertson and Isabel Karpin, Eds. *Mothers in Law: Feminist Theory and the Legal Regulation of Motherhood.* New York: Columbia UP, 1995.

Ginn, Diana E. "Pregnant Women and Consent to Medical Treatment." *Health Law in Canada* 15.2 (1994):41–48.

Grant, Isabel. "Forced Obstetrical Intervention: A Charter Analysis." *University of Toronto Law Journal* 39 (1989):217–257.

Hanigsberg, Julia E. "Power and Procreation: State Interference in Pregnancy." *Ottawa Law Review* 23.1 (1991):35–69.

Jackman, Martha. "The Canadian Charter as a Barrier to Unwanted Medical Treatment of Pregnant Women in the Interests of the Foetus." *Health Law in Canada* 14.2 (1993):49–58.

Jost, Kenneth. "Mother Versus Child." *American Bar Association Journal* April (1989):84–88.

MacIntosh, Constance. "Conceiving Fetal Abuse." *Canadian Journal of Family Law* 15.2 (1998):178–220.

Martin, Sheilah and Murray Coleman. "Judicial Intervention in Pregnancy." *McGill Law Journal* 40 (1995):947–991.

Marshall, Harriette. "The Social Construction of Motherhood: An Analysis of Child-care and Parenting Manuals." Phoenix, Woollett, and Lloyd 66–85.

Phoenix, Ann, Anne Woollett, and Eva Lloyd, eds. *Motherhood: Meanings, Practices and Ideologies*. London: Sage Publications, 1991.

Phoenix, Ann and Anne Woollett. "Motherhood: Social Construction, Politics and Psychology." Phoenix, Woollett, and Lloyd 13–27.

Planned Parenthood Federation of America. "Fact Sheets." 27 June 2000. *<http: //www.plannedparenthood.org/abortion/chooseabort2.html#When are>* and *<http: //www.plannedparenthood.org/library/ABORTION/afterfirst.html>*.

ProChoice Connection. "Abortion Information FAQs" and "Choosing Abortions— Questions and Answers." 27 June 2000 *<http://www.prochoiceconnection.com/ aic02.html#03>*. July 2000.

Rich, Adrienne. *Of Woman Born: Motherhood as Experience and Institution*. New York: Norton, 1976.

———. "When We Dead Awaken: Writing as Re-Vision." *Adrienne Rich's Poetry and Prose: Poems, Prose, Reviews and Criticism*. Eds. Barbara Charlesworth Gelpi and Albert Gelpi. New York: Norton, 1993:166–177.

Seager, Joni. Introduction. *The State of Women in the World Atlas: Women's Status Around the Globe: Work, Health, Education and Personal Freedom*. Second ed. New York: Penguin, 1997:9–10.

Smart, Carol. "Feminist Interventions and State Policy." *Women and the Canadian State*. Eds. Caroline Andrews and Sanda Rogers. Montreal: McGill-Queen's UP, 1997:110–115.

Statistics Canada. 2000. "Therapeutic Abortions, 1996 and 1997." 27 June 2000 *<http://www.statcan.ca/Daily/English/000407/d000407c.htm>*.

———. 1997. "Therapeutic Abortions, 1995." 27 June 2000 *<http://www.statcan.ca/ Daily/English/971105/d971105.htm#ART2>*.

———. 1996. "Therapeutic Abortions, 1994." 27 June 2000 *<http://www.statcan.ca/ Daily/English/960925/d960925.htm#ART1>*.

———. 1995. "Therapeutic Abortions, 1993." 27 June 2000 *<http://www.statcan.ca/ Daily/English/950712/d950712.htm#ART1>*.

Women's Health Clinic Incorporated, Metis Women of Manitoba Incorporated, Native Women's Transition Centre Incorporated, Manitoba Association for Rights and Liberties Incorporated, "Factum of the Intervenors."

Women's Legal Education and Action Fund. "Factum of the Intervenor."

Winnipeg Child and Family Services (Northwest Area) v. D.F.G., [1997] 3 S.C.R. 925.

Woollett, Anne and Ann Phoenix. Afterword. Phoenix, Woollett, and Lloyd 216–231.

TWO

Of Party-State Born

Motherhood, Reproductive Politics, and the Chinese Nation-State

SARAH E. STEVENS

My individual, seemingly private pains as a mother, the individual, seemingly private pains of the mothers around me and before me, whatever our class or color, the regulation of women's reproductive power by men in every totalitarian system and every socialist revolution, the legal and technical control by men of contraception, fertility, abortion, obstetrics, gynecology, and extrauterine reproductive experiments—all are essential to the patriarchal system, as is the negative or suspect status of women who are not mothers.
—Adrienne Rich, *Of Woman Born*

It is the misfortune of women that it is their reproductive power and their bodies which are being fought over in this struggle between the State and the still patriarchal family.
—Delia Davin, "Gender and Population in the People's Republic of China"

IN MY USE OF Adrienne Rich's groundbreaking work to examine motherhood and reproductive politics in twentieth-century China, I will be tiptoeing between two equally deep theoretical chasms. On the one side, this chapter seeks to avoid the Western feminist-centric pit of assuming some sort of essential womanhood, which naturally transcends all barriers of nation, color, sexuality, and the historical specificity of individual experience. On the other side, this work resists the pull of the void that labels all use of Western theory as Orientalist, colonialistic, and patronizing to the Chinese subject. I endeavor to show how Rich's discussion of the institution of motherhood can be used to trace the evolution of political control over women's bodies in twentieth-century China, while firmly placing these political movements in the context of their historical, China-centered reality.

Following Rich's example of blended experience and scholarship, I will situate myself and explain why I have chosen to write this chapter. I am not (yet) a mother. Nonetheless, when I first read Rich's *Of Woman Born,* her words spoke to me, to my experiences as a woman living in a patriarchal world, and to my scholarly work on women in China. This chapter is a direct result of who and what I am: a white, feminist, American, woman graduate student, immersed in a tangle of exploitative discourses, studying female sexuality in China—and discovering more exploitative discourses in the process. My anxiety over the future of reproductive freedom in the United States, my readings on the current situation of women in the People's Republic of China, and my dissertation research on eugenics, reproduction, and sexuality have contributed in equal parts to the formation of these thoughts.

The most helpful theoretical construction in Rich's work is her recognition of the dual meanings encompassed in the word "motherhood." Motherhood is the potential relationship women have to reproduction and to their children. In this way, motherhood may represent a source of female power and authority. Motherhood is also an institution, a human invention. "Motherhood—unmentioned in the histories of conquest and serfdom, wars and treaties, exploration and imperialism—has a history, it has an ideology, it is more fundamental than tribalism or nationalism" (Rich 1976, 34). Through creating the institution of motherhood, patriarchal culture seeks to confine and limit women by defining their role in reproduction and their role in society. This chapter will explore the ways in which the Chinese nation-state has shaped the institution of motherhood in order to limit its potentialities.

Within the last twenty years, scholarship on reproduction in the People's Republic of China has revolved around the controversial one-child family policy, initiated in 1978–79. This scholarship has ranged from praise for effective population control to accusations of extreme abuses of human rights, including women forced into abortions and sterilization procedures, female infanticide, selective abortion of female fetuses, and physical abuse of women who give birth to daughters.[1] I am not going to engage in a full-fledged investigation of the policy in this limited space. Instead, I will look at some of the ways in which the one-child family policy fits into the context of patriarchal control of women's bodies and the institution of motherhood. To do so, I will first place PRC policies within the framework of early twentieth-century Chinese theories of reproduction, motherhood, and eugenics. The one-child family policy, while representing the pinnacle of political power over reproduction, is merely one link in a long chain of patriarchal control over motherhood.

Arguably, throughout history Chinese women have never had control of their own reproduction. In premodern times, women's childbearing was strictly circumscribed by the power of the family and the (always male) head of the household. Beginning in the late 1800s, this locus of power over reproduction shifted away from the family toward the Chinese state. Rhetoric both before and after the 1949 founding of the People's Republic of China addressed reproductive issues in nationalistic language. This nationalistic rhetoric made formerly private spaces (the womb, the household, and the temporal space of childhood) into public spaces, where the interests of the nation-state are preeminent.[2] The consonant blurring of the public/private boundary resolidified patriarchal control over motherhood. In other words, even though twentieth-century China has seen much discussion of women's rights and the equality of the sexes, the basic fact of patriarchal control over reproduction has not changed. The location of that patriarchal power has merely shifted from the family to the nation-state, from the male head of the household to the male head of the Chinese Communist Party (CCP). The Chinese nation-state has used the rhetoric and ideology of nationalism to appropriate the ideological power of motherhood.

SAVING THE CHINESE NATION:
MOTHERHOOD IN THE 1920s AND 1930s

During the Republican decades of the 1920s and 1930s, intellectuals of all political persuasions were focused on the need to reform China, to modernize society, and to improve the Chinese people so as to compete with Western nations. The transformative power of Western science was embraced with fervent faith, resulting in a widespread "scientism" (Kwok 1965). Among other scientific notions, evolutionary theory—specifically, a belief in linear evolution progressing through a clear hierarchy of stages—played a crucial role in Republican era ideas of sex, race, nation, and reproduction (Dikötter 1992, 99–102). Spencerian ideas of group evolution influenced the development of eugenic theories that dominated discussions of reproduction. Racial evolution was conceptualized as a crucial element of national strengthening.[3] Discussions of eugenics (in Chinese, *youshengxue*, literally "the study of superior births") included many texts on fetal education *(taijiao)*, a traditional concept that was newly clothed in biological and evolutionary terms.

The concept of fetal education that was popular during the 1920s and 1930s is very different from the current Western notion of prenatal education. In addition to encompassing ideas of proper nutrition and health for the pregnant woman and fetus, fetal education also includes the idea that the mind, body, and spirit of the fetus can be influenced and molded by the outside world while it is still in the womb. Articles on hygiene and fetal education warn pregnant women against feeling extreme emotions, watching movies, reading "popular" books, eating spicy foods, and engaging in "debauched" sexual activity.[4] In other words, pregnant women were viewed as vessels whose main purpose was the proper cultivation of the fetus. In traditional China, women who cared for their unborn children were praised as "virtuous wives, good mothers." In the Republican decades, the rationale for fetal education was stripped of this familial context and explained in terms of "saving the nation" (jiuguo).

Texts in popular journals like The Ladies' Journal claimed that fetal education "has an important significance for the evolution of the human race" (Zhu 13). The hygiene of pregnant women and their efforts of fetal education were closely linked to "the preservation of the race" and "the strengthening of the people's health" (Yun 257). After pregnancy ends with the birth of a eugenically desirable child, the duties of motherhood are described with the same nationalistic rhetoric. Children are configured as a national resource that needs to be carefully trained and preserved for the good of the nation-state. One metaphor commonly used equates children with "blank paper" (baizhi), saying: "If you write with black ink, they turn black; if you write with red ink, they turn red" ("Hopes for children's year" 1). While the caregiver, in particular the mother, is granted the responsibility of writing on the paper, texts assert the right of the nation-state to mandate what type of ink should be used, in order to create the final, ideal citizen. This connection between the household and the country is semantically exemplified by the term guojia, used to translate the idea of the modern nation and literally meaning "nation-family."

Such views of pregnancy and motherhood exert a paternalistic control over women's reproductive capacities. Regardless of the gender of their authors, 1920s and 1930s texts on pregnancy and motherhood largely act for the male state, advising the female citizen how to act, how to feel, how to reproduce, and how to rear children. Using the language of race and nation, women's wombs are reconfigured as a space that must only be used for the public good. The texts discussed above would largely be classified as socially conservative, supportive of a strictly nationalistic view of modernism and critical of the decadent cosmopolitanism visible in some other cultural forms like movies, pictorial magazines, and experimental fiction. Political discourse of the Republican decades, including rhetoric of the early CCP, also identifies reproduction and motherhood as concerns of the nation-state.

One interesting rhetorical example of this equation of motherhood and nation is the use of the term tongbao, literally "same-womb," as a political form of address indicating solidarity. The traditional meaning of the term tongbao is "brother," specifically referring to brothers born of the same woman. By the first decades of the twentieth century, the term picks up the additional meaning of "person from the same nation" and was often used to open political pamphlets.[5] This political meaning—while gender neutral at first appearance—has the deeper, gendered significance of rhetorically linking the nation with the womb. *Tongbao* is both "brother from the same womb" and "person from the same nation." The nation thus becomes the mother, the womb, which produces the people. The notion of people (or citizenry) also becomes gendered as male, because of the overlying male connotations of the word *tongbao*, "brother." This semantic development is representative of the general slippage between family and nation, woman and country, where the Chinese nation becomes the producer of the people and the power of motherhood is appropriated by the state.

OF PARTY-STATE BORN: SOLIDIFYING CONTROL IN THE PEOPLE'S REPUBLIC OF CHINA

Keeping this historical context in mind, I will now turn to look at the institution of motherhood in the People's Republic of China. One of the key rhetorical planks of the People's Republic of China has been the establishment of equality between the sexes, illustrated in Mao Zedong's popular slogan "women hold up half the sky." Harriet Evans, in her provocative work *Women and Sexuality in China: Female Sexuality and Gender Since 1949*, looks at trends in thinking about female sexuality and reproduction. Evans links rhetoric of the 1950s and 1980s and shows how both time periods emphasized women's physical, reproductive functions, thus essentializing women and locking them within the reproductive body (Evans 1997). As clear from my earlier discussion, this use of science and physiology to rationalize a system of hierarchical gender relationships is not new to the People's Republic of China, but is a continuation of the pre-1949 discourse of evolution, biology, and eugenics. In contrast, during the decade of the Cultural Revolution (1966–1976), gender differences were masked by a Party policy that encouraged the androgynous ideal of the revolutionary worker. Regardless of shifts in rhetoric that essentialized or masked gender differences, PRC policy in all time periods clearly links the production of children to nationalistic goals and appropriates the power of motherhood for the state. I will first discuss the period of the Cultural Revolution, then examine the 1980s and the one-child policy.

The decade of the Cultural Revolution encompassed an extremely unified and widespread propaganda campaign. One of the most visible (and visual) forms of propaganda was posters—bright posters of every size, shape, and color, plastered on walls in streets, in classrooms, and in homes, published in huge numbers, and distributed to both urban and rural areas. On a superficial level, women in these posters are depicted as model workers and revolutionaries, supporting the Party line that declared women and men were equal.[6]

Their clothes, comportment, and occupations visually accord with Party policy, which tried to erase gender differences and disrupt traditional images of women. Although terms like socialist androgyny have been used to describe the depiction of women during the Cultural Revolution, it is important to note that this androgynous model is actually a *male* model. An androgynous appearance meant male dress, a short haircut, and dark colors.

How do these representations deal with issues of reproduction and motherhood? Most Cultural Revolution posters depict women engaged in various revolutionary activities, for instance, joining their male comrades in agricultural work, military drill, and even technical work on high-in-the-sky electrical power lines (Evans 1999). One subset of posters that directly addresses issues of motherhood are posters that promote birth control. One such poster "Practice birth control for the Revolution"[7] shows a vibrantly healthy woman holding a medical manual and a bottle of pills. Behind her, smaller pictures depict women studying Mao's thought, performing scientific experiments, and participating in revolutionary performance art. Among these other "red" activities are two scenes illustrating proper motherhood. In one, a woman and her small daughter engage in calisthenics. In the other, a woman is teaching her daughter about history—presumably about the history of the Revolution—in front of what appears to be a museum exhibit.

Three things are immediately apparent in an examination of this poster. First, as Evans and Donald note, the position of the medical manual in this poster echoes the ubiquitous presence of Mao's "little red book" in other posters. Hence, "the everyday concerns of reproductive health and fertility control are linked with a broader project of political authority, present in the title as well as the symbolic place of the manual" (1999a, 11). In other words, the poster contains visual and textual markers indicating that reproduction is a political issue. The (female) viewer receives the message that birth control and motherhood are issues of national importance.

Second, the fact that both of the children on the poster are girls is not accidental. This poster was published during the "later, sparser, fewer" *(wan xi shao)* birth control campaign, which foreshadowed the one-child policy of 1978–1979. Part of this campaign—and indeed a crucial point of the later one-child policy—was to work against the traditional bias toward male children and increase the desirability of daughters. Because of this aim, much propaganda about the one-child policy also centers on the figures of a mother and daughter.

Third, the smaller pictures in the background clearly indicate that motherhood is one more form of revolutionary work, like the study of Mao's thought. The depictions of mother and child teach the poster's viewer that the proper performance of motherhood must center around inculcating a revolutionary spirit in the next generation. Mother and daughter show their loyalty to the nation by exercising their minds and their bodies, following the popular philosophy that strong people make a strong nation.[8] The Party-state thus sets itself in a supervisory mode, positing itself as the arbiter of good parenting. Women give birth to children, but the Party-state tells them how and when, and how to rear them.

The *potential* power of the mother-child bond is thus overshadowed by the *institution* of motherhood, which emphasizes the relationship between the Party-state and the future revolutionary citizen. This proprietary move is clearly visible in other posters that depict children. Stephanie Donald has shown that children in propaganda posters are most often depicted without a parental figure (1999). The space left by the parent's absence is filled by the presence of nationalistic content. The state thus replaces the parent on a crucial visual level. As Donald concludes, "Posters of the 1960s and 1970s are organized around a notion of the revolutionary family, and the logical progress in the quotation, from child to family to state, is replaced by an elision of family and Party, and of Party and state" (1999, 97). Just as in the earlier use of *tongbao* to indicate political solidarity, the use of these images posits the nation as the true family of its people. The Party-state steps in as the main producer of citizens, usurping the power of motherhood. In lieu of women reproducing children, the state produces citizens.

The epitome of state-controlled reproduction occurs under the one-child policy, first implemented in 1978–1979. The original codification of the policy mandated that all couples should produce only one child, regardless of the child's sex. Following an initial period of strict enforcement, beginning in the late 1980s the policy has seen an increase in exceptions that allow for a second birth. Currently, these exceptions allow the majority of rural families to have two children (Milwertz 57–58). Use of birth control is supervised at the local level by birth control workers assigned to each work unit and a sanctioned number of official "birth permits" are distributed each year. Birth control workers keep records of women's contraceptive methods and menstrual cycles.

While enforcement of the policy has varied over time and across regions, codification of the policy clearly establishes the right of the state to control the production of children. Wasserstrom points out that the one-child family policy is an intensification of earlier PRC birth control programs, rather than a marked departure from these programs.[9] He points to consistent strategies that link family planning to other health care issues and that use peer group pressure to help enforce population policy (1984, 351). In the same way, the one-child family policy is an intensification of earlier twentieth-century efforts to appropriate the institution of motherhood and replace the family with the Party-state.

The one-child family policy has both physical and social consequences for women. Some measurable consequences that drew international attention during the 1980s include an increase in female infanticide, a higher mortality rate for girl babies, and physical abuse of women who give birth to daughters.[10] The policy has also resulted in changes in contraceptive practices, as the majority of Chinese women are fitted with an IUD after their first child is born (Milwertz 106–110).[11]

Changes in the social role of motherhood are not as easily defined. Some scholars have tried to find possible advantages of the one-child family policy for women that might compensate for the strengthening of patriarchal control over reproduction. These works have looked at whether or not the policy has resulted in an expansion of the roles open to women, accompanied by a move away from traditional stereotypes of the "virtuous wife, good mother."[12] However, such studies have concluded that a decrease in the size of the family has been accompanied neither by a lessening of women's domestic responsibilities, nor by a decrease in the burdens of motherhood. The results of a survey conducted in the early 1990s concludes that there is no obvious correlation between being a one-child mother and spending less time on domestic work (Milwertz 162). Instead, many women are doubly burdened by responsibilities at home and at the workplace, resulting in an overload "second shift" situation.[13]

In addition, Jean Robinson has shown that having a single child actually *increases* the responsibility felt by mothers to ensure the child's health, happiness, education, and future success (1985, 54–55). Instead of being freed from the duties associated with a household full of children, women are increasingly held responsible for rearing a single, perfect child. Croll's work on women's self-identity concludes that women still face tremendous pressure to marry, to become mothers, and to produce a perfect child (1995, 158–171).[14] Generally speaking, it is the mother (not the father) who is burdened with the responsibility of the child's welfare, and maternal care is seen as the foundation of the child's success.[15] In Rich's words, "The physical and psychic weight of responsibility on the woman with children is by far the heaviest of social burdens" (1976, 52).

It is clear from these studies that the usurpation of reproductive control by the Party-state has not resulted in a positive loosening of social expectations for women. Instead, the appropriation of women's rights by the state has been accompanied by an *increase* in pressure on women. Women are burdened with the expectations of motherhood, but are unable to control their own reproduction, since the Party-state regulates the timing and number of births. Government economic policies have not recognized reproduction as a legitimate from of production (Robinson). Therefore, women are expected to participate fully in the workplace, and yet still provide the perfect home and the perfect child.

In the 1980s and 1990s, under policies of economic reform that encourage families to participate in capitalist ventures, a successful child is one who is educated, driven to achieve, and able to provide future economic security for the family. This picture of the perfect child is different than the perfect "red" child of the Party-state during the Cultural Revolution. Yet the policy that limits family size clearly posits children as future citizens and reproduction as a national concern. The tug of war between the patriarchal family and the patriarchal Party-state thus continues, to the detriment of women and mothers.

THE PUBLIC, THE PRIVATE, AND THE PATRIARCHY

As I mentioned when discussing early twentieth-century China, the concepts of private and public can be used as a keyhole through which to approach these issues of motherhood and reproductive politics. The idea of the private-public divide is crucial to Adrienne Rich's analysis of motherhood. Rich states:

> This institution [of motherhood] has been a keystone of the most diverse social and political systems. It has withheld over one-half the human species from the decisions affecting their lives; it exonerates men from fatherhood in any authentic sense; it creates the dangerous schism between "private" and "public" life; it calcifies human choices and potentialities. In the most fundamental and bewildering of contradictions, it has alienated women from our bodies by incarcerating us in them. (1976, 13)

Rich theorizes that the oppressive institution of motherhood is inextricably linked to definitions of the private and the public, the inner domestic sphere *(nei)* and the outer world *(wai)*.[16] The institution of motherhood constructs a domestic realm that physically and metaphorically confines women, isolating them from the fellowship of other people, from participation in society at large, and from recognition in public discourse.

Rich rightly points out the dangers in such a strict division of private and public, motherhood, and the "outer" realm. A rigid distinction between the public and the private is often used by the ideology of male supremacy as a means to exclude important matters from political debate. This type of exclusion almost always works to the advantage of dominant groups and individuals.[17] This model aptly describes the situation in traditional China, where women were under the supervision of the male head of the household and were sometimes even physically unable to leave the home.[18]

The feminist call that "the personal is political" is in large part a call to interrogate matters of the "private" realm. Making the personal into the political is an effort to direct public attention to matters of gender inequity, which are hidden by the public-private dichotomy, such as domestic violence and marital rape. However, the act of making matters "public" in and of itself is not always a path to empowerment (Benhabib 1993). In a socialist country, often the act of making "private" matters "public" means increasing state domination of the domestic sphere.[19] The Chinese case thus illustrates both the dangers of a strict public-private divide and the dangers inherent in a complete conflation of private and public, individual and Party-state. Both of these theoretical extremes reinforce patriarchal control over reproduction and undermine motherhood as a site of female power.

How then does this danger of conflating the two realms relate to Rich's reminder of the "dangerous schism between 'private' and 'public' life"? Rich's discussion of the false boundaries between "inner" and "outer" is a beginning step to recognizing the patriarchal nature of such dichotomies. Rich observes: "The dominant male culture, in separating man as knower from both woman and from nature as the objects of knowledge, evolved certain intellectual polarities which still have the power to blind our imaginations" (1976, 62). Rich proceeds to explode one of these false polarities. She breaks down the boundary between inner and outer, showing how the female embodied experiences of sexuality and reproduction contradict with the idea of an inner-outer divide. For women, the realms of the inner and the outer are "continuous, not polar" (1976, 64).

In the same way, the split between public and private is false and destructive to female existence. If patriarchy defines and controls both the public and the private, then the dichotomy is meaningless. If both realms are under patriarchal supervision, the potential of motherhood in either realm is crushed under an institutional burden. The call to make the personal political is meaningless if public dialogue is shaped by patriarchal values. When motherhood is locked into the private domain, women are isolated in the home, their talents and labor unrecognized. In the process of making motherhood public, however, individual women are subordinated to the needs of society, or the nation. The case of Chinese mothers reveals that the distinction between private and public is negligible in a patriarchal culture.

What we need is to explode the categories. Or to wrest control of the definitions from patriarchal culture. Instead of echoing the schisms of private and public, personal and political, we must find some way to express the fact that these divisions are meaningless to our actual experience as women, as people. To our multiple *lived* and *embodied* experiences. Perhaps then we can loosen the hold of the motherhood-as-institution and realize the potential of motherhood. And this power of motherhood would not lie in *power over others*, but in *the power of the self*, to live with wisdom, generosity, integrity, and strength.

NOTES

1. The most balanced accounts that deal with the one-child family policy include those of Elisabeth Croll (1983 and 1995), Delia Davin (1987), Cecilia Nathansen Milwertz (1997), and Jeffrey Wasserstrom (1984). Croll's latest work on the self-identity of

Chinese women aptly emphasizes the specific experiences of living with Chinese political rhetoric. Davin addresses the struggle for control between the state and the patriarchal family that is illustrated by PRC reproductive policies. Milwertz's work on urban women examines the cultural equation of care, concern, and control in China and looks at the cultural differences in the idea of what is "voluntary." Wasserstrom's article looks at the contradictions between the stated goals of the one-child family policy and the Deng era reformist economic policies of the 1980s, which act to undercut the one-child goal.

2. My use of "public" and "private" loosely accords with the work of Nancy Fraser (1990). "Public" is generally defined as accessible by all, for the common good of all, related to the state, and/or of concern to everyone. "Private"—in addition to meaning the opposite of these definitions—also designates things related to private property and "pertaining to intimate, domestic or personal life, including sexual life" (70–71). In the Chinese case, I must emphasize that the formerly private spaces of the womb and the household were private in the sense that they were areas of familial concern, as opposed to areas where the individual woman had full control.

3. Although Chinese notions of racial evolution were based on Spencerian ideas of group evolution, there are some similarities between this drive to improve the Chinese race and the pre-1933 racial hygiene movement in Germany, which was based on social Darwinism. For instance, both campaigns focused on instilling a sense of reproductive duty in its citizens, by calling on the need to safeguard the collective health of the nation (Dikötter 1998; Weiss 1987).

4. The best examples of these types of warnings can be found in Fan 1927, He 1915, Yun 1937, and Zhu 1931. For more information about hygienic texts and fetal education in particular, see my dissertation, "Making Female Sexuality in Republican China: Women's Bodies in the Discourses of Hygiene, Literature, and Education," chapters 1–4, 2001.

5. For one example, see Wasserstrom 1991, illustrations following page 124. Wasserstrom also notes that other familial and gendered images show up in many pamphlets from the political movements of 4 May 1919 and 30 May 1925 (personal communication, 9 May 2000).

6. Harriet Evans (1999) has shown that this superficial reading misses key visual and textual clues within the posters that negate the supposed equality of women and privilege the male position.

7. "Practice birth control for the Revolution" (Wei geming shixian jihua shengyu) was printed in 1974 and is labelled H8 in the University of Westminster Collection, on exhibit at Indiana University September through October 1999. A black and white reproduction of the poster appears in Evans and Donald (1999b), 12.

8. For more information on the link between physical culture and nationalism in twentieth-century China, see Brownell 1995, Morris 1998, and Stevens 2001. Susan Brownell notes, "Physical education as a way of linking individual bodies to the welfare of the nation is a historically recent phenomenon and must be viewed as one of the disciplinary techniques that developed with the rise of the nation-state. In China, it developed alongside efforts to turn a dynastic realm into a modern nation-state according to the political ideas of the times" (46).

9. One interesting difference that Wasserstrom mentions occurs in the style of birth control propaganda, with propaganda in the mid-1980s emphasizing the personal and national economic benefits of birth control in lieu of need to prove one's "redness" by following the policy (351).

10. For more information on female infanticide, see Davin, 117–118.

11. Demand for contraceptives and access to abortions was a key issue in the 1950s and 1960s, as women fought for the right to control their reproduction. Ironically, the use of birth control is now mandated by the Party-state and accompanied by a certain level of coercion. See Milwertz, 62–64.

12. Among the works that explore issues of motherhood, the one-child policy, women's economic productivity, and women's self-identity as "virtuous wives, good mothers" are Croll (1983 and 1995), Milwertz, and Robinson.

13. Rita Mae Kelly addresses this issue in the United States and discusses the "role strain" and "role spillover" that occur because of second shift work (1991, especially 78–95). Croll's interviewees also mention this double burden of familial and work responsibility (1995, 171–176). See also Rich on patriarchal socialism and its role in supporting women's double burden (1976, 54–55).

14. For further support of Croll's findings, see Milwertz's account of the cultural assumptions of motherhood among urban one-child mothers (150–182). The results of her surveys and interviews also reveal that the expectations of mothers are strengthened by the one-child policy.

15. This assumption that women are responsible for the birthing and rearing of a proper child is also visible in the—biologically erroneous—belief held by many people that the sex of the child is determined by the mother. See Davin 1987, 117–118, on female infanticide and wife abuse.

16. In traditional China, husbands called their wives *neiren*, "inner people," alluding to their strict segregation in the domestic realm. Women called their husbands *waizi*, "outer ones."

17. See also Fraser 1990, 73; 1992, 609.

18. One commonly told story from traditional China involves a family searching for a wife for their son. In order to discern the virtue of a prospective bride, the matchmaker asked the household's neighbors their opinion of the daughter. When the neighbors did not even know that a girl lived in the household (because she never left the domestic realm), the matchmaker could be assured of the future bride's virtue. In addition to this sheltered feminine ideal, the actual practice of footbinding also greatly reduced women's mobility in traditional China, as the resulting three-inch "golden lotus" feet prevented women from excessive movement.

19. For a chilling look at the politics of reproduction and the dangers inherent in state domination of the domestic sphere, see Gail Kligman's account of Ceausescu's Romania (1998).

WORKS CITED

Benhabib, Seyla. "Feminist Theory and Hannah Arendt's Concept of Public Space." *History of the Human Sciences* 6.2 (1993):97–114.

Brownell, Susan. *Training the Body for China: Sports in the Moral Order of the People's Republic.* Chicago: U of Chicago P, 1995.

Croll, Elisabeth. *Changing Identities of Chinese Women: Rhetoric, Experience and Self-perception in Twentieth-Century China.* London: Hong Kong UP, 1995.

———. *Chinese Women Since Mao.* London: Zed, 1983.

Davin, Delia. "Gender and Population in the People's Republic of China." *Women, State, and Ideology: Studies from Africa and Asia.* Ed. Haleh Afshar. Albany: State U of New York P, 1987:111–129.

Dikötter, Frank. *The Discourse of Race in Modern China.* Stanford: Stanford UP, 1992.

———. *Imperfect Conceptions: Medical Knowledge, Birth Defects, and Eugenics in China.* New York: Columbia UP, 1998.

Donald, Stephanie. "Children as Political Messengers: Art, Childhood, and Continuity." *Picturing Power in the People's Republic of China: Posters of the Cultural Revolution.* Eds. Harriet Evans and Stephanie Donald. Lanham: Rowman and Littlefield, 1999:79–100.

Evans, Harriet. "'Comrade Sisters': Gendered Bodies and Spaces." 63–78.

Evans, Harriet and Stephanie Donald. *Women and Sexuality in China: Female Sexuality and Gender Since 1949.* New York: Continuum, 1997.

———, eds. *Picturing Power in the People's Republic of China: Posters of the Cultural Revolution.* Lanham: Rowan and Littlefield, 1999b.

———. "Introducing Posters of China's Cultural Revolution." Evans and Donald 1–26.

Fan, Xuqin. "The hygiene of pregnancy *(Renshenzhi weisheng).*" *Hygiene Journal (Weishengbao)* 1.13 (1927).

Fraser, Nancy. "Rethinking the Public Sphere: A Contribution to the Critique of Actually Existing Democracy." *Social Text* 25/26 (1990):56–80.

———. "Sex, Lies, and the Public Sphere: Some Reflections on the Confirmation of Clarence Thomas." *Critical Inquiry* 18 (1992):595–612.

He, Xishen. "About the relationship between body, mind, and descendents *(Shenxinyu sixuzhi guanxishuo).*" *Women's Journal (Funü zazhi)* 1.7 (1915).

"Hopes for children's year *(Ertongniande qiwang).*" *Mass Hygiene (Dazhong weisheng)* 1.2 (1935):1–2.

Kelly, Rita Mae. *The Gender Economy: Work, Careers, and Success.* Newbury Park: Sage, 1991.

Kligman, Gail. *The Politics of Duplicity: Controlling Reproduction in Ceausescu's Romania*. Berkeley: U of California P, 1998.

Kwok, D. W. Y. *Scientism in Chinese Thought, 1900–1950*. New Haven: Yale UP, 1965.

Milwertz, Cecilia Nathansen. *Accepting Population Control: Urban Chinese Women and the One-Child Family Policy*. Richmond, Surrey: Curzon, 1997.

Morris, Andres. "Cultivating the National Body: A History of Physical Culture in Republican China." Diss. U of California, San Diego, 1998.

Rich, Adrienne. *Of Woman Born: Motherhood as Experience and Institution*. New York: Norton, 1976.

Robinson, Jean C. "Of Women and Washing Machines: Employment, Housework, and the Reproduction of Motherhood in Socialist China." *China Quarterly* 101 (March 1985):32–57.

Stevens, Sarah E. "Making Female Sexuality in Republican China: Women's Bodies in the Discourses of Hygiene, Literature, and Education." Diss. Indiana U, 2001.

Wasserstrom, Jeffrey. "Resistance to the One-Child Family." *Modern China* 10.3 (July 1984):345–374.

———. *Student Protests in Twentieth-Century China: The View from Shanghai*. Stanford: Stanford UP, 1991.

Weiss, Sheila Francis. "The Race Hygiene Movement in Germany." *Osiris* second series, 3.193–236 (1987).

Yun, Qin. "Hygiene during pregnancy and fetal education *(Renshenzhongde weishengyu taijiao)*." *Far Eastern Miscellany (Dongfang zazhi)* 34.7 (1937):257–260.

Zhu, Wenyin. "Fetal education and eugenics *(Taijiao yu youshengxue)*." *The Ladies' Journal (Funü zazhi)* 17.8 (1931):11–19.

THREE

Murderous Mothers

Adrienne Rich's Of Woman Born and Toni Morrison's Beloved

EMILY JEREMIAH

THE FIGURE OF THE murderous mother is profoundly disquieting. If a culture rests upon the assumption of women's innate passivity and selflessness, it must be unsettled by the assertion that this is not necessarily so. Myths and tales of mothers who kill their children can thus be seen as repositories for anxieties that are perhaps predominantly, but by no means exclusively, masculine. In feminist terms, such narratives are no less unnerving, but they may also be instructive, offering as they do valuable insights into the constraints that have historically been placed on mothers and into the desperation of individual women subjected to those constraints. In addition, as we will see, they raise the complex questions of choice, power, and agency, terms that will be discussed in the course of this chapter.

The notion of mothering as an ambivalent, even hostile undertaking has been a significant focus of recent feminist thinking about maternity. Such thinking owes an important debt to Adrienne Rich's *Of Woman Born*, a groundbreaking[1] fusion of personal reflection on maternal experience and scholarly examination of what Rich terms the "institution" of motherhood, a body of practices and assumptions governing maternity, which Rich views as pernicious. Maternal hostility and violence are emphasized in Rich's account, an aspect of her text that she defends against criticism in a later introduction (1997:26–27, my pagination).[2] According to Rich, mothers are not naturally or exclusively loving, and to perpetuate this view serves no useful feminist aim. As well as lending weight to traditional essentialist assumptions regarding women as docile and affectionate, such a gesture may also serve to obscure or romanticize what Rich perceives as their victimization. In Rich's view, "oppression is not the mother of virtue" (1997, 27, my pagination); it can, instead, bear violence and death.

This chapter is concerned to analyze and develop these important insights, in particular by means of a comparison of Rich with the novelist Toni Morrison. I look first at Rich's conception of maternal ambivalence and violence, and link it to more recent feminist perspectives on the issues. As well as posing a challenge to a key strand of masculinist thought that holds mothers to be naturally and rightly selfless, such perspectives also raise the issues of choice and power, which are crucial as far as feminist conceptions of mothering are concerned. I deploy the ideas raised and anticipated by Rich in this regard to examine Toni Morrison's 1987 novel *Beloved,* and I argue that Morrison's novel both complements and extends Rich's thesis.

In *Of Woman Born,* the institution of motherhood is defined by Rich as violently oppressive, and as giving rise to violent behavior on the part of mothers. The "anger and tenderness" of Rich's own experience of mothering was not sanctioned by popular views of mothers, and she was made to feel monstrous and unnatural (1997, 32). Rich's maternal ambivalence is largely depicted as resulting from the conditions in which her mothering took place; she is concerned with mothering *"as defined and restricted under patriarchy"* (1997, 14, Rich's emphasis). And she suggests that outside of "patriarchy," defined here as a "familial-social, ideological, political system in which men [. . .] determine what part women shall or shall not play," mothering would be quite different, as her evocation of a summery idyll with her children is intended to demonstrate (Rich 1997, 57, 194–195). Rich views the institution of maternity as leading to "the mutilation and manipulation" of the mother-child relationship (1997, 33); while offering up harmonious images of mother and child, it in fact distorts and, in some cases, fatally disrupts the relationships between them.

There is a problem here. Rich's conception of mothering as corrupted by patriarchal constructions of femininity occasionally suggests that there is an authentic type of mothering behavior that lies outside of patriarchy; Rich thus falls into an essentialist trap common in radical feminist thought, which frequently takes refuge in ideas of a fixed female or maternal self. For in attributing maternal ambivalence to the influence of patriarchy, Rich is suggesting that mothering is actually and essentially loving. In addition, to posit a utopian space outside of patriarchy, and thereby suggest a potential untarnished maternal subjectivity, is to ignore the complex psychological interaction betwen subject and ideology that later feminist thought has been able to probe more subtly. Poststructuralist feminism, in particular, has offered nuanced and helpful theoretical models that, crucially, allow for the possibility of change on the part both of social institutions and of individual agents (see Weedon 1987).

However, Rich does offer a complex and subtle interpretation of the phenomenon of infanticide. She writes of the "numberless women" who in the past have killed children they knew they could not rear, identifying as a chief historical reason for infanticide Christianity's demonization of unmarried motherhood (1997, 258 and 259). Rich emphasizes the social, economic, and legal factors that have led to infanticide (1997, 260–262), being concerned to contextualize it. Her treatment of the story of Joanne Michulski, who murdered two of her eight children in 1974, shows this awareness of social and ideological context. The beginning of Rich's account focuses on the newspaper coverage of the murders, that is, on the reaction to and construction of the event (1997, 257). Rich views Michulski as a scapegoat, "the one around whom the darkness of maternity is allowed to swirl," on whom blame can be easily pinned (1997, 276). Her treatment of the case is careful; on the one hand, she presents Michulski as a victim of "the violence of the institution of motherhood," whose love for her children was warped by despair; on the other, she acknowledges that Michulski's problems were not easily explicable or soluble (1997, 262 and 264). She is above all concerned with the issue of choice, with the enforced and constructed nature of motherhood in 1970s America that, in her view, means that women like Michulski are forced into motherhood and then silenced and trapped.

Despite the occasional lapse into a risky kind of essentialism, then, Rich poses an important challenge to traditional ideas regarding maternity as an instinctive and unproblematic affair. Her concern, as we have seen, is to show that mothering is by no means inevitably or wholly loving and harmonious; she mentions other women's revelations of maternal hostility and criticizes the association of women with pacifism (1997, 24 and 16, my pagination).[3] Rich also offers a complex view of mothering as a process involving change and ambivalence, an idea which anticipates more recent poststructuralist views of maternity. She affirms, for example, that motherhood must be "earned," and that the mother is not merely a given, but a changeful subject (1997, 12, 36, 37), thereby lending weight to the recent idea of mothering as something one does, rather that something one is (see Rothman, 1989, 22). Mothering, in Rich's view, is an activity that involves change and contradiction, "anger and tenderness."

Such a view is echoed and supported by later examinations of motherhood. Elisabeth Badinter's historical survey of motherhood also suggests that mothering is shaped by social and political contexts and is not necessarily or unambiguously loving. Badinter, similarly, points to the numerous incidents of infanticide in seventeenth- and eighteenth-century France, to demonstrate that "maternal instinct" is a highly questionable and unstable notion.

Philosopher Sara Ruddick's *Maternal Thinking* also makes the point that "in any given culture, maternal commitment is far more voluntary than people like to believe" (22). And a recent examination of motherhood from a socio-biological perspective confirms the contingent nature of maternal commitment; in animals and in humans, mothers' investment in their offspring is extremely variable and dependent upon numerous factors (Hrdy xv).

These views bear out Rich's insights into mothering as complex and ambivalent, and, crucially, they highlight the constructed and changeable nature of maternity, as an experience and as an idea. This idea is significantly shaped by prevalent ideas of women, as Estela V. Welldon demonstrates. Welldon detects an ideological bias operating in traditional psychoanalytic discourse, which has meant that maternal hostility has been deemed unthinkable and glossed over. Rich herself makes clear that motherhood as an experience and an idea is not static. Her notion of the "institution" of motherhood performs such a gesture. It highlights motherhood as a construct with its own history (and, therefore, with the capacity to change and be changed). In addition, Rich points out the way in which ideology masks its own constructedness (1997, 43), a notion that allows for the possibility of unmasking and unfixing conventional practices, of choosing alternatives.

Choice is an important notion in Rich's account, signifying here the decision making involved in becoming a mother. Rich points out that "most women in history have become mothers without choice," and she spells out the psychological effects of this entrapment: "Motherhood without autonomy, without choice, is one of the quickest roads to a sense of having lost control" (1997, 13 and 264). Infanticide, in her view, is an extreme and terrible manifestation of such a sense. Rich locates the solution to mothers' traditional lack of "autonomy" (here understood as the prerequisite for "choice") in the repossession by women of their bodies, which in Rich's view have been wrested away from them by patriarchy. In particular, she foregrounds the issue of birth control as a vital factor in this proposed reclaiming of female corporeality (1997, 76). Rich's stress on the body is an important and productive one, as recent debates surrounding new reproductive technologies would suggest (see Raymond 1994). At the same time, however, it leads her to a neglect of the complexity of individual psychology and its interdependence with social structures and institutions, as Rich herself acknowledges in her later introduction (1997, 9–10, my pagination). Female corporeality, she admits, can only be liberated and validated if women are granted meaningful social status, and it is only in such a context that "choice" can occur.

And while Rich offers a nuanced view of maternal power, an issue inevitably raised by infanticide, her conclusions on the subject are a little weak. Rich regards mothering as involving both power and powerlessness; the mother is oppressed by society, but has immense power over her child, not least the capacity to nourish or to deny nourishment, to sustain life or to destroy it (1997, 38 and 67). Rich's awareness of the ambiguous power of mothers is echoed in the work of psychoanalysts Dorothy Dinnerstein and Jessica Benjamin, who argue that it is fear of maternal power that is at the root of male oppression of women, an idea that underscores the fearful, unsettling nature of infanticide, which I mentioned earlier. Rich's view of power is not developed, however; her productive ideas concerning the body and, another solution to mothers' oppression proffered here, female community and collective action, are somewhat undermined by her problematic proposal that we need to "destroy" the institution of motherhood (Rich, 1997, 280), rather than, as poststructuralist feminism would argue, subvert it from within by means of discursive challenges. "Power" is understood by Rich as something that is either possessed or denied, and not, as in feminist poststructuralism, as polymorphous and performative.[4] Rich's treatment of infanticide and the issues linked to it is thus both useful and limited. While she fruitfully (and, in her time, originally) reveals motherhood to be a shifting ideological construct and a complex experience, and while she highlights the need for choice in maternity, her conclusions bear refinement.

Morrison's novel *Beloved* does validate Rich's conclusions in several ways. Morrison's protagonist Sethe murders her baby girl out of desperate love, wanting to keep her safe from the horror of slavery. Like Rich, Morrison suggests that maternal love is shaped, or, as here, distorted by the context in which it takes place, and that it has historically been bound up with loss of control and despair. But unlike Rich, who offers a sometimes sweeping view of the "institution" of motherhood, Morrison deals here with a particular type of oppression and its particular effects upon a mother. Specifically, she locates infanticide in the context of the "institution" of slavery, demonstrating its workings upon one mother. As one critic points out, "the slave mother is interpellated first and primarily into the institution of slavery" (Hirsch 95). Morrison's concern here is not with the (white, middle-class) institution of motherhood, but with black maternal experience as constructed by slavery, an "institution" that, in the present of the novel, is coming to an end. Morrison's deployment of historical sources means that the experience of motherhood is implicitly yet significantly historicized.[5]

Morrison's black perspective is of itself challenging. Rich makes fleeting mention of motherhood under slavery (1997, 35, 44, 203), and she is aware of class as a factor in defining mothering (1997, 81–82); she is, however, more concerned to underplay differences between women (1997, 34, 58). As Morrison points out in an essay, "the act of enforcing racelessness [. . .] is itself a racial act" (1993, 46); Rich, then, is open to criticism on the grounds of white color blindness. In this, she is again of her time; throughout the past two decades, feminism has become increasingly aware of its own white, middle-class bias.[6] A powerful corrective to this bias has come from black feminism. By thematizing motherhood under slavery, Morrison contributes to this correction.

Nonetheless, Rich's conception of maternal murder provides a useful way of reading *Beloved*. The novel, in its turn, challenges and extends Rich's notion of a fixed and damaging "institution" that needs to be destroyed for a happier form of motherhood to emerge, by offering a complex and, I would contend, potentially liberating depiction of maternal subjectivity as shifting, relational, and communal. Where Rich occasionally ignores or simplifies the links between psychology, society, and politics, Morrison puts forth compelling suggestions on the issues. My examination of *Beloved* focuses first upon the ways in which Rich's and Morrison's treatments of maternal murder resemble each other, then points out and elucidates how Morrison can be seen to go further than Rich in terms of the strategies of liberation that she offers.

In *Of Woman Born*, Rich had written of the "Great Silence" surrounding motherhood (61). Her concern with infanticide forms a significant part of her uncovering of the taboos with which motherhood is "hedged" (15). In *Beloved*, Morrison is similarly concerned with that which has been hushed up. Central to this novel is absence, not least the absence of Sethe's murdered daughter, now present only as a ghost. This sad, jealous, disruptive presence is, on one level, a symbol of a "Great Silence" that has been violently achieved—the muteness of black slave women and their children. Like Rich, Morrison exposes the gaps and silences in traditional accounts of the world, which are constructs of the powerful. The narrator asserts: "definitions belonged to the definer—not the defined" (1997, 190), a statement reminiscent of Rich's reference to "the makers and sayers of culture, the namers, [. . .] the sons of the mothers" (1977, 11).[7]

Like Rich, Morrison shows how maternal subjectivity and corporeality have been abused, setting infanticide in the context of such abuse. The "tree" of scars on Sethe's back, from the whipping inflicted upon her when she was pregnant, is a visible imprint of slavery. The maternal body under slavery was, as Rich also points out (1997, 35), viewed as a resource, as "property that reproduced itself without cost," as it is expressed in the novel (1997, 228). The theft of Sethe's milk is of great significance in the novel, as her repeated lament "And they took my milk" (1997, 17) suggests. Both Rich and Morrison, then, are concerned with the maternal body as a site of oppression, and both affirm female corporeality in defiance of the violence to which it has been subjected. Sethe is motivated in her escape journey by the desire to nurse Beloved, for example; the biological act of breastfeeding is a provocation to action.

Rich and Morrison are both concerned with how oppression distorts maternal love, which thus emerges as contingent and manipulable, though powerful. In *Beloved*, slavery renders love, particularly maternal love, a risk (23, 45, 92). At one point, it is spelled out: "Unless carefree, motherlove was a killer" (132). In the case of Sethe it leads to a literal killing. Elsewhere, Paul D recalls a "witless coloredwoman" jailed and hanged for stealing ducks that she took for her children (66); the rupture of the mother-child bond brought about by slavery here leads to a punishable insanity. That insanity, that despair, is subject to white interpretation. The murder of Beloved is narrated from the point of view of the schoolteacher and his nephew, that is, from a white, racist perspective (149–150); Morrison shows by means of her narrative technique how black experience is appropriated and constructed by dominant perspectives. And by means of ironic citation, she parodies these perspectives, in a manner reminiscent of Bhaktin (Morrison 1997, 151; Bhaktin 1988, 132). There is a parallel here with Rich, who also focuses on the reaction to infanticide, upon its construction by dominant (male) interpretations, and who also offers an alternative reading, one that concentrates on both the powerlessness and the love of the mother.

Murder signifies rupture, disturbance, but Sethe's act is also one of resistance and love: "And if she thought anything, it was No. No. Nono. Nonono. Simple" (163). Morrison's evocation of despairing love is again reminiscent of Rich, who cites Michulski's view of the murder of her children as a "sacrifice," and describes the suffering that prompted the act as "honorable" (262, 264). In *Beloved*, Sethe's act of murder represents both her attempt to protect her child from slavery and her desire to "outhurt the hurter" (234). According to Sethe, the real abomination is not murder, but "that anybody white could take your whole self for anything that came to mind" (251). Like Rich, then, Morrison is concerned with how individuals are interpellated by institutions in violent and oppressive ways, and with maternal murder as a desperate reaction to this interpellation. Neither Rich nor Morrison are concerned with condemnation or with easy exculpation of the murderous mother; rather, they seek to delineate the background against which her crime takes place and to reveal mothering as an ambivalent and complicated process.

In several ways, then, Morrison's novel resembles Rich's text in its exploration of murderous maternity. But Morrison's novel expands upon a strategy of empowerment touched on but not developed by Rich: collectivity. While Rich makes a powerful case for what might be termed a strategically essentialist (see Spivak 176)[8] view of mothers as an oppressed group who must come together to combat "patriarchy," her arguments are, as I have argued, undermined by her occasional overlooking of important differences between mothers and her somewhat reductive view of the "institution" of motherhood as homogeneous. Morrison, on the other hand, offers in her tale of maternal murder a more nuanced depiction of the mothering subject, one that allows for the notion of a feminist-maternal community founded upon difference and multiplicity, and which, in its complexity and promise, echoes the work of Judith Butler, as we will see.

It would be possible to read the ghost of Beloved and her relationship with Sethe as occupying a "semiotic" realm, in Kristevan terms (1980), that is, as situated in and participating in a repressed, pre-oedipal, prediscursive space.

The sensual, lyrical monologues of Sethe, Beloved, and Denver, the living daughter, are reminiscent of such ideas, recalling, in particular, Irigarayan notions of plenitude and connection between mother and daughter (1981b). The murder of Beloved could be viewed as symbolic of the violent operations of the Law of the Fathers, which serves to rupture the mother-daughter bond. Such a view would, in addition, tie in with Rich's notion of the "Kingdom of the Fathers" (1977, 56) as oppressing mothers.

But such psychoanalytic theories, it has been pointed out, rest on traditional Western European notions of kinship (see Plasa 133), and it is just such notions that Morrison can be seen to challenge, as I will show a little later. In addition, Sethe and Beloved do not exist "outside" of history, memory, and culture. Indeed, Beloved embodies both the collective experience of slaves and the act of recollecting this experience (Barnett 73). As has been pointed out, Morrison engages in a revision of history, revealing accepted accounts of the past to be contingent and partial (Edwards 19). In doing so, she does not reject the necessity of "history," abandoning the category; rather, she opens it up for scrutiny. And while this is "not a story to pass on" (Morrison 1997, 275)—such is its unspeakable horror—it *has* been passed on. Sethe and Beloved are thus implicated in "the symbolic order," to borrow from Lacan.

Like Rich, Morrison examines infanticide as a manifestation both of power and powerlessness. But she also challenges the power-powerlessness dichotomy, going further than Rich's (albeit important) stress on the issues of "choice" and "power," to develop what might be termed a notion of maternal "agency," where agency is defined as "a reiterative or rearticulatory practice, immanent to power, and not a relation of external opposition to power" (Butler 1993, 15). That is to say, Morrison is concerned not to identify slave mothers as a group at the mercy of an oppresive institution, as Rich does with mothers in general, but rather to open up space for a notion of maternal subjectivity as operative within institutions (which are themselves in flux), and as relational and communal, in complicated ways.

In *Beloved*, the relationship between Sethe and her murdered daughter is characterized by connection and separation, nourishment and withdrawal. Beloved's fierce desire for her mother recalls Butler's speculation, prompted by Lacan, that "it may be that we desire most strongly those individuals who reflect in a dense or saturated way the possibilities of multiple and simultaneous substitutions, where a substitution engages a fantasy of recovering a primary object of love lost—and produced—through prohibition" (1993, 99). In this case, the "prohibition" on love is the result not (only) of oedipal constraints, but (also) of slavery. Morrison thus demonstrates the violence of such prohibitions *and* the potentially subversive nature of the desire they produce. While slavery led Sethe to murder her daughter, it cannot remove memory and love. The idea that "nothing ever dies" (36), borne out by the ghostly presence of Beloved, strengthens this notion.

The shifting relationships between Denver, Sethe, and Beloved point to a view of subjectivity as relational, as defined by interaction with others, an idea reminiscent of recent conceptions of maternity (Benjamin; Everingham). Beloved, it has been noted, has to be willed into being by Sethe; her existence depends upon the recognition of others (Boudreau 114). While Rich and Morrison both stress autonomy, the latter's view of it is more complex. Sethe may be her own "best thing," an idea that recalls Rich's search for an identity beyond motherhood (1977, 31), but it takes Paul D to acknowledge that fact (273). This view of subjectivity as defined by others is, however, problematized and complicated by the destructive nature of Sethe's intensely symbiotic relationship with Beloved, who begins to drain her. Paul D's anxious reflection that "this here new Sethe didn't know where the world stopped and she began" (164) implies the need for a kind of autonomous maternal self that exists alongside or within the relationships in which the individual mother is engaged.

Butler, referring to the problematic nature of identity politics, which can tend to enforce rigid identity categories, points out, on the other hand, that "None of us can fully answer to the demand to 'get over yourself.'" (1993, 117), and nor, she adds, should we. Morrison too is concerned with collective identities and strategies, an aspect of the novel that has been convincingly examined by April Lidinsky. Lidinsky argues that Morrison develops here a postmodernist[9] notion of identity as communal, arguing that the figure of Baby Suggs, in particular, is used to call for "a conceptual shift from the totalized to the multiplicitous subject" (192). The support given to Sethe on her escape journey, Denver's increasing contact with the world outside, the community's shared memories of Baby Suggs, and the collective effort to exorcise the ghost lend weight to this reading. In particular, I would argue, we can fruitfully read this postmodernist identity as a feminist one. In the echoes and connections between Baby Suggs, Sethe, Denver, and Beloved, Morrison suggests the existence of an Irigarayan "female genealogy" (Irigaray 1981a; see also Horvitz 60–61). When Denver tells the story of her birth to Beloved, reference is made to Baby Suggs's quilt, which Beloved likes to have near her: "It [the quilt] was [. . .] feeling like hands—the unrested hands of busy women" (78). Here, storytelling, birth, female labor, and creativity are linked to each other and to the ideas of intergenerational female connection and the sharing of memory, key themes of the novel.

But while Morrison may focus upon female experience, insisting upon gender as a key category in shaping lives, she also illustrates the ways in which gender is unstable, open to revision, in particular in the scene in the clearing: "It started that way: laughing children, dancing men, crying women and then it got mixed up. Women stopped crying and danced, men sat down and cried; children danced, women laughed, children cried" (1997, 88). Marianne Hirsch has usefully pointed out how Morrison disrupts traditional Western notions of the patriarchal family in her novel (1994); in this quotation, the roles of men, women, and children merge and cross, to suggest a liberating view of gender roles within family units as open to change, as shifting. Where Rich views the patriarchal family as serving a key role in the oppression of mothers (1977, 60), Morrison is concerned with a revision of the very notion of "family." In her novel, women like Baby Suggs, Ella, and Amy Denver "nurture across biologically and racially constructed borders," and men are shown acting in "maternal" ways (Lidinsky 212). In addition, Morrison challenges the boundaries between public and private by means of her stress on collectivity.

Morrison's novel echoes and supports Rich's *Of Woman Born* in several ways, then, but it also goes beyond it. Morrison thematizes maternal murder in order to raise and explore the questions of maternal subjectivity and agency, offering, as we have seen, complex and compelling insights on the issues. Here it is worth noting again the contingent nature not only of mothering, but also of conceptions of maternity. For example, it is only recently, with the advent of widely available birth control and women's increased financial independence from men, that the (Western) mother can be construed as an agent; as both Rich and Morrison show us, motherhood has, in many cases, spelt insanity and despair. Rich's text, then, must be viewed in context. While there are problems with it, in particular the notion of motherhood as a fixed and monolithic "institution," these problems are both understandable and forgivable, given the novelty of Rich's thesis. Rich's project was one of defiance and assertion; at the time of its gestation, it was important, and even necessary, to affirm women as mothers and to define the forces that constructed and curtailed their experience, even if that meant risking essentialism. As Diana Fuss recommends, we should not, in any case, dismiss essentialism out of hand, but rather consider what motivates its deployment (xi). In addition, Rich's awareness of the constructed nature of maternity tempers aspects of her account that might be considered essentialist. It anticipates a central insight of poststructuralism—the mutability of social structures and of the self—and it allows for the possibility of change, for the continuous fulfillment of Rich's prediction that "thinking itself will be transformed" (1997, 286).

NOTES

1. Before *Of Woman Born* (1976), motherhood had largely been dismissed or sidestepped by second wave feminists (as in de Beauvoir 1997 [1949], Firestone 1979 [1970], Friedan 1992 [1963], and Millett 1977 [1970]).

2. This introduction was written in 1986, for the tenth anniversary edition. It appears without pagination; hence, "my pagination."

3. But compare Sara Ruddick, who defends the notion on the grounds that "there are maternal practices in which ideals of nonviolence actually govern" (183).

4. These terms are taken from Foucault (1990, 11) and Butler (1993, 20).

5. See Rushdy, 142–143 on the sources of the story.

6. Rich herself exemplifies this development (1997, 16–17, my pagination).

7. Compare Morrison's statement: "I am a black writer struggling with and through a language that can powerfully evoke and enforce hidden signs of racial superiority, cultural hegemony, and dismissive 'othering' of people and language" (1993, xii). Compare also Rich, 1979, 35: "the very act of naming has been till now a male prerogative."

8. But see also Butler: "strategies always have meanings that exceed the purposes for which they are intended" (1990:4).

9. A consideration of the term "postmodernism," and its relationship to "poststructuralism," is beyond the scope of my enquiry.

WORKS CITED

Note: Where the first date of publication differs from that of the edition used, the former is given in parentheses at the end of the reference.

Badinter, Elisabeth. *The Myth of Motherhood: A Historical View of the Maternal Instinct.* Trans. Roger DeGaris. London: Souvenir, 1981 (1980).

Bakhtin, Mikhail. "From the Prehistory of Novelistic Discourse." Trans. Caryl Emerson and Michael Holquist. *Modern Criticism and Theory: A Reader.* Ed. David Lodge. London and New York: Longman, 1988:125–156 (1967).

Barnett, Pamela E. "Figurations of Rape and the Supernatural in *Beloved*," Plasa 73–85 (1997).

Beauvoir, Simone de. *The Second Sex.* Trans. H. M. Parshley. London: Penguin, 1997 (1949).

Benjamin, Jessica. *The Bonds of Love: Psychoanalysis, Feminism and the Problem of Domination.* London: Virago, 1990 (1988).

Boudreau, Kristin. "Pain and the Unmaking of Self in Toni Morrison's *Beloved.*" Extract in Plasa 105–115 (1995).

Butler, Judith. *Gender Trouble: Feminism and the Subversion of Identity.* New York and London: Routledge, 1990.

———. *Bodies That Matter: On the Discursive Limits of Sex.* New York and London: Routledge, 1993.

Dinnerstein, Dorothy. *The Mermaid and the Minotaur: Sexual Arrangements and Human Malaise.* New York: Harper Perennial, 1991 (1976).

Edwards, Thomas R. "Ghost Story." Extract in Plasa 19–21 (1987).

Everingham, Christine. *Motherhood and Modernity: An Investigation into the Rational Dimension of Mothering.* Buckingham: Open UP, 1994.

Firestone, Shulamith. *The Dialectic of Sex: The Case for Feminist Revolution*. London: The Women's Press, 1979 (1970).

Foucault, Michel. *The History of Sexuality, Volume One: An Introduction*. Trans. Robert Hurley. London: Penguin, 1990 (1976).

Friedan, Betty. *The Feminine Mystique*. London: Penguin, 1992 (1963).

Fuss, Diana. *Essentially Speaking: Feminism, Nature and Difference*. New York and London: Routledge, 1989.

Hirsch, Marianne. "Maternity and Rememory: Toni Morrison's *Beloved*." *Representations of Motherhood*. Eds. Donna Bassin, Margaret Honey, and Meryle Mahrer Kaplan. New Haven and London: Yale UP, 1994:92–110.

Horvitz, Deborah. "Nameless Ghosts: Possession and Dispossession in *Beloved*." Extract in Plasa 59–66 (1989).

Hrdy, Susan Blaffer. *Mother Nature: Natural Selection and the Female of the Species*. London: Chatto & Windus, 1999.

Irigaray, Luce. *Le corps-à-corps avec la mère*. Montreal: Les éditions de la pleine lune, 1981a.

———. "And the One Doesn't Stir Without the Other." Trans. Hélène Vivienne Wenzel. *Signs* 7, 1 (1981b):60–67 (1979).

Kristeva, Julia. *Desire in Language: A Semiotic Approach to Literature and Art*. Trans. Thomas Gora, Alice Jardine, and Leon S. Roudiez. Ed. Leon S. Roudiez. Oxford: Blackwell, 1980 (1977).

Lidinsky, April. "Prophesying Bodies: Calling for a Politics of Collectivity in Toni Morrison's *Beloved*." *The Discourse of Slavery: Aphra Behn to Toni Morrison*. Eds. Carl Plasa and Betty Ring. New York and London: Routledge, 1994:191–216.

Millett, Kate. *Sexual Politics*. London: Virago, 1977 (1970).

Morrison, Toni. *Playing in the Dark: Whiteness and the Literary Imagination*. London: Picador, 1993 (1992).

———. *Beloved*. London: Vintage, 1997 (1987).

Plasa, Carl, ed. *Toni Morrison: "Beloved." A Reader's Guide to Essential Criticism*. Cambridge: Icon, 2000.

Raymond, Janice G. *Women as Wombs: Reproductive Technologies and the Battle over Women's Freedom*. North Melbourne: Spinifex, 1994 (1993).

Rich, Adrienne. *Of Woman Born: Motherhood as Experience and Institution*. London: Virago, 1997 (1976).

———. "When We Dead Awaken: Writing as Re-Vision." *On Lies, Secrets, and Silence: Selected Prose 1966–1978*. New York and London: Norton, 1979:33–49 (1972).

Rothman, Barbara Katz. *Recreating Motherhood: Ideology and Technology in a Patriarchal Society*. New York and London: Norton, 1989.

Ruddick, Sara. *Maternal Thinking: Toward a Politics of Peace*. Boston: Beacon, 1995 (1989).

Rushdy, Ashraf H. A. "Daughters Signifying History: The Example of Toni Morrison's *Beloved.*" *Toni Morrison: Contemporary Critcal Essays.* Ed. Linden Peach. Houndsmill: Macmillan, 1998:140–153.

Spivak, Gayatri Chakravorty. "Three Women's Texts and a Critique of Imperialism." *The Feminist Reader: Essays in Gender and the Politics of Literary Criticism.* Eds. Catherine Belsey and Jane Moore. Basingstoke: Macmillan, 1989:175–195.

Weedon, Chris. *Feminist Practice and Poststructuralist Theory.* Oxford and Cambridge, MA: Blackwell, 1987.

Welldon, Estela V. *Mother, Madonna, Whore: The Idealization and Denigration of Motherhood.* New York and London: The Guilford Press, 1993 (1988).

PART TWO

Mothering as Experience

Empowerment and Resistance

FOUR

"We Have Mama but No Papa"

Motherhood in Women-Centered Societies

MARIA-BARBARA WATSON-FRANKE

WHEN ADRIENNE RICH decided to write "a book on motherhood because it was a crucial, still relatively unexplored, area for feminist research" (Rich 1976, 15) she opened the door for scholarly discourse on a topic that many felt uncomfortable with and therefore had ignored. Analyzing motherhood under patriarchy and calling for change, she encouraged us "to imagine a world in which [. . . s]exuality, politics, intelligence, power, motherhood, work, community, intimacy will develop new meanings; thinking itself will be transformed. This is where we have to begin" (286).

One way of following Rich's call is to study motherhood in a global context with a focus on women-centered ethnic groups who have developed ideologies on maternity and women's roles that lack the patriarchal concepts that she analyzes. A dramatic example of such societies is provided by the Mosuo from Southwest China, whose women-centered social structure and lifestyle has astonished the patriarchal West. The Russian explorer Peter Goullart who traveled in China during the 1940s describes the Mosuo as "entirely matriarchal. The property passed from mother to daughter. Each woman had several husbands and the children always cried, 'We have mama but no papa'" (49). Anthropologists identify people like the Mosuo as matrilineal, which means that descent is traced in the female line. As a consequence, the mother is the central figure in such a system, and it is she and not the father who determines the child's place in society and her or his citizenship. This scenario is clearly different from the West where men, and especially men in the role of father, are the central figures, which has affected perceptions of and scholarship on motherhood.

In earlier Western feminist discourse motherhood is perceived as the barrier to all those other things women could accomplish if they were not mothers (cf. De Beauvoir). Western feminism, just like Western patriarchy, has been, clearly, uncomfortable with the body, and, especially, the maternal body. Firestone suggested technology as the solution to biological mothering. Women, just like men, should be unburdened by reproduction. It was in this ideological climate that Adrienne Rich brought *Of Woman Born* into the world. The book challenged people to understand the personal and political aspects of motherhood by studying it "as experience and institution." Rich positioned motherhood within the larger Western sociopolitical framework when she closes the book with a call for "the repossession by women of our bodies" (285). Yet, the majority of scholars continued to ignore motherhood as a research topic. In 1978 Chodorow takes up the issue, but focuses on the male-dependent mother in the nuclear Western family, which can serve as an illustration of Rich's claim that "the mother serves the interest of patriarchy" but she ignores Rich's plea for women to take control of their Selves. The patriarchal character of motherhood appears as an unquestioned given. The debates of the 1980s ultimately rediscovered the issue. However, the patriarchal framework remains essentially intact with the mother being idealized (cf. Kristeva) or being portrayed as a powerless figure (cf. Ruddick). The burgeoning feminist literature on the female body of the 1990s seemed to suggest that scholars finally responded to Rich's call to women to reclaim their bodies, but this newly found interest in the body was not necessarily linked to the maternal body and to mothers. As Stivens (1996, 53) notes: "Mothers' bodies (and children's bodies) even seem to be less common than we might expect in writing about the body, which has often concentrated on a narrow understanding of sexuality." The 1990s, however, created a new interest in mother as person and Self, which includes the issue of maternal agency (cf. Bassin et al.; Glenn et al.). This was accompanied by a critique of the Western middle-class framework, which defined the discussion up to this point. Now critical voices called for a multicultural perspective on motherhood (cf. Glenn et al.) and the debate became also, at last, internationalized (e.g., Rausch; Ram and Jolly).

But Rich did not only discuss the mother in patriarchy. She raises the issue of "gynocentric" cultures, which are characterized by a "woman-centered social organization." Rich depicts this situation as a matriarchy of the past (1976, 93; chapter 4) and does not pursue this phenomenon in a contemporary context. While anthropology has perceived matriarchy with good reason as a controversial and historically undocumented stage, societies with woman-centered social organizations, that is, matrilineal societies, have existed and do so to this day as mentioned earlier. Rich (1976, 58–59) makes brief reference to matriliny but follows the standard anthropological position that categorizes these cultures as male-dominant, not acknowledging the gynocentric aspect of these societies. This chapter discusses in how far matrilineal motherhood, which has not been studied systematically at this point, reflects gynocentric features.

THEORETICAL ISSUES

The study of gynocentrism is problematic in a cultural context like Western society, which is opposed to it, as can be demonstrated by looking at such different sources as children's literature or ethnohistorical studies. The seemingly innocent *Tale of Peter Rabbit* by Beatrix Potter shows us a single mother caring for her four young children. However, she is not a single woman but a widow, as we learn in the very beginning of the story when she admonishes her little ones: "Now my dears [. . .] you may go into the fields or down the lane, but don't go into Mr. McGregor's garden: your father had an accident there; he was put in a pie by Mrs. McGregor." The significance of the once present father is upheld even though he has been irresponsible and is ultimately absent. That women should not act or be perceived as agents of their own and others' destiny is dramatically demonstrated through Inge Kleivan's ethnohistorical study of a woman's rebellion against the Danish colonial powers represented by men from both Greenland and Denmark in the late nineteenth century in Western Greenland. In 1874 a young Inuit woman claimed that she had given birth to the Infant Jesus who had given her several messages that "she was to have social and economic advantages equal to those enjoyed by the Danes, and if she did not, the world would come to an end" (221). The women in the community supported her and the authorities became obviously concerned about potential social unrest. They punished the young woman physically and placed various restraining orders on her to restrict her social movements and contacts. The father of the child remains unnamed and unidentified except for the fact that the young woman had stated he was a Dane. But without the presence of the father, the mother had no power. Kleivan concludes that she "must have finally given up her protests and her search for a new identity when she received her punishment for her attempt to go against the male clerical and secular authorities" (236). Her efforts to use her motherhood to initiate social change and doing so by identifying with the Virgin Mary were seen as blasphemy and could not be tolerated by the male authorities who determined the ethnic and gender hierarchies in Western Greenland at the time.

The picture is different when we look at women-centered systems. The fact that women and especially mothers are the structurally central figures in matrilineal societies makes them important players in the motherhood debate.

They are those "active and admired participants in all of culture" mentioned by Rich (1976, 85), though she imagines such roles for women only as a possibility for the ancient past. Today, however, several million people adhere to matrilineal principles. Still, in traditional as well as feminist scholarship, matriliny is at the sidelines. As Stivens (1996, 11) has pointed out, "Anthropology [for example] had problems with matriliny precisely because it concerned social arrangements which called into question the male-female relations expected by western discourse." Stivens refers here to the fact that in matrilineal systems women build strong socioeconomic bonds with their brothers and the cross-sex sibling relationship is, indeed, more important than the marital link. Men as fathers have no, or extremely limited, authority over their children and are instead the male disciplinarians in their sisters' children's lives. As a result of these social dynamics, men are not powerful in their sexual persona as father or husband. Their authority derives instead from their roles as brother and uncle. No doubt, this leads to family dynamics different from the Western stereotype and also to different views of heterosexuality. This, of course, makes matrilineal mothers a dramatic subject in western scholarship, and especially so when we follow Glenn's (5) suggestion "to [attend] to the variation [of mothering] rather than searching for the universal, and to shift what has been on the margins to the center."

It is difficult to assess the number of people who live in matrilineal systems today. In the contemporary world they constitute ethnic minorities and subgroups in their respective nation states. The Akan in Ghana and the Minangkabau in Indonesia represent probably the largest matrilineal systems in the modern world. Scholars have presented different views with regard to their survival. Gough represents the mainstream view that increasing globalization will lead to disintegration of matrilineal systems with the nuclear family becoming their basic social unit just like in Western society. A different view is offered by Douglas, who sees the flexibility of matrilineal systems as an adaptive strategy that can prove to be successful in an expanding market economy. In this discussion I draw on examples from matrilineal groups in North and South America, Africa, Asia, and Oceania.

MOTHERS AS BUILDERS OF GENERATIONS

The matrilineal custom to trace descent through the mother has a myriad of consequences for peoples' interaction and outlook on life that go far beyond the traditional Western notion that the matrilineal mother is just a womb that connects generations in the biological and technical sense. As Stoeltje (1995, 18) explains with respect to the Akan of Ghana: "The position of mother takes on a value beyond its biological function and becomes an important symbol because of its power to define persons, to situate a person within the

larger system, and also because of the knowledge associated with that power."
"The significance of the mother in a person's life is thus not only based on the
emotional bond but also on the impact the mother has on the child's public
identity. This interplay of identity and political system prepares the basis for
the role of mother" (Stoeltje 1997, 377, translated from the German original).
Burke (256) makes the same point with respect to the Kongo of Zaire when
she states that while "a woman is primarily valued as a life-bearer [. . .] this
valuation is not limited to mere biological production" and she points out the
importance of the concept of social maternity among the Kongo. The maternal power of defining a person is expressed, for example, in the mother's
authority to name the children and to bestow citizenship, social rank, and economic status upon them. Thus the children find their publicly acknowledged
place in the world through the mother and they will be reminded of it if necessary even in adulthood as in the case of a young Navaho man in the American Southwest, whose mother scolded him for being stingy, a great wrong-
doing in this culture: "Your name goes by my name. Everybody knows me, and
everybody knows you through me. Everybody calls you Son of Abaa. I think
you have got such a nice name. When you have such a nice name why do you
want to be stingy? You mustn't be stingy. They will call you stingy after a
while, instead of calling you by my name. You will make yourself a name if you
don't look out" (Dyk and Dyk 16).

Now let us compare this account with the following case, which portrays
a son's close identification with his mother as unacceptable closeness. When
former Black Panther Leader Elmer "Geronimo" Pratt, upon leaving prison
after twenty-five years of wrongful incarceration, announced his immediate
plans, the *Los Angeles Times* (11 June 1997) reported this event as follows: "He
told [his supporters that he planned] to . . . visit his 94–year-old mother. 'I need
to see . . . my mother,' said the decorated Vietnam War veteran. 'I am a mama's
boy.'" The reporter offers a catchy phrase by combining images that are perceived to be incongruent in the patriarchal West: "War Hero" and "Mama's
Boy." In a matrilineal society such a statement would certainly not be news but
expected behavior, as Fortes (265), for example, explained with regard to the
Ashanti from West Africa: "For a man, his mother is his most trusted confi-
dant, especially in intimate personal matters." The same sentiment is expressed
by Pedro Gonzalez, an eighty-year-old Guajiro from South America: "The
man who listens to his mother and obeys her is going to be all right, just
because he obeyed her" (Watson 1970, 46). In matrilineal systems men's matu-
rity is obviously not measured by their ability to distance themselves from
mother and their natal home. As Roscoe (134) observes with respect to the
Zuni in the Southwest of the United States, with adulthood comes "a realign-
ment of the original mother-child relationship rather than its repudiation."

But the strength of mothers as structure-building agents goes beyond the
bond with their children. Matrilineal people's view of women as the builders

of generational networks imbues them with a sense of history that is lacking in the ahistorical essentialist Western perspective on mothers. As a Minangkabau man in Indonesia put it (quoted in Sanday, 144): "Women and men are the same, but women are more respected and given more privileges [. . .] because people think that women determine the continuation of the generations. Whether the next generation is bad or good depends on women. Women's role will determine future generations, because children stay most of the time with their mother and mothers are responsible for teaching children." Among the Ashanti the queenmothers, who were members of the royal lineage, were seen as "[contributing] significantly to Akan identity" (Stoeltje 1995, 15), a belief expressed in the proverb: "It is the queenmother who builds the nation" (19). Rich (1976, 45) speaks to this important and all-encompassing role of mothers when she states "[The mother] exemplifies in one person religion, social conscience, and nationalism. Institutional motherhood revives and renews all other institutions." She places this observation in the Western context and thus comes to the conclusion that "the mother [certainly] serves the interest of patriarchy." Yet, as the matrilineal examples mentioned above illustrate, Rich's idea of women as system-renewing forces applies also to matrilineal societies, only that here it reaches its full meaning in a positive and constructive sense as it is expressed in the expectations and the confidence matrilineal systems demonstrate with regard to women.

Even colonial observers came to appreciate this aspect of matrilineal thinking. Commenting on the strong economic role of matrilineal women in Malaysia, Moubray (218), a former colonial official praises the importance of women as builders of the future: "Men exert an effect only on the immediate future. Women through their children affect the distant future. Should we by analogy with those well-beloved of economic theorists, who discount present in favour of future gains and pleasures, discount progress in the immediate future as against progress in the distant future, we would concentrate our attention on women and girls rather than on boys and men." Matrilineal systems undoubtedly do pay close attention to girls and women. Thus, it is not surprising and actually widely documented in the literature that female births are usually highly desirable. Hrdy (343) reports in a worldwide context that "outright daughter preference is unusual," but interestingly enough, her example of daughter-preference comes from a matrilineal group, the Tonga from Zaire. "Daughters," Hrdy writes, "are essential for perpetuating the matrilineage." Zhang Weiguo, doing research among the Mosuo writes: "In 1986 I found out that Mosuo people prefer girls." In Africa the same sentiment has been widely reported: "Among matrilineal groups such as the Chewa and Yao, a girl is especially welcome, not only does she bring a new source of labor to female relatives but she will continue the fertility of her lineage through the birth of future children. A mother with several daughters is considered blessed" (Davison 42). The importance of female offspring, expressed through the desirability of female births reflects the importance of women as builders of the social structure and with that comes pressure, if not anxiety, to produce daughters. Mosuo women, for example, worried and feared social rejection when they had not yet borne a daughter even when they were already mothers of sons (Knoedel 196–197). And to this day a woman and her family will rejoice when finally a long-awaited girl is borne (Lakshmanan 2000). The Trobrianders are equally concerned with female offspring. While they believe that a man's death weakens the kingroup, they feel "even greater fear . . . when girls or women of child-bearing age die, for then the villagers believe that someone desires the destruction of the entire matrilineage itself. Without women to bear children, the matrilineage dies out" (Weiner 36). Among the Tonga mentioned previously, "the mother comes in for criticism from kin" in case of "too many sons" (Hrdy 343). These examples suggest that matrilineal people are most acutely aware of women's finite capacity to create and sustain life, and perhaps this is one reason that makes women such important citizens in these systems, because, unlike in patrilineal groups here the women from within the system are responsible for the group's survival. They cannot easily be replaced by outsiders. If this becomes necessary for lack of female births, the Mosuo, for example, solve the problem through adoption or even through an outsider woman joining the group through marriage, the latter being, however, in Mosuo opinion a less desirable option (Knoedel 122–123).

MOTHERS AS PROVIDERS

In matrilineal systems the woman is not dependent on the father of her children nor does she produce goods or children for his kingroup. Women's economic role is usually seen as very important and as closely connected to her mothering. Among the Akan in Ghana to this day a woman's economic role matches that of mothering and is therefore part of her reproductive role: "A woman's gender identity depends on her financial independence as well as her fertility, just as a man's does. A woman without an income is not a real woman [. . .] the foolish [is] the type of woman who depends solely on her husband for sustenance" (Clark 107). As an Akan market woman sees it, working outside the home makes her a better mother and she looks at "intensive trading as a sacrifice made for the children, not a betrayal of them" (Clark 368). These women question "European women's intelligence in sharing common bank accounts with their husbands. 'She would never do such a foolish thing,'" one woman told an anthropologist, instead she was "very careful to keep her finances a secret from her husband because if he knew she had enough money to feed herself and their child, he would not provide this customary support" (Gott 22). And while separate finances are also desired among other West African groups who are not necessarily matrilineal, the descent system and the philosophy accompanying it make obviously a difference as is apparent from Brenzel's (1) comparative study of female decision-making power in Ghana. She observed that "women belonging to matrilineal groups are posited to have greater decision-making power, and consequently more influence over resource allocation for child medical care and food, than women belonging to patrilineal groups." Brenzel comes to the conclusion (153) that "female decision-making power is derived from descent group norms and standards of behavior."

Among the Guajiro from South America, the mother's authority rests not only in her central position in the social structure but also strongly in her economic power. This is especially interesting because the Guajiro practice pastoralism, that is, an economic structure that has been traditionally associated with strong male dominance (Watson-Franke 1987). However, the Guajiro display many women-centered features. The Guajiro mother, for example, can withhold inheritance and gifts in livestock and thus control her children's behavior (Watson 1968a; 1968b). She, not her husband, is responsible for the economic well-being of the household. Within such a setting children learn from early on to acknowledge the significance of maternal actions. Guajiro women are usually highly critical of Venezuelan housewives with a husband as the sole bread winner and are quick to point out that the Guajira of the desert owns her own animals and manages her financial affairs (Watson-Franke and Watson). These examples clearly show that these societies believe that the good mother is the economically independent and resourceful woman and they live by rules that enable women to achieve this role.

Western industrial society by contrast experiences much difficulty with mothers' employment. Countless examples could be cited. An especially compelling case was the decision of an Arkansas Baptist church to close its childcare center "saying working mothers neglect their children, damage their marriages and set a bad example" (*Los Angeles Times* 5 April 1997). Members of the board of the church reminded parents that "God intended for the home to be the center of a mother's world," and that women should be "discreet, chaste, keepers of the home, good and obedient to their own husbands." The instructions suggest that the woman's maternal role is an appendage to her wifely role with the husband as economic leader. Such thinking is directly opposed to matrilineal philosophies. These tensions will be further explored in the following section.

MOTHERS, HETEROSEXUALITY, AND THE "SEXUAL FAMILY"

We must always be cognizant of the fact that women do not mother in a vacuum and not in isolation. Their mothering is informed by their relations to others, including men, within a particular context: "Mothering is constructed through men's and women's actions within specific historical circumstances" (Glenn 3). Traditional Western scholarship has acknowledged this fact as the famous example of Freudian theory demonstrates. But the West has also assumed that women and men can only be efficient agents within the family in their roles as husband and wife. Fineman (3) refers to the resulting family pattern as the "sexual family" because "at its core [is the] sexual tie" between mother and father. It has been this type of family that "has been invested by our culture and society with exclusive legitimacy" and discussions of mother-hood, traditional or feminist, usually use this family model as their defining framework. Different family modes are often referred to as anomalies, deviant in character and not well functioning.

This mindset creates cognitive dissonance when looking at mothering and the family in matriliny. Traditional scholarship has framed matrilineal issues in Western patriarchal terms. According to the Western view of matriliny, women and men are still agents in their maternal and paternal roles, the difference being that the mother's brother plays the paternal role rather than the husband. Accordingly, the mother's brother as the male figure most closely resembling the Western father has received much attention from scholars because the West emphasizes paternal agency. However, this approach ignores the reality that matrilineal family dynamics are not as closely embedded in heterosexuality as is the "sexual family" of the West. This becomes obvious as soon as we analyze the roles of the mother's brother vis-à-vis other family members. Toward his sister's children, as their male disci-plinarian, he displays behavior that resembles very much that of the Western father, but his relationship toward the mother is completely different since he has no sexual tie with her. Therefore, though heterosexuality is a part of matriliny, it does not play the central role it has in the West where, as Rich (1980, 633) puts it, heterosexuality becomes "a beachhead of male dominance" as expressed by men's power "to deny women sexuality, or to force it upon them, to command or exploit their labor to control their produce, and to con-trol or rob them of their children" (cf. 638f.). Rich of course does not discuss heterosexuality in general terms, but in a context of specific power relations, that of patriarchy, which creates male heterosexual authority. The matrilineal reality is clearly different as we have seen and one might actually ask if matri-lineal families are, indeed, heterosexual institutions. The matrilineal context gives support to Whisman's (364) supposition that "heterosexual institu-tions . . . are probably not [universal]." Therefore, it can be argued that moth-erhood in matrilineal systems is not as strongly defined by heterosexuality, if at all, as it is in the "sexual family." Matrilineal women mother in spite of being wives, Western women mother because they are wives. Clark (368) dis-cusses this point with regard to the Akan, where motherhood is, to some extent, in conflict with wifehood. An Akan woman's loyalty to her lineage might win out in times of conflict since "the strength of [women's] lineage position primarily enables them to do without marriage, rather than modify relations within it." Such conflicts of loyalty, however, do not present the problem they would in Western society, because matrilineal mothering is not legitimized by the mother's heterosexual attachment to a male partner but by her affiliation with her own kingroup. While heterosexual contact is necessary for the survival of the matrilineage, it is the birthing and life-sustaining activities of women that are considered central, and men's most important role as family members is to support these female efforts. The sexual potential and power of men has less significance by comparison and therefore cannot be used to gain authority within the conjugal unit.

Considering the wide range of matrilineal systems in the world today, there is, of course, much variation with respect to the argument presented here. Also, with globalization and Western concepts intruding, not all women in matrilineal systems perceive the "sexual family" as an undesirable arrangement. As a sixty-five-year-old Nayar woman told an anthropologist, some women might see the opportunity for sexual manipulation as an advantage: "In a way I think the system today is much better. It is easier to talk with and persuade a husband, rather than a brother. I think most women have some degree of power over men in a situation where they are sexually involved and that is not the case with brothers. There is always a distance and it is impossible to talk with them beyond a point" (Menon 140). Of course, it is this power that patriarchy has denounced in many contexts. And at the same time, patriarchy also fears the marginalization of heterosexuality in matrilineal systems that this Nayar woman alludes to in her statement. The patriarchal "solution" has been to make mothers allies of patriarchy and to deny them autonomy and agency. The matrilineal data in general suggest that manipulation on the basis of sexual factors has little or at least less impact on decision making affecting the family as compared to the West. What is needed is to study the implications of this fact for women, men, and children.

The matrilineal model is relevant to the debate on female-headed families in the West due to its marginalization of heterosexuality. It should be a discussion point in the creation of policies affecting these families. Patriarchy is critical of mothers who "cannot keep a man" and end up divorced and it condemns lesbian mothers who chose a life without a central father figure. The overwhelmingly negative perception of single motherhood in the West is based in the cultural paradigm of mothers being defined by their relationship to the father of their children because it is this definition that upholds the principles of heterosexuality. The important issue here is that the father has the opportunity to exercise his authority in the family, even if he is frequently or permanently absent. Due to such thinking even lesbian families in the West are frequently not free of paternal authority as Slater (100) has pointed out in her discussion of lesbian mothers who "gave birth within the context of an ongoing heterosexual relationship with the children's father." Once the mother leaves the marriage and the man, "homophobia embellishes the father's power," which can have a powerful impact in custody cases. "Even primarily absent biological fathers [. . .] represent an enduring danger to lesbian families" (100) because these fathers represent the "heterosexual alternative" and thus "enjoy a powerful advantage in court." Fumia (91) has argued that "In order to begin to think about alternative family structures, or households headed by mother-lesbians, it is necessary to find an entry point into motherhood outside the North American ideal of womanhood." This chapter introduces such an alternative through families in matrilineal systems. These families, by principle, do include the father, and children usually have in their early life a strong emotional bond to him. But, as we remember, he has no authority over them or over their mother. And in a case like the Mosuo's, the father is actually not even part of the family (cf. Cai Hua). Goullart most likely prompted Mosuo toddlers to cry "We have mama but no papa" because in their world such a statement really does not make any sense, since they are taken care of by women and these women's brothers.

As the foregoing discussion documents, cultures displaying gynocentric features do exist. They are represented in the matrilineal reality, which is based on a woman-centered social organization. Female and male roles as well as gender dynamics vary across these cultures but the matrilineal model in all its variations can provide viable alternatives to the "[hetero]sexual family" and allows us to envision "a wholly different way for women to exist in the world" (Rich 1976, 85).

WORKS CITED

Bassin, Donna, Margaret Honey, and Meryle Mahrer Kaplan, eds. *Representations of Motherhood*. New Haven: Yale UP, 1994.

Beauvoir, Simone de. *Le deuxieme sexe*. Paris: Gallimard, 1949.

Brenzel, Logan Elaine. *Female Decision-Making Power and the Intrahousehold Allocation of Food and Child Medical Care Resources in Ghana*. Diss.; The Johns Hopkins U School of Hygiene and Public Health, 1995. Ann Arbor: UMI.

Burke, Joan F. "These Catholic Sisters Are All Mamas! Celibacy and the Metaphor of Maternity." *Women and Missions: Past and Present*. Eds. Fiona Bowie, Deborah Kirkwood, and Shirley Ardener. Providence: Berg, 1993:251–266.

Cai Hua. *A Society Without Fathers or Husbands: The Na of China*. New York: Zone Books, 2001.

Chodorow, Nancy. *The Reproduction of Mothering: Psychoanalysis and the Sociology of Gender*. Berkeley: U of California P, 1978.

Clark, Gracia. *Onions Are My Husband: Survival and Accumulation by West African Market Women*. Chicago: Chicago UP, 1994.

Davison, Jean. *Gender, Lineage, and Ethnicity in Southern Africa.* Boulder: Westview Press, 1997.

Douglas, Mary. "Is Matriliny Doomed in Africa?" *Man in Africa.* Eds. Mary Douglas and Phyllis Kaberry. London: Ravistock, 1969:121–135.

Dyk, Walter and Ruth Dyk. *Left Handed: A Navajo Autobiography.* New York: Columbia U, 1980.

Fineman, Martha Albertson. *The Neutered Mother, the Sexual Family and Other Twentieth Century Tragedies.* New York: Routledge, 1995.

Firestone, Shulamith. *The Dialectic of Sex: The Case of Feminist Revolution.* New York: William Morrow, 1970.

Fortes, Meyer. "Kinship and Marriage Among the Ashanti." *African Systems of Kinship and Marriage.* Eds. A. R. Radcliffe-Brown and Daryl Forde. London: Oxford UP, 1950:252–284.

Fumia, Doreen. "Marginalized Motherhood and the Mother-Lesbian Subject." *Journal of the Association for Research on Mothering* 1.1 (1999):86–95.

Glenn, Evelyn Nakano. "Social Constructions of Mothering: A Thematic Overview." Glenn et al. 1–29.

Glenn, Evelyn Nakano, Grace Chang, and Linda Rennie Forcey, eds. *Mothering, Ideology, Experience and Agency.* New York: Routledge, 1994.

Gott, Edith Suzanne. *In Celebration of the Female: Dress, Aesthetics, Performance and Identity in Contemporary Asante.* Diss., Department of Folklore, Indiana U, Bloomington, 1994.

Gough, Kathleen. "The Modern Disintegration of Matrilineal Descent Groups." *Matrilineal Kinship.* Eds. David M. Schneider and Kathleen Gough. Berkeley: U of California P, 1961:631–652.

Goullart, Peter. *Forgotten Kingdom.* London: John Murray, 1955.

Hrdy, Sarah Blaffer. *Mother Nature: A History of Mothers, Infants, and Natural Selection.* New York: Pantheon Books, 1999.

Kleivan, Inge. "The Virgin Mary of Tasiussaq: A Case of Feminism." *Arctic Anthropology* 23.1–2 (1986):221–238.

Knoedel, Susanne. *Die matrilinearen Mosuo von Yongning. Eine quellenkritische Auswertung moderner chinesischer Ethnographien.* Muenster, 1995.

Kristeva, Julia. *The Portable Kristeva.* Ed. Kelly Oliver. New York: Columbia UP, 1997.

Lakshmanan, Indira A. R. "Where Women Rule." *The Boston Globe Magazine,* 27 April 2000.

The Los Angeles Times, 11 June 1997.

Menon, Shanti. "Male Authority and Female Autonomy: A Study of the Matrilineal Nayars of Kerala South India." *Gender, Kinship, Power: A Comparative and Interdisciplinary History.* Eds. Mary Jo Maynes, Ann Waltner, Birgitte Soland, and Ulrike Strassner. New York: Routledge, 1996:131–146.

Moubray, George, Alexander, de Chazal de. *Matriarchy in the Malay Peninsula and Neighbouring Countries.* London: Routledge, 1931.

Ram, Kalpana and Margaret Jolly, eds. *Maternities and Modernities: Colonial and Post-colonial Experiences in Asia and the Pacific.* Cambridge: Cambridge UP, 1998.

Rausch, Renate, ed. *Frauen, Sexualitaet und Mutterschaft in der Ersten und Dritten Welt.* Forum Wissenschaft und Studien 22. Marburg: BdWi-Verlag, 1993.

Rich, Adrienne. *Of Woman Born: Motherhood as Experience and Institution.* New York: Norton, 1976.

———. "Compulsory Heterosexuality and Lesbian Existence." *Signs* 5.4 (1980): 631–660.

Roscoe, Will. *The Zuni Man-Woman.* Albuquerque: U of New Mexico P, 1991.

Ruddick, Sarah. *Maternal Thinking: Toward a Politics of Peace.* London: Beacon, 1989.

Sanday, Peggy Reeves. "Androcentric and Matrifocal Gender Representations in Minangkabau Ideology." *Beyond the Second Sex: New Directions in the Anthropology of Gender.* Eds. Peggy Reeves Sanday and Ruth Gallagher Goodenough. Philadelphia: U of Pennsylvania P, 1990:139–168.

Slater, Suzanne. *The Lesbian Family Life Cycle.* New York: The Free Press, 1995.

Stivens, Maila. *Matriliny and Modernity. Sexual Politics and Social Change in Rural Malaysia.* Sydney: Allen and Unwin, 1996.

———. "Modernizing the Malay Mother." Ram and Jolly 50–80.

Stoeltje, Beverly, J. "Asante Queenmothers: A Study in Identity and Continuity." *Gender and Identity in Africa.* Eds. Mechthild Rehaud and Gudrun Indwar-Eue. Muenster: Lit Verlag, 1995:15–32.

———. Spuren weiblicher und maennlicher Macht im Koenigreich der Ashanti in Westafrika." *Sie und Er. Frauenmacht und Maennerherrschaft im Kulturvergleich.* Ed. Gisela Voelger. Cologne: Rautenstrauch-Joest-Museum, 1997:375–380.

Watson, Lawrence C. *Guajiro Personality and Urbanization.* Latin American Studies, 10. Los Angeles: Latin American Studies Center, U of California, 1968a.

———. "The Inheritance of Livestock in Guajiro Society." *Antropologica* 23 (1968b):3–17.

———. 1970. *Self and Ideal in a Guajiro Life History.* Acta Ethnologica et Linguistica, vol. 21, Series Americana 5. Vienna: Stiglmayr, 1970.

Watson-Franke, Maria-Barbara. "Women and Property in Guajiro Society." *Ethnos* 52.1–2 (1987):229–245.

Watson-Franke, Maria-Barbara and Lawrence C. Watson. "Conflicting Images of Women and Female Enculturation among Urban Guajiro." *Journal of Latin American Lore* 12.2 (1986):141–159.

Weiguo, Zhang. Email message, 29 January 1997, Institute of Social Studies, The Hague, The Netherlands.

Weiner, Annette B. *The Trobrianders of Papua New Guinea.* New York: Holt, 1988.

Whisman, Vera. "Heterosexuality." *Lesbian Histories and Cultures: An Encyclopedia.* Ed. Bonnie Zimmerman. New York: Garland, 2000:364–365.

FIVE

Mother as Transformer

Strategic Symbols of
Matrilineage Recuperation in
Princess Pocahontas and the Blue Spots

DANNABANG KUWABONG

IN *OF WOMAN BORN: Motherhood as Experience and Institution,* Adrienne Rich writes that women's "relationship to the past has been problematical" because "in the written records we can barely find ourselves"(84). Confronted with what she aptly terms "this 'Great Silence,'" women have been constrained into choosing between either "anatomizing our oppression, detailing the laws and sanctions ranged against us; [or] . . . searching out those women who broke through the silence, who, though often penalized, misconstrued, [. . .] still embodied strength, daring, self-determination; [. . .] in short, exemplary" (84). Rich proceeds to argue further that this desire for female voice recuperation and reinscription of a matrilineage in a patriarchal world history clearly defines the "search for a tradition of female power," which would be used to validate the past and justify a future in which women's roles are no longer negated by a warped social system afraid of women's potentials (85) and contributions to world civilization.

Ultimately, as Rich advises in "When We Dead Awaken: Writing as Re-Vision" (1982), this can be achieved only through a re-visionary reading of history. Re-visionary reading involves an "act of looking back, of seeing with fresh eyes, of entering an old text from a new critical direction," which for women in general, and for Native women in particular, transcends a casual and causal reinterpretation of their "cultural history," if they want their works to become acts of survival (1996). Through re-vision women writers can unravel the "assumptions in which we are drenched," and enter into a "radical" and "feminist" reappraisal of literature for clues "to how we live, how we have been living, how we have been led to imagine ourselves, how our language has trapped as well as liberated us, how the very act of naming has been till now a male prerogative, and how we can begin to see, and name—and therefore live—afresh" and progress to self-knowing, and new identity re-formation (1996).

On the one hand, Rich's analyses may not have taken account of the differences of degree to which European patriarchal constructions of history affect white women and Native American women (85). On the other hand, what Rich articulates is applicable, with some modifications, to Native women's projects of group recodification and race reclamation through re-visionary reading of written history. In order to achieve this goal, Native women writers enter into a much more rigorous navigation of the labyrinthine nuances of the colonizing Euro-American language(s), which Rich claims to have been both imprisoning and liberating to women in general. However, none of the language(s) to which Rich refers, including English, French, Spanish, Dutch, Portuguese (all languages of Native peoples' colonization), has ever really been liberatory to Native women. Nevertheless, Rich's proposition does provide hints through which Native women can explore history and language as ways of reconstituting themselves. Through a re-visionary reading of the history of Pocahontas, Mojica's play, *Princess Pocahontas and the Blue Spots,* therefore aims to restore the humanity of Pocahontas and claim her as a foremother in Native women's struggle for voice in North American society.

In *Princess,* Mojica intervenes in the histories of the Americas to expose and contest the negation or idolization of her Native foremothers, which invariably results in their absence from history. Using the dramatic rhetoric of retrieval, redefinition, and reconciliation of the "scattered pieces" (LaRoque xxvii) in these histories, Mojica speaks to "the voices of despair among" Native women with a new "dream [and a] new [set of] visions to bring hope for the future" (xxvii). Beth Brant has similarly praised Mojica for her exciting woman-centered re-visionary writing in which she lays "bare the lies perpetuated against Native women [. . .] with laughter *and* anger—a potent combination in the hands of a Native woman" (15). Mojica's re-visioning enterprise is embedded in and framed by the Sioux proverb: "no people go down until their women are weak and dishonored, dead upon the ground" (Tobias 9). Similarly, Mojica's ideological bent is underpinned by Cheyenne philosophy, which underscores the centrality of women to the stability and continuous existence of any nation: "Una nación no será conquistada hasta que los corazones / de sus mujeres caigan a la tierra. / No importa que los guerreros sean valientes o que sus armas / sean poderosas!" (A nation is not conquered until the hearts of its women / are on the ground. Then, it is done, no matter how brave / its warriors, nor how strong its weapons) (*Mojica* 1998, 60). Collaborating with this woman-centered philosophy, Arthur Solomon (12) emphatically then proclaims: "It's time for the women to pick up their medicine in order for the people to continue." In a letter to J. B. Custer, Solomon (19) stresses that as the last teachers of Native cosmogony, the possibility of "harmony with creation" and intergender and intergenerational harmony exists only within a framework of a universal submission to women's wisdom. He stresses that society must allow "women to take their rightful place in the human family, because they are the real leaders and the best leaders in the human family. We as men have to begin to honor and respect our women again and hear what they are trying to say to us. They also must take the garbage out of their heads and put good things back in."

Kathleen Donovan defines this act of taking up the medicine baskets as Native women's strategic retrieval and repossession of their "agency in their dealings with the dominant, patriarchal culture." Donovan (25) writes: "given the prominence of women in Métis society, it is only natural that literary texts by Métis women feature strong female characters who resist and subvert domination to effect personal and political change." As a corollary, Mojica (1991, 3) has stated, "it is significant that the healers as [women] artists are in the vanguard of this critical time. We are fertile minds from a living culture—ancient as well as contemporary." Similarly, Margo Kane (27) traces the sources of the influences that defined and clarified her vision in *Moonlodge* to "the women at the center of the Native community, strong and enduring women," "who provided me with the answers to questions not yet formulated and ones that plagued my senses. They showed me that it is possible to survive genocidal attempts on their lives with dignity and sensitivity and humor. They were my role models [. . .] they keep the ancestral fires burning." By implication, if the present groups of Native peoples want to survive and grow, they must recognize and submit to the transformative wisdom of their women as mothers of the tribe. Indeed, as Maria Gonzalez (156) has pointed out, Native people (especially the men) must translate the veneration of the mother into a veneration of all motherhood via womanhood, and retreat from the restrictive duality of Madonna-whore imposed on women.

Mojica in *Princess* engages ceremony and other nonverbal sensibilities (Cowan 26) to create space for Pocahontas to revisit her story, and to consolidate that ceremony within the cosmology of ritual reconceptualization of group selfhood. Ceremony, writes Allen (227), is the ritual dramatization of human relations with the divine and cosmic world, as myth is the narrative recording of that ritual relationship. Thus, Princess-Buttered-On-Both-Sides (or more appropriately, Princess-Buffeted-on-Both-Sides) opens the play with a ritual ceremony of invocation and libation. In pouring libation of corn to the four corners of Mother Earth, and in inviting all the elements of creation to join in

the journey through ceremony to healing, Mojica establishes a female geomorphologic foundation for her play. Corn growing and land guardianship was a
woman's provenance prior to European colonization of the Americas. It is
appropriate therefore that agriculture, which was associated with Native
women, and which also was linked to nature as goddess and mother, should
become the opening movement for the drama of matrilineage reclamation.

The maternal geomorphologic foundation, which encompasses the whole
of the Americas (*Mojica* 1998, 9), simultaneously localizes and internationalizes
Mojica's characters even as it historicizes their narratives of re-vision. Mojica
invokes the presences of foremothers both as historical figures and tropes of
Native female recovery. She also facilitates her revisionary writing through what
Allen (31–47) calls the "folkloric techniques of transfigurations and transformations." These techniques dissolve the borders between human and nonhuman
worlds. They also uphold the Native concept of the intertwining of the four
worlds—spirits, plants, animals, earth—as reflected and refracted in the play's
four-section structure. The four sections parallel the four directions of the com-
pass from which Native peoples believe the "four major human races" originated. Alan R. Sandstrom (31) has also observed that in Nahua cosmology,
from which Mojica has borrowed some ideas, the universe has four spheres: the
surface earth, the sky, the ancestral world or the area beneath the earth's surface,
and the watery deeps in which live those who die violent deaths and by drown-
ing. It is important therefore that a ceremonial libation of corn be offered in
these directions to the various gods and ancestors dwelling therein.

The libation of corn creates a multidimensional space for Mojica to stage
the ritual reclamation of her Native foremothers through thirteen lunar transformations and transfigurations. These lunar transformations encode Native
cosmogony in which the Moon is worshiped as Grandmother goddess. As
Grandmother goddess, she is mystically responsible for the thirteen transformations of the year and their correspondence to the proactive and procreative
transformations of women's bodies during menstruation. Rich (103) touches
on this relationship between the woman's menstrual cycle, and its mysterious
correspondence to "the cycle of the moon" in her interpretation of what
Robert Briffault, Bruno Bettelheim, and Joseph Campbell describe as the
male's fear, and probably envy, of this ability of the female's body to gestate,
bring forth, and nourish new life, indeed perform an act which only gods are
capable of doing. M. Ester Harding (70) has also traced this relationship
between the moon and women to prepatriarchal religious beliefs, in which the
feminine principle in the cosmos was recognized, deified, and then worshiped.

Nevertheless, as Rich (107–108) postulates, "the moon was merely one
aspect of the female presence once felt to dominate the universe. Prepatriarchal thought gynomorphosed everything. Out of the earth-womb vegetation
and nourishment emerged, as the human child out of the womb." Each menstrual cycle then becomes a new psychoemotional, spiritual, and biological

transformation. In this process of transformation the woman's somatic, psychical, emotional, and cosmic worlds prepare her for the creative process of a new life. Mojica weaves into her meaning certain aspects of Aztec spiritual beliefs in a "divine pair, 'Lord and Mistress of Our Flesh,' and in other Native cultures, Lord and Mistress of corn and regeneration" (Neumann 181). Mojica then uses the correspondence between lunar cycles and women's menstruation periods to construct umbilical links between present-day Native women and their foremothers. Through these links, contemporary Native women can repossess a selfhood recuperated through the mysteries of their bodies, tracing back to a period of prepatriarchal and pre-European conquest in which Native mother right was recognized in the worship of Native goddesses.

Matoaka's (also known as Pocahontas) first experience of menstruation begins her transformation; not only into a woman, but also into the role she is to play in the unfortunate history of the relationship between European invaders and Native Americans in the United States. She is transformed from a cartwheeling, nubile Matoaka into a woman who assumes her training and responsibilities as a healer, a wife, a mother, a leader, and a woman (*Mojica* 1998, 33–34). In this stage of puberty, she recognizes and accepts her changing role in society, even as she regrets the loss of her age of innocence. The puberty rites, suggested in the play, help prepare Matoaka's transition from girlhood to womanhood. Through these rites, she is taught to appreciate and to love her body's biology and its divine functions, including its ability to provide a safe passage for ancestral reincarnation.

Thus, unlike what Rich (107–108) calls the "tendency to flesh-loathing" laid on women in so called "advanced" societies, the so-called primitives had ways to instruct their women toward "flesh-loving," not only during premenstrual days, but also during their menses. Menstruation to Matoaka then is seen as the genesis of an awakening sexuality and its link to the life-giving force in her womb. It means exuberance, and a future of possibilities:

> Becoming woman/child—open up/Look!
> All around your world, everything's alive!
> Everything is growing, *(embraces tree)* everything has spirit,
> everything is breathing, *(kneels, washes hands in basin of tree)*
> everything needs water, everything needs sunlight,
> everything needs rest. (*Mojica* 1998, 34)

Subsequently, Matoaka joins Ceremony unreservedly to welcome her first menstrual blood. In this celebration of her puberty, both Ceremony and Matoaka recognize the four zones of the universe that combine to form the human person: Sky, earth above, earth below, and watery deeps.

Every ritual ceremony has its symbols. Thus, Matoaka's celebration of her coming of age as a woman, and as a potential mother, has its own ceremonial symbols: red paint, pot, tree. For instance, the red paint, which is used to decorate her arms and feet, indicates her menstrual blood. The pot, from which the paint is taken, is linked symbolically to her maturing womb, which is now preparing to gestate life and transform her from a young girl into a woman, a mother, a creator. The tree is a representational icon of the connection between the Earth and the life it generates as vegetation, and woman/mother as the life-giving force without which humanity would perish. All these symbols coordinate to insist that menstruation is a natural and divine process and there is nothing evil about it. It encodes the phenomenon of the continuity of human existence. Thus, when Ceremony tells Matoaka to "Look around [her] world woman / child," she wants Matoka to recognize the significance of menstruation and its divine link to the cosmic world of clouds, stars, and moon: "Dark skies, the moon is mine / stars travel / woman's time" (*Mojica* 1998, 34–35). From then on there is a new voice of confidence, which is heard declaring that women's time has come. The voice is not one of supplication, but one of empowering authority. It summons Native women to acknowledge and appreciate the potentiality of their transformative powers through motherhood as an experience of their divinity, creativity, and femininity.

Potential motherhood then is represented as an experience in which Matoaka's transformative power is enunciated in the symbolic act of staged childbirth (*Mojica* 1998, 20). This symbolic theatrical maneuver is a representational fleshing and speechifying of the gaps, silences, and distortions of Native femininity in phallocentric Euro-American historiographies. The ritual of childbirth becomes a trope of transubstantiation. It consolidates the faith in motherhood as the divine path toward the creative reconstruction of Native peoples. As female descendants of Matoaka, Contemporary Woman #1 and #2 are linked to their foremother through this act of divine creativity. Through this linkage, in both the context of biology and social role as potential mothers, they inherit Native mother right privileges, together with the responsibilities of becoming the new mothers of a new nation of recuperated Native peoples. Thus, the symbolic childbirth is a cultural and feminist trope of re-centering the mother for race re-invention. Moreover, childbirth as a trope formulates the journey motif and defines the motives of Contemporary Woman #1 and #2 as they undertake their journey of retrieval of their matrilineage. The journey itself is a trip to personal reconnection with the historical mothers for the purpose of a personal rebirth.

In arguing this way, I am by no means oblivious to the position of several feminist writers, including Rich, who see motherhood as sometimes disempowering to women, considering the ways patriarchal discourses have used this biological function of women to overessentialize, objectify, and negate women's intellectual and spiritual importance, and thus to undermine their logical centrality in society (Sacks 25). But I am also aware that often, anti-innatist feminist rhetoric has overdetermined the interpretations of mother-

hood, even when the cultures examined, or majority of women perceive motherhood differently. Hence, I situate my reading of *Princess* within Native
matricentricity, which is the foundation of most Native American cultures.
Several anthropologists, including Grumet (43–62); Leacock (25–43); Klein
(88–108); Rothenberg (63–87); Medicine (65–73); Bourgeault (129–150) testify to the matricentric structures of most Native communities. This awareness, coupled with concrete facts of traditional precontact positions of Native
women in most Native societies, informs my reading of matrilineage reclamation in *Princess*.

In addition to childbirth, the matricentric ideology of the transformative
powers of mothers/women in *Princess* is ritualized through other symbols and
ceremonies. The pot, as one such symbol in the play, relates to Rich's idea of
a woman as a radical and proactive caldron of transformation (98). The pot,
from which Matoaka takes red paint to ritually mask and thus strengthen and
purify her body and spirit, evokes the idea of the woman's womb as an active
and sacred caldron with transformative powers. Like the vessel image representing the feminine principle discussed by Neumann (1972:282–291), the
pot in *Princess*, which contains the symbol of menstrual blood, and ritual
blood of sacrifice for spiritual healing, is Mojica's play with the idea of the
woman's womb as an active, powerful, and a transformative vessel. The pot
also is representative of woman as the traditional retainer of the knowledge of
healing, and therefore preservation of society. For instance, Matoaka is taught
about the medicinal properties of herbs: "Name of the flower, name of the leaf,
which one for headaches, / which one for broken bones, which one to pray,
which ones never to touch" (*Mojica* 1998, 34). In Neumann's (288) words, "the
magical caldron or pot is always in the hands of the female mana figures, the
priestess," who then, writes Briffault, uses her position to ensure the survival
of the clan, not through dictatorship, but through transformative and regen-
erative use of that power (Briffault 490, 513). Ana Castillo (108), among others, has written on the link between a woman's fertility, potency, and divine
power, which are symbolized in the menstrual flow, pregnancy, childbirth, and
nurturance through the woman's body in the form of breast milk. If this is
understood, we can then accept a mother's/woman's indispensable transformative role in our continued existence, and not perceive women/mothers as a
threat to civilization.

Neumann (1971:466–467) postulates further that pottery in many cultures reflect those cultures' belief systems in the magical procreative cycle. He
writes that through the magic "in pottery making . . . the essential features of
the feminine transformation character are bound up with the vessel as a symbol of transformation." Likewise, in writing about the Zuni of North America, Biffault (473–474) contends that "the manufacture of pots [. . .] partakes
of a ritual [. . .] and the pot's identity with the Great Mother is deeply rooted
in ancient belief through the greater part of the world." The pot image in

Princess can therefore be seen as a very crucial symbol in Mojica's program of using Native concepts of motherhood as her recuperation trope. It is through the pot symbol that Mojica is able to articulate the mother's womb as a proactive caldron from which the continuation of the Native people is guaranteed. The pot as mother/woman provides the enclosed, unknown, and secure space in which a new generation of people is gestated and birthed. It also symbolizes the uterine connection between Contemporary Woman #1 and #2 and their foremothers, and a sibling connection between Native men and women. For example, after Contemporary Woman #1 (*Mojica* 1998, 39) *"Moves to pot of paint upstage right and in one deliberate gesture, paints the center part in her hair; returns downstage center,"* she immediately proclaims that she can now "recognize my lifeline in your face when you bow your head in respect to hold a single kernel of corn in your hand" (39).

These observations demonstrate that Mojica's Pocahontas, as the foremother of a new generation of Native people, should not be regarded as a traitor to her people, but should be venerated as the mother of racial and social transformation, whose wisdom and actions have ensured the transformation and, consequently, the survival of her people. Brant (88–89) therefore sees Pocahontas as a holy woman—shaman and priestess—who, being in tune with the Creatrix Spirit, foresaw the devastating consequences Native contact with Europeans was to have on her people. As shaman, Pocahontas adapted the measures necessary to preserve her people, even if it meant a radical transformation of their racial structure and composition. However, as Contemporary Woman #1 and #2 re-traverse the Americas seeking empowerment from the spirits and wisdom of their foremothers, they ignorantly, but not maliciously question the actions of these foremothers: Would a real Indian Princess betray her people? If so, how come she is said by male historians to have betrayed her "race / through sex and / sexual politics" (*Mojica* 1998, 21). The answer is an evasive silence from Princess-Buttered-On-Both-Sides. Her silence invites a critical reexamination of the historical data from which Contemporary Woman #1 and #2 derived their knowledge about Pocahontas. It indicates the depths of the silencing, distortions, and exclusions of Native women's achievements in mainstream American history.

In refusing to respond directly to the impatient inquiry and implied condemnation by Contemporary Woman #1 and #2, Princess-Buttered-On-Both-Sides dramatizes her rejection of futile discourses based on fallacies. According to Susan Bennet (19), some of these fallacies lead to the appropriation and misrepresentation of Native women's voices by some Euro-American female writers. These writers may desire new territories of intellectual, cultural, and artistic colonization. Hence, they assume the positions as spokespersons for Native women. In the process, they create Native women who fit Euro-American concepts of who, what, and how Native women are and feel. Silence as demonstrated here is a strategy of resistance to the noisy words of a false discourse on authenticity. Barbara Goddard (135–158) has shown how silence in Native women's writing performs the dual function of Native self-recuperation and differentiation. Also, Jordan Wheeler (10) has shown that "for the Aboriginal person, silence and stillness are as important as sound and action." Silence evokes the voice of sorrow beyond words and hope and restitution foreseen, but not foretold. Hence, Ana Castillo (111) has argued for the need for contemporary Native women to "reconstruct our history with what is left unsaid and not with what has been by those who have imposed their authority on us" especially "as women and Native people" (111).

Strangely, but also predictably, the strategy for Native women's recuperation through silence ends in an unexpected opening through the answer given by Princess-Buttered-On-Both-Sides: she is here to show the new race of Native people the path to recovery, which is the art of making fry bread. Fry bread, a Native American ceremonial food, becomes the material and symbolic tool of instruction and restitution in Native ways toward a rebirth. The art of making fry bread is a ritual of new beginnings for contemporary Native women who seek to rediscover their ways and roles. Fry bread is both a sacrament of cultural remembrance and meal of physical recovery. It is emblematic of both the cosmic and physical retrieval and survival of the people. In the ritual of making fry bread, cultural roots are regenerated. The ritual also establishes the ancient role of the Native woman as healer, transformer, activist, teacher, provider, nurturer, wife, and mother. Learning how to make fry bread will help Contemporary Woman #1 and #2 to regain insights into their cultural and spiritual roots. It will liberate them from the physical and ideological junk that surrounds and beckons to them to eat and enter into a world of amnesia. Fry bread making is an act in exorcism that will purify them from the demons of colonialism and misogyny. Thus, the ritual of making fry bread is linked to the rituals of menstruation and childbirth, both of which are necessary for matrilineage recuperation. The symbol of making fry bread also echoes the connection between woman and hearth/oven and, hence, nourishment as shown diagrammatically by Rich (1976, 1985:98).

These ritual movements enable Mojica to excavate and revise the Anglo-American textbook stories of Pocahontas, which were variously celebrated in sixteenth- and seventeenth-century settler ballads (Green 1990:17). Through a duet between the English troubadour and Pocahontas, Mojica questions the cultural and historical bases of the romanticized and negative representations of Pocahontas. For instance, the emblazoned words "CAPTAIN JOHN WHITEMAN" (*Mojica* 1998, 19) compels further exploration of the word Whiteman, not only as a racial referent, but also as a cultural and historical trickster figure representing European conquistador imposition of European patriarchal social structures on Native communities. The duet is the vehicle for Pocahontas to verbalize, vocalize, and personalize her plight, hitherto spoken over by the romanticized narratives. The silenced voice of Pocahontas becomes audible as she laments her betrayal by both her people and by the English. Her indignation is perfectly in order when she says: "What owe I to my father? Waited I not one year in / Jamestown, a prisoner? One year before sent he my / brothers to seek me" (*Mojica* 1998, 31). Powhatan, her father, was more concerned with maintaining good ties with the colonists, and he was therefore not very enthusiastic about rescuing his daughter. Thus, we can understand Pocahontas's pain as she further asks: "If my father had loved me, he would / not value me less than old swords, guns or axes: therefore I / shall dwell with the Englishmen who love me" (31). Pocahontas's bitterness is backed by historical accounts (Barbour 106–131). Hence, a re-visionary reading of the transformation of Pocahontas from Matoaka into Lady Rebecca (Barbour 128–179) teaches us that this transfiguration has its roots in the use of women by men as chattel in their transactions and negotiations for power sharing.

Through humor, Mojica satirizes the way Pocahontas is supposed to have fallen insanely in love with Captain John Smith, when history tells us that she was actually captured (Barbour 106–109). Unable to return home to her people, she chose the man who seemed to show some kindness to her. Mojica uses the parallel structure of the duet to destabilize Captain John Smith's diary entries about Pocahontas. She questions the whole narrative in which an eight- to eleven-year-old Pocahontas was so enamored of John Smith, and his nobility of character, that she risked her life and the survival of her race to protect his own. Rayna Green (1990:15–21) in "The Pocahontas Perplex: The Image of Indian Women in American Culture, Retrospect and Prospect," has also challenged the insidious manner in which most dominant Euro-American historians treat the Pocahontas story. These historians refuse, or fail, to see or accept that Pocahontas was a trophy in the exchange of gifts in the contact zone, where Native and European males gave and received daughters and rusty swords as pawns in a game of political and sexual brigandy (*Mojica* 1998, 31). Like the Women of the Puna, Malinche, Wapithe/oo, who are "betrayed by our own fathers brothers uncles husbands" (36), but collectively keep the flames of maternal ways burning and demand their purity be reclaimed (36), Pocahontas feels betrayed by her own menfolk and contests the validity of Native American males' representation of her role in the history of European conquest of North America.

In *Princess*, Mojica sculptures a performance-based text, which revises Anglo-American narratives about Pocahontas, and subsequently then reestablishes Pocahontas and other key Native historical mothers. Her revisionary writing provides the framework for the development of an ongoing discourse of recovery of Native matrilineage. The political and philosophical conclusion, which is couched in Spanish and English, and derived from Sioux and Cheyenne philosophies, legitimates the centrality of the Native mother/woman in the project of recuperation of Native personhood and traditions. The womanist project validates the actions of Pocahontas and restores her as the precursor to a new generation of Native women activists, who accept the challenge of the philosophy that sees women as the strongest and final defense of any nation. Mojica, like other contemporary Native writers in North, Central, and South America and the Caribbean, critiques dominant culture while also building a bridge between "archaic and modern ways of knowing" (Sequoya-Magdaleno 91). Like the foremothers she reclaims, Mojica's legitimates her Indianness by fulfilling the conditions delineated by Allen above, and which Sequoya-Magdaleno describes as entailing "claims of authority vis-à-vis tribal traditions that transgress the customary modes of self-representation based on those traditions" (91). *Princess* mediates the "principle between contesting social formations" (91) in the same way that the reclaimed Pocahontas stood as the interpreter and caldron of transformation between her people and the new conquering European peoples. In acting as a re-visionary cultural interpreter, Mojica draws upon the courage and vision of Pocahontas as a foremother, and in turn, she also becomes the intellectual caldron of transformation of Native people's perception of themselves and their foremothers.

Mojica's *Princess Pocahontas and the Blue Spots* is a direct response to Rich's call for women writers to engage in re-visionary reading and writing of history. The play, therefore, as a re-visionary performance text of history involving several Native women's roles in the history of the Americas, legitimates its own energy and ideology in the future of possibilities suggested at the end for Native peoples through their women in the following words: "Una nación no sera conquistada que los corazones de sus mujeres no caigan a la tierra. No importa que los guerreros sean valientes o que sus armas sean poderosas!" (60). Native people are yet to be conquered because the daughters are taking up the strength, vision, and transformative courage of their foremothers. Through a uterine connection, Contemporary Woman #1 speaks on behalf of all Native women writers when she promises "to return to / Love you always" (57). The "you" here, of course, refers to her foremothers, her culture, her history, and her people through the reclaimed image of Pocahontas. Her promise to return marks the turning point in the search of Native women for a rhetoric and that "tradition of female power" (Rich 1976, 1985:85), which Donovan (25) has observed exists already in the historical locations and roles of Native foremothers. Her promise signals her readiness to assume her rightful position as a healer of her people through the reclamation of her role as a Native woman, a role that the play's central theme endorses and advocates.

WORKS CITED

Allen, Paula Gunn. "The Sacred Hoop: A Contemporary Indian Perspective on American Indian Literature." *The Remembered Earth: An Anthology of Contemporary*

Native American Literature. Ed. Geary Hobson. Albuquerque: U of New Mexico P, 1981:222–239.

———. "'Border' Studies: The Intersection of Gender and Color." Palumbo-Liu 31–47.

Bachofen, J. J. *Myth, Religion, and Mother Right.* Trans. Ralph Manheim. Princeton: Princeton UP, 1967.

Baker, Marie Annharte. "An Old Indian Trick is to Laugh." *Canadian Theatre Review* 68 (Fall 1991):48–49.

Barbour, Phillip L. *Pocahontas and Her World.* Boston: Houghton, 1970.

Bennet, Susan. "Who Speaks? Representations of Native Women in Some Canadian Plays." *Canadian Journal of Drama and Theatre* 1.2 (1991):13–28.

Bourgeault, Ron. "Race, Class, and Gender: Colonial Domination of Indian Women." *Racism in Canada.* Saskatoon: Fifth House, 1991:129–150.

Brant, Beth. *Writing as Witness: Essay and Talk.* Toronto: The Women's Press, 1994.

Briffault, Robert. *The Mothers.* New York: Johnson, rp. 1969.

Castellano, Marie Brant. "Women in Huron and Ojibwa Societies." *Canadian Woman Studies/Les Cahiers De La Femme.* 10.2 and 10.3 (Fall/Spring 1990):45–51.

Castillo, Ana. *Massacre of the Dreamers: Essays on Xicanisma.* New York: Penguin, 1995.

Cowan, Cindy. "The Trap of Cultural Specificity: Seeking Intercultural Solidarity." *Canadian Theatre Review* 73 (Winter 1992):24–28.

Donovan, Kathleen M. *Feminist Readings of Native American Literature: Coming to Voice.* Tucson: U of Arizona P, 1998.

Etienne, Mona and Eleanor Leacock. *Women and Colonization: Anthropological Perspectives.* New York: Praeger, 1980.

Goddard, Barbara. "Listening for the Silence: Native Women's Traditional Narratives." *The Native in Literature.* Eds. Thomas King, Cheryl Calver, and Helen Hoy. Toronto: ECW Press, 1987:133–158.

Gonzalez, Maria. "Love and Conflict: Mexican American Women Writers as Daughters." *Women of Color Mother-Daughter Relationship in 20th-Century Literature.* Ed. Elizabeth Brown-Guillory. Austin: U of Texas P, 1996:153–171.

Green, Rayna. "The Pocahontas Perplex: The Image of Indian Women in American Culture, Retrospect and Prospect." *Unequal Sisters: A Multicultural Reader in US Women's History.* Eds. Dubois E. and Ruiz V. London: Routledge, 1990:15–21.

———. "Contemporary Indian Humor." *Words of Today's American Indian Women: Ohoyo Makachi.* Cited by Kate Stanley. "Thoughts on Indian Feminism." *A Gathering of Spirit: A Collection by North American Indian Women.* Ed. Beth Brant (Degonwadonti). Toronto: The Women's Press, 1988, 1984:213–215.

Grumet, Robert Steven. "Sunksquaws, Shamans, and Tradeswomen: Middle Atlantic Coastal Algonkian Women During the 17th and 18th Centuries." Etienne and Leacock. New York: Praeger, 1980:43–62.

Harding, M. Esther. *Woman's Mysteries*. New York: C. G. Jung Foundation, 1971.

Johnson, Emily Pauline. *The Moccasin Maker*. Tucson: The U of Arizona P, 1913.

Kane, Margo. "From the Centre of the Circle the Story Emerges." *Canadian Theatre Review* (Fall 1991):26–29.

Kelly, Jennifer. "The Landscape of Grandmother: A Reading of Subjectivity(ies) in Contemporary North American Native Women's Writing in English." *World Literature Written in English* 31.2 (1991):112–128.

Klein, Laura F. "Contending with Colonization: Tlingit Men and Women in Change." Etienne and Leacock. New York: Praeger, 1980:88–108

LaRoque, Emma L., ed. Preface. *Writing the Circle: Native Women of Western Canada*. Eds. Jeanne Perreault and Sylvia Vance. Edmonton: NeWest Pubs., 1991:xv–xxx.

Leacock, Eleanor. "Montagnais Women and the Jesuit Program for Colonization." Etienne and Leacock. New York: Praeger, 1980:25–43.

——— . "Women's Status in Egalitarian Society: Implications for Social Evolution." *Current Anthropology* 19.2:247–275.

Medicine, Beatrice. "Indian Women: Tribal Identity as Status Quo." *Woman's Nature: Rationalization of Inequality*. Eds. Marian Lowe and Ruth Hubbard. New York: Pergamon, 1983:65–73.

Mojica, Monique. *Princess Pocahontas and the Blue Spots*. Toronto: Women's Press, 1998:11–62.

——— . Preface. *Canadian Theatre Review* (Fall 1991):68.

Neumann, Erich. *The Great Mother: An Analysis of the Archetype*. Trans. Ralph Manheim. New Jersey: Princeton UP, 1972.

——— . *The Origins and History of Consciousness*. New Jersey: Princeton UP, 1971.

Palumbo-Liu, David, ed. *The Ethnic Canon: Histories, Institutions and Interventions*. Minneapolis/London: U of Minnesota P, 1995.

Pérez, Emma. "Sexuality and Discourse: Notes from a Chicana Survivor." *Chicana Critical Issues: Mujeres Activas en Letras y Cambio Social*. Eds. Norma Alarcón et al. Berkeley: Third Woman Press, 1993:45–69.

Pratt, Mary Louise. *Imperial Eyes: Travel Writing and Transculturation*. London: Routledge, 1992.

Rich, Adrienne. *Of Woman Born: Motherhood as Experience and Institution*. New York, London: Norton, 1985.

——— . "When We Dead Awaken: Writing as Re-Vision." *The Norton Anthology of Literature by Women: The Traditions in English*. Eds. Sandra M. Gilbert and Susan Gubar. New York, London: Norton, 1996:1953–1992.

Rothenberg, Diane. "The Mothers of the Nation: Seneca Resistance to Quaker Intervention." Etienne and Leacock. New York: Praeger, 1980:63–87.

Sacks, Karen. *Sisters and Wives: The Past and Future of Sexual Equality*. Westport: Greenwood Press, 1979.

Sandstrom, Alan R. "The Tonantsi Cult of the Eastern Nahua." *Mother Worship: Theme and Variations.* Ed. James J. Preston. Chapel Hill: The U of North Carolina P, 1982:25–50.

Sequoya-Magdaleno, Jana. "Telling the *difference:* Representations of Identity in Discourse of Indianness" *[sic].* Palumbo-Liu 88–116.

Solomon, Arthur. *Eating Bitterness: A Vision Beyond The Prison Walls.* Eds. Cathleen Kneen and Michael Posluns. Toronto: NC Press, 1994.

Stanley, Kate. "Thoughts on Indian Feminism." *A Gathering of Spirit: A Collection by North American Indian Women.* Ed. Beth Brant (Degonwadonti). Toronto: The Women's Press, 1988, 1984:213–215.

Tobias, Leonore Keeshig. "My Grandmother Is Visiting." *Canadian Woman Studies* 4.1 (Fall 1982):8–9.

Wheeler, Jordan. "Our Own Stories: A Revolution in Aboriginal Theatre." *Canadian Theatre Review* 66 (Spring 1991):8–12.

SIX

Of Woman (but Not Man or the Nuclear Family) Born

Motherhood Outside Institutionalized Heterosexuality

KATE McCULLOUGH

> The history of institutionalized motherhood and of institutional-
> ized heterosexual relations . . . converge[. . . .] The institution of
> motherhood is not identical with bearing and caring for children,
> any more than the institution of heterosexuality is identical with
> intimacy and sexual love. Both create the prescriptions and the
> conditions in which choices are made or blocked; they are not
> "reality" but they have shaped the circumstances of our lives.
> —Rich, *Of Woman Born*

REREADING ADRIENNE RICH'S landmark 1976 critique of the institution of motherhood, *Of Woman Born*, at the turn of the twenty-first century, much of the originally quite radical and revolutionary analysis on Rich's part might appear somewhat banal today.[1] "Yes, yes," today's feminist rereader might think, "we already know all this: motherhood as social institution that works to circumscribe women and protect the status quo of patriarchy; motherhood is not simply a personal experience but one deeply shaped by the forces of the state, defined by legal systems, controlled by the medical system, linked to the production and protection of the nuclear heterosexual family and a capitalist economy; motherhood as the vehicle by which children are gendered and the family is reproduced; motherhood as an ideological ideal to which all women are taught to aspire but that none can achieve; motherhood and birth as yet further terrain on which women's bodies are coerced and controlled by the structural institutions of patriarchy. And perhaps this alleged banality is in fact something to be celebrated, for it suggests that feminists have learned something in the past three decades. That is, thanks precisely to the work of feminists like Rich, we now understand much more about the workings of patriarchy and the social constructions of gender and sexuality; we are now able to see motherhood as a cultural institution that is itself imbricated in many other cultural institutions, institutions that, for the most part, have not served women's interests.

Yet a broader historical impact than this becomes apparent when *Of Woman Born* is viewed in conjunction with Rich's 1980 "Compulsory Heterosexuality and Lesbian Existence," an article that opened up a critique of heterosexuality as a cultural institution and helped pave the way for a generation of queer scholarship. In their analyses of institutionalized motherhood and institutionalized heterosexuality respectively, *Of Woman Born* and "Compulsory Heterosexuality" arguably provide Rich's most important contributions to twentieth-century North American feminist thought. Her observation (in the chapter opening) that the histories of these two institutions "converge" and that both create the conditions that shape our lives provides the starting point of this chapter, as I explore subsequent feminist efforts to detach institutionalized "motherhood" from institutionalized "heterosexuality." How have women, in the three decades since Rich's book appeared, attempted not simply to rework/reclaim motherhood, but to do so specifically outside the dictates of heterosexuality and its institutionalized location within the nuclear family unit? To what extent has Rich's analysis, now commonplace in academic feminist circles, entered the realm of popular or material culture in the United States?[2] Turning first to the popular genre of pregnancy and motherhood guides (mainstream guides like Arlene Eisenberg et al.'s 1984 *What to Expect When You're Expecting*, as well as Rachel Pepper's 1999 *The Ultimate Guide to Pregnancy for Lesbians*, a lesbian reworking of the maternal, and Ariel Gore's 1998 *The Hip Mama Survival Guide*, a heterosexual reworking that explicitly challenges a model of motherhood grounded in the middle-class, marital, domestic sphere), and then to two memoirs of a new mother's experience (Anne Lamott's 1993 bestseller *Operating Instructions: A Journal of My Son's First Year* and Cherríe Moraga's 1997 *Waiting in the Wings: Portrait of a Queer Motherhood*), I will examine the degree to which Rich's feminist critique has translated into popular change.

Perhaps one of the most powerful legacies of Rich's analysis of motherhood is its enactment of second-wave feminism's contention that "the personal is political." That is, the book provides a detailed anatomy of motherhood as a cultural institution in addition to a personal experience, arguing that women's individual experiences have historically been subsumed into motherhood as a cultural institution defined and controlled by patriarchal forces. Rich notes that motherhood has a history and an ideology that are "essential to the patriarchal system" and she succinctly notes that "Certainly the mother serves the interests of patriarchy: she exemplifies in one person religion, social conscience, and nationalism. Institutional motherhood revives and renews all other institutions" (45).

Crucial to this function is motherhood's location within the marriage contract. Rich reminds us that, with this contract, the legal system creates in one swift move a position of ownership of husband over wife and an officially approved context for the production of motherhood and children, legal heirs (260). This, in turn, produces not simply a measure of "good" and "bad" mothers, but an approved venue for the reproduction of the family and gender system, as the "good" mother performs the labor of gendering her children. Furthermore, the image of the mother in the home, Rich notes, "has haunted and reproached the lives of wage-earning mothers," while at the same time this ideal functions as a disciplinary mechanism for even the woman who most closely emulates the ideal—the full-time at-home mother—for by definition she can never quite embody the ideal (52). Held responsible for both the reproduction of the family and the heterosexualizing and gendering of children, mothers can then be blamed for myriad social ills, just as women who choose not to reproduce are simultaneously castigated for being failed women and bad citizens.[3]

Drawing on her personal experience, the specific version of this structurally located, idealized maternal that Rich critiques emerges from a Cold War model of white, middle-class, U.S. suburban domesticity. As Betty Friedan did some thirteen years earlier, Rich provides an analysis of this white, class-privileged, privatized, maternal isolation, an analysis that is simultaneously cuttingly perceptive and universalizing. Much to her credit, in an introduction written for the 1986 tenth-anniversary edition of her book, Rich recognizes that a reliance on a broad concept of patriarchy led her, as it led so many white feminists of that historical moment, to universalize from her own experience in a way that elided important differences (particularly those based on class and race) among women. From the vantage point of 1986 she notes that while "Patriarchy is a concrete and useful concept," it cannot be viewed as "unrelated to economic or racial oppression" (xxiii; xxiv).[4]

Concurrent with the class and racialized bias of Rich's original perspective, however, there is a great deal of important and persuasive analysis. Reading motherhood as imbricated in other social institutions—the legal system, the family—is certainly one of the strengths of Rich's analysis, and nowhere is this more apparent than in her discussion of women as literal bearers; that is, in her analysis of the history of childbirth and of the medical industry's pathologizing of birth.[5] In what is perhaps the most powerful section of her book, Rich traces the struggle between midwives and the emerging medical profession over birthing practices, a struggle that resulted in the medical industry's claiming control of birth and redefining it as a near-pathology to be "managed" by professionals to their own economic profit. This battle over authority, augmented by the twentieth-century rise in the use of painkillers, led to a situation by mid-century in which most U.S. women gave birth in hospitals in a state of drugged unconsciousness,[6] what Rich calls "complete passivity" (158).

By the time Rich began *Of Woman Born,* growing opposition to this vision of birth and to the broader abuse of women by the medical industry had intersected with the rise of second-wave feminism in the United States, and produced the feminist health care movement in general and the "natural" or "homebirth" movement in particular. In her 1986 Introduction, Rich locates the newly emergent second-wave feminist movement as the context for the original production of her text, then notes that by 1986, "a vigorous and wide-spread women's health-care movement has grown up, challenging a medical industry [. . .] notable for its arrogance and sometimes brutal indifference toward women, and also toward poverty and racism as factors in illness and infant mortality" (x). This movement, perhaps most famously exemplified in the United States by the Boston Women's Health Collective and their now classic 1970 text *Our Bodies, Ourselves,* in turn provides a context for the emergence of the U.S. homebirth movement, a movement begun largely by Ina May Gaskin.[7] Gaskin's work as a midwife on "The Farm," as well as the publication in 1977 of her tremendously influential *Spiritual Midwifery,* embodies the originary and most radical form of the homebirth movement. In her preface to the third edition of *Spiritual Midwifery* Gaskin claims that the book's contents are "almost exclusively derived from women by women. This fact alone makes this information rare and unique," then she goes on to state that her hope is that the book "will aid women in attaining the insight that can lead to power that equals that of men" (8, 9).[8]

Rich notes that the homebirth movement (predictably, given its ties to second-wave feminism) was in its origins at least "a middle-class phenomenon" (174),[9] and in her 1986 retrospective introduction she observes that while the "movement to demedicalize childbirth [. . .] became a national one, with an increase in homebirths, alternative birthing practices, and the establishment of 'birth centers' and 'birthing rooms' in hospitals" it swiftly became "a reform easily subsumed into a new idealism of the family. Its feminist origins have been dimmed along with its potential challenge to the economics and practices of medicalized childbirth and to the separation of motherhood and sexuality" (xi, xii). This co-optation of the radical feminist politics fueling these reforms can certainly be seen in the mainstream adoption, in massively diluted form, of some of the general principles of the feminist health care movement. Mainstream middle-class health care now offers women more information about the birth process and encourages them to take a more active role, if only to the extent of monitoring their diets and bodily "symptoms." Meanwhile, the publishing industry has turned a feminist desire for medical self-education into a profitable market niche by generating an ever-increasing number of handbooks on pregnancy and mothering. Located within this market economy, to what extent can or do these handbooks challenge or reinforce the patriarchal scripting of motherhood so clearly detailed by Rich?

To the extent that all of these books offer a range of information on the physical and emotional transformations inherent in pregnancy and childbirth, as well as information on early childhood development, they offer a corrective to the abuses of the medical system so thoroughly detailed by Rich.[10] At the same time, however, many of these texts reinscribe motherhood within a patriarchal marital unit that naturalizes heterosexuality and, like Rich's original analysis, universalizes a class-privileged white experience. One of the United State's best selling and most popular of these books, *What to Expect When You're Expecting,* for instance, embodies the worst excesses of this kind. A generally pro-AMA-style-medicine guide, *What to Expect* furnishes a huge amount of information packaged with a walloping dose of white, middle-class heterosexual normativity that naturalizes the nuclear middle-class family. Presuming class privilege and economic choice, for instance, the authors council pregnant women to stop working outside the home after the twenty-fourth week, particularly if they "stand on the job" (177). Specifically mentioning "salespeople, cooks, waitresses, nurses, and so on" the authors thus not only assume a dual family income but also target precisely the segment of working women—service industry laborers in particular—who can least afford to quit working months before the birth of their child (177). The naturalizing of class privilege is accompanied by an assumption of a heterosexual married life as well. The opening section on choosing a practitioner, for instance, begins "Assuming you and your husband have already taken care of conception, the next challenge" is choosing a doctor (23), a comment that both locates conception within the marital contract and presumes a heterosexual basis for it. The privileging of the husband/father and indeed the reinforcement of his position of ownership over both wife and fetus/child resurfaces toward the end of the text in a chapter wholly devoted to fathers. This chapter addresses the father's fear of "feeling left out" and soothes his impatience with his "wife's hormonal changes"—"I don't know how much longer I can be patient," he says—by assuring him that "pregnancy is *not* a permanent condition" (323). Thus the authors implicitly normalize and support his desire for a wife focused fully on his needs rather than her own (an image evoked by Rich's description of woman as "healer, helper, bringer of tenderness and security. The roles (or rules) are clear: nowhere [. . .] is it suggested that a man might

do this for a woman" [190]).[11] The overall effect of *What to Expect* is not simply to privilege a heterosexual married context for a woman's pregnancy, but
also to render a woman as simply a body, either sexual or reproductive but
never both, and a body, moreover, under the control of, indeed the property of,
first, her husband, and second, a seemingly benign medical industry. That this
is the ideological message of one of the United State's best selling and most
widely read pregnancy guides suggests that Rich's decades-old critique is far
from obsolete.[12]

Against this backdrop of mainstream maternity guides, however, both
Rachel Pepper's *The Ultimate Guide to Pregnancy for Lesbians* and Ariel Gore's
The Hip Mama Survival Guide attempt to contest at least certain aspects of an
institutionalized motherhood grounded in a heterosexual, middle-class
nuclear family. Both Pepper's discussion of conception to just postbirth and
Gore's more wide-ranging pregnancy and parenting guide are the daughters
of the feminist health care movement and its contention that knowledge is
power: both assume their reader is a woman capable of learning about her own
body and making informed decisions about how to best care for both herself
and her offspring.[13] Although Pepper is writing primarily to a middle-class
lesbian audience and Gore addresses a younger, single, working-class (or some
combination thereof) mother, both have produced books that are less pre-
scriptive than tomes like *What to Expect* while also (like Rich) to some extent
denaturalizing both the nuclear family and the authority of other institutions—primarily the medical industry—that buttress that family.

The two writers most clearly echo Rich in their discussion of the med-
icalization of birth and the politics fueling it. Recalling Rich's observation on
the results of extensive medical intervention that "so often, medical technology creates its own artificial problem for which an artificial remedy must be
found" (178), Pepper cautions that the routine use of drugs (like epidurals or
pitocin) means "you will no longer be as active a participant in your own baby's
birth" (159). She also suggests that lesbian moms hire a doula to "advocate on
the mother's behalf and ward off any homophobic attitudes from hospital
staff, as well as [ensure] that you are respected as a couple and family throughout the birthing experience" (121).[14] This comment suggests the rampant
homophobia of the medical industry and its ongoing investment in controlling birth, at the same time as it echoes Rich's naturalizing of class privilege:
clearly not all women can afford to hire a doula.

Gore is more self-conscious in her discussion of the politics of birth,
commenting, "Despite the natural childbirth movement, many hospitals still
routinely employ [. . .] unnecessary intervention that can actually complicate
your labor, rather than help things along. [. . .] Not surprisingly, low-income
moms and women who go into labor without a doula or midwife advocate are
most vulnerable to hospital policies that are motivated by pressure from insurance companies, fear of malpractice suits, and general misogyny" (54). Like

Rich and Pepper, Gore critiques the pathologizing of birth, but goes on to contexualize this in terms of both classism and racism, as well as the economic interests of doctors and the insurance industry. She quotes family advocate Julie Bowles, who contends, "It comes down to rights. A lot of doctors, especially those on the white, male side of things, think they have the right to make decisions for you and tell you what to do. Poor women are at particular risk because, especially if you've been poor all your life, you haven't had a lot of practice demanding quality, and labor is a very hard time to start" (65). The politics of birth, suggest Gore and Bowles, haven't changed that much since Rich's day: The medical industry is still driven by doctors' convenience and economic profit motives, coupled with doctors' resistance to the idea, as Rich put it, "of the mother's right to decide what *she* wants" (182).[15]

Both Pepper and Gore also follow Rich's lead in critiquing the naturalized image of the heterosexual mother isolated within a normalized nuclear family unit. This critique is inherent in Pepper's focus on lesbian mothering, as, for instance, when she denaturalizes even the biology of conception by providing four chapters on the myriad details of conception. Her detailed focus on the reproductive technology (whether high- or low-tech) necessary for lesbian conception not only strips away romanticized images of conception, it also denaturalizes biology itself, suggesting not simply the cyborgian nature of lesbian reproduction but, by extension, the degree to which medical technology intervenes in and thus helps to produce nearly all human reproduction in the United States.[16] Moreover, Pepper consistently contests the naturalized yoking of reproduction and a spontaneous, naturalized family unit. She comments in her introduction, "Getting pregnant is usually harder than we ever think it's going to be before we get started. There's a lot to learn about issues of fertility and conception. There are so many decisions that have to be made about donors, sperm banks, and how we're going to define our family" (ix). Both the bodily processes and the family unit often associated with it are thus from the start denaturalized, as "getting pregnant" raises, rather than answers, the question of how to define a family. This reformulation underscores Rich's point that the naturalizing of motherhood shores up the institution of the family just as the notion of biology as destiny has "buttressed the structure of patriarchy from the first" (76).[17] But Pepper goes beyond detaching reproduction from the family to query the terms of family itself. For lesbians, of course, the nuclear heterosexual family is always an unnatural unit, and even the most yuppified lesbian attempts to replicate it entail a reshaping of it. Pepper registers this lesbian reshaping,[18] observing, "Some coupled lesbians who have trouble getting pregnant will switch roles, with the second woman attempting pregnancy. And some women will donate an egg to their partner for her to carry, allowing both women to share in the pregnancy experience" (74). On the one hand, these scenarios both force the rethinking of the category "family" as constructed rather than natural, and simultaneously radically recast the meaning of motherhood, detaching it from an individual's biology and casting it instead as a sort of collective female biological endeavor. At the same time, however, in Pepper's vision even this recast family is dependent on economic privilege and, moreover, betrays the limits of white experience. Put another way, this is an instance of what Rich describes as "one of the lines on which, in the United States, American Indian and Black women [among others] have had a very different understanding [than white women] rooted in their respective community history and values" (Introduction xxiv): the non-white U.S. family has been remade numerous times—both nineteenth- and twentieth-century-African-American women, for instance, have reworked the maternal and the family—a fact that ironically escapes Pepper's view.

Pepper is thus radical simply by virtue of her identity category (lesbian) but simultaneously articulates an unacknowledged class/race blindness that replicates that of Rich's original analysis. Gore, on the other hand, is much more explicitly radical in her critique of both the institution of motherhood and its pervasive interconnections with what she sees as a corrupt patriarchal system.[19] Gore rarely misses an opportunity to link motherhood and its uses to this larger system, but like Rich, is careful also to draw a distinction between the individual experience and potential of motherhood and the oppressive institution surrounding it.[20] Gore explicitly links the institution of motherhood to the nuclear family and critiques both by contextualizing her experience within the rise of the Radical Right and its program of "Family Values": "I completely forgot that 'Family' no longer refers [did it ever?] to a group of people who love each other but to something a little more limited like, say, a wealthy, white Christian Republican heterosexual married nuclear group of people who may or may not love each other. And I'm just some chick who got herself knocked up a few years back. [. . .] My daughter and I are a family, but we are not, according to Mr. [Pat] Robertson and his friends, a capital-F *Family*" (2).[21]

Both Gore and Pepper spend considerable time underscoring the extent to which the mother's power operates only within the sanctioned confines of the family as an institution produced by the legal system. Their discussions confirm Rich's claim that "Motherhood is 'sacred' so long as its offspring are 'legitimate'—that is, as long as the child bears the name of a father who legally controls the mother" (42). This same father also generally retains legal control of the children, a situation that both Pepper and Gore rightly read as dangerous for the non-normative mother. Pepper cautions, "Whether you use fresh or frozen sperm, you should know the legal ramifications of using the type you choose, and plan accordingly with eyes wide open" (xi). She tells various stories to illustrate the courts' stripping of rights from lesbian moms, and cites the National Center for Lesbian Rights' chilling statement that "when in doubt, the courts will grant donors full parental rights in cases involving single mothers" (37). Gore, meanwhile, reminds us that "Men win seven out of ten contested custody cases. The reason that most children live with their mothers is that fewer men want custody." She also broadens this analysis, commenting, "Family courts vary widely [. . .] but most are misogynist institutions with little or no understanding of alternative family structures and more interest in patriarchal social engineering than in your individual child's best interest" (35, 33). Motherhood located outside of the normative marital unit, in other words, continues to be punished.

But while these institutionalized forms of power and the narrow definitions of motherhood and family that emerge from them attempt to pathologize and punish mothers like Gore and Pepper and their families, both authors also see life and possibility in the non-normative location. Pepper notes that lesbians' need for intentional proactive reproductive strategies means that "we have the advantage of really thinking through our decision to parent and its ramifications" (2), and closes her book by asserting, "Remember that straight people have these same problems [adjusting to the new family configuration that a child brings] and that it takes time to grow a family. But being queer, we have the freedom to create new kinds of family situations, without the rigid boundaries straight married couples face" (182). Gore also refers to gay and lesbian families as on the "cutting edge" in part because our procreative circumstances demand, as sociologist Judith Stacey tells Gore, "a much more conscious and reflective process" (155, 156). More broadly, Gore ridicules the idea that the "notorious white heterosexual Christian nuclear capital-F Family [. . . is] the best and only structure in which to raise a kid," contending instead that "all kinds of families are working" (156).

This is a contention with which Cherríe Moraga and Anne Lamott would clearly want to agree, given the experiences each recounts in her memoir of her son's first year of life in what is not a "capital-F Family." Both Moraga and Lamott have written texts that participate in the current North American boom in women's memoir; the current popularity of the genre (as well as the fact that Lamott's book sold so well that it appeared on the *New York Times*'s bestseller list for several weeks[22]), makes it another productive site at which to investigate the absorption into mainstream culture of Rich's critique. Lamott's account of her pregnancy and maternity as a single woman fast became the sort of book pregnant women passed around to one another,[23] while Moraga's more recent account of what she labels her "queer motherhood"—her decision as a partnered lesbian to have a child, and his subsequent birth and first few years—has already attained celebrity among lesbian mothers. Both books celebrate non-normative versions of motherhood and versions located outside of institutionalized heterosexuality. Both also interrogate the relationship of motherhood to patriarchy, in large part through an analysis of what it means to bear a son within patriarchy, and both attempt to construct alternative forms of family, even as they continue to react to dominant models.

Moraga's and Lamott's narratives simultaneously critique ideals of motherhood and, by their very existence, testify to the possibility of less normative forms of it. This double move occurs as early as their accounts of conception and pregnancy, a process that for both of them took place outside of the sanctioned heterosexual family and, perhaps even more significantly, as the result of a conscious choice. Lamott, pregnant as the result of a heterosexual affair, and a strong defender of women's right to abortion, frames this pregnancy as a free choice: despite "extraordinary" pressure to have an abortion, she decides to bear the child (3). For Moraga, as a lesbian, not simply the decision to bear a child but the entire process of conception is an active decision. Lillian Faderman, in an account of her experience as a lesbian mother, notes that "It was the dual proliferation [in the 1970s] of the pill and donor insemination that finally led me to understand there was no reason I couldn't be both a lesbian and a mother: Women no longer had to get pregnant as a result of having heterosexual intercourse, and women no longer had to have heterosexual intercourse in order to get pregnant" (62). Her comment suggests that the very recasting of the relationship of sexuality and motherhood that Rich called for has finally become possible, although still mainly only for women of some class privilege. Moraga and Lamott embody this sense of agency: neither feels forced into heterosexual marriage in order to become a mother; they choose to bear a child rather than either remaining childless or bearing a child because they have no other option.

Partly by simply recounting the authors' self-chosen relationship to the institution, both these narratives represent motherhood as a constructed institution rather than a natural state, but both do so in a variety of other ways as well. In her accounts of the hospital where her son, born prematurely, spends the first months of his life, Moraga, for instance, underscores the degree to which motherhood as institution continues to imply heterosexual married life. As her interactions with the medical industry illustrate, a nonbiological comother simply does not exist within the institution of motherhood. Even in San Francisco, a city containing one of the most visible gay/lesbian populations in the United States, Moraga and her partner Ella encounter what Moraga labels "the usual deterrents" (63). Calling the hospital for information on the baby, for instance, Ella is met with erasure and suspicion, leading Moraga to wonder "how many times Ella has had to succumb to questioning when [. . .] a new receptionist answers. 'Who are you? What is your relationship to Rafael Moraga?'" (76). Even as the biological mother, Moraga is recognized only when she appears alone: "As Rafael's biological mother, I am surrounded by acceptance at the hospital, until Ella walks in and we are again the lesbian couple, the queer moms—exoticized or ostracized" (76). By raising what Karleen Pendleton Jiménez calls "questions that heterosexuals never even consider, but which become serious decisions and potentially logistical nightmares for queers," Moraga makes it clear that motherhood continues to be narrativized within a heterosexual family unit.

And just as Moraga shows how motherhood is defined in relation to the heterosexual nuclear family, her text also explicitly and repeatedly grounds motherhood and family in a specific ethnic and cultural context, thus standing as a corrective to *Of Woman Born*'s original tendency to universalize a white, middle-class, postwar family. Moraga discusses growing up in an "huge extended Mexican family" in which "the *we* of my life was always defined by blood relations. *We* meant family" (17). But because she felt that her lesbianism could not be "fully expressed there," her "search for a *we* that could embrace all the parts of myself" took her "beyond the confines of heterosexual family ties" (17). Noting that "the need for familia, the knowledge of familia, the capacity to create familia remained," Moraga explains that rather than advocating lesbian marriage, she has "always longed for something else in my relationships—something woman-centered, something cross-generational, something extended, something sensual, something humilde ante la creadora. In short, something Mexican and familial but without all the cultural constraints" (18). Her contextualizing of motherhood and family in this way thus uses the specifics of her identity as both Chicana and lesbian, making clear by contrast the institution of motherhood's white racialized and heterosexualized vectors.

Lamott, meanwhile, uses the specifics of her identity and situation as a single mother to deconstruct ideals of maternity. With a savage hilarity that links her to Gore, she deromanticizes maternity by detailing the isolation, the tedium, and the sense of being "crazy . . . mind-numbingly wasted . . . all the time" (101). More explicitly, she notes that "I am certainly not Donna Reed," invoking a U.S. television icon of idealized maternity (235). But where in Rich's journals of decades past an invocation of a similar ideal functioned to produce a sense of guilt and failure in the young Rich, who compared herself to this ideal and found herself lacking, in Lamott's narrative there is more critical irony, as the narrative voice represents her distance from the ideal but suspends judgment. She notes, for instance, "I wonder if it is normal for a mother to adore her baby so desperately and at the same time to think about choking him or throwing him down the stairs. It's incredible to be this fucking tired and yet to have to go through the several hours of colic every night" (59). Both the tone of the memoir and the repeated passages in which Lamott rhapsodizes about her son suggest that indeed she is not, as she describes herself, "Lady Macbeth as a nanny" but that, instead, this conjunction of love, anger, and exhaustion is indeed "normal," more normal than the selfless devotion of the fictional Donna Reed (49). Her choice of a fictional television character to represent the idealized maternal further suggests the artificiality and constructed nature of this image. An even more pointed instance of this occurs in an interview, where Lamott recalls, "When I was pregnant [. . .] all the mothering books made it sound like a 'normal' mother goes around feeling like Melanie Wilkes in 'Gone With the Wind.' Well, I felt like Squeaky Fromme"

(Holt E5). Her reference to the fictional, fragile, idealized Southern mother of *Gone With the Wind,* a mother who fulfills her culture's highest imperatives to both womanhood and motherhood yet still dies young, suggests the extent to which this ideal serves the interests of patriarchy at the costs of individual women. Lamott's reference to Squeaky Fromme, a woman who made U.S. national news in the 1970s because of her connection to Charles Manson and her failed assasination attempt on then President Ford, offers in place of Melanie Wilkes the image of a woman made famous precisely because of her inability or unwillingness to live within her prescripted gender role and because of her attempt to kill the most important symbolic patriarch in U.S. culture: the president.

Lamott further denaturalizes the universality of idealized motherhood by revealing its dependence on class privilege and heterosexual marital stability, both noticeably absent in her family. She comments that "I do sometimes wish I had a husband and a full-time nanny," adding later, "I wish I had an armed husband or at least a dog. Everything would feel safer" and "It is clear to me that we need a breadwinner. Also, servants" (80, 157, 177). Taken together, these one-liners suggest the distance between institution and individual embodiment of it: Although Lamott is certainly a mother (a doting one, even, given her repeated meditations on her son's beauty and intelligence), she lacks the cultural authority of the family—the literally or figuratively armed husband and dog—to protect her, financially support her, and provide her with a showcase for her material success. Moreover, Lamott's comments suggest a resistance to the punitive coding of that position within contemporary U.S. culture; like Gore, she implies that the problem is not with her version of motherhood but with the institution's.[24]

Even more explicitly, both Lamott and Moraga explore the way motherhood as institution serves patriarchy by producing its sons. In this, they suggest the ongoing relevance of Rich's claim, in her retrospective introduction, that "Perhaps the most overtly painful and divisive issue in the 1970s was that of sons" (xxxi), and certainly some of the most moving writing in *Of Woman Born* chronicles the tensions between Rich's deep love for her sons as individuals and her analysis of the institution of motherhood as working to reproduce the system of patriarchy by training sons to take up male privilege within it.[25] While Rich is referring specifically to lesbian communities in her comment above,[26] Robin Morgan, in a discussion of raising a son in this period, points out that sons were—and are—an issue for feminists of various sexual orientations: "Few subjects so provoke anxiety among feminists as the four-letter word *sons,*" yet raising sons "goes to the heart of practicing what we claim to believe, that 'the personal is political.' It goes to the crux of power and of patriarchy" (38). Both Lamott and Moraga specifically interrogate the ways the violence of patriarchy might affect their relationship with their sons. Lamott, from the heterosexual perspective, notes that she has seen the penis as "the

root of all my insanity, of a lot of my suffering and obsession" (8), then goes
on to explain this by commenting that "we internal Americans of the hetero
persuasion have really, really conflicted feelings about you external Americans
because of the way you wield those things, their power over us, and especially
their power over you" (8). She later links this directly to her mothering of her
son Sam by stating, "Part of me loves and respects men so desperately, and part
of me thinks they are so embarrassingly incompetent at life and in love . . . part
of me is so afraid of them. . . . I want to clean out some of these wounds,
though, with my therapist, so Sam doesn't get poisoned by all my fear and
anger" (83). Rich's contention that the work of mothers is to raise the next
generation of patriarchs even at the mothers' own expense echoes in Lamott's
comment, suggesting both that this danger stills exists for mothers and that
efforts to avoid it are possible, but difficult. Interestingly, Moraga articulates
nearly the same fear as Lamott, recalling, "I prayed that I would learn how to
raise a male child well, that the wounds men have inflicted on me, even in
their absence, will not poison me against my son" (41). More eloquently than
Lamott, Moraga also ponders the intersection of institutional imperatives
with personal experience, asserting, "I feared that there was no place for my
reckoning with his maleness. [. . .] It is not mere feminist rhetoric that makes
a woman stop dumbfounded in the face of a life of raising a son. It is the living woman-wound that we spend our lives trying to heal" (33). If contemporary feminists are aware, then, of the complicity with patriarchy that the institution of motherhood demands, our strategizing of resistance remains a work
in progress.[27]

One means by which both Lamott's and Moraga's narratives attempt to
resist patriarchal uses of motherhood is by recasting maternity within alternative forms of family or kin. Both draw on notions of nonbiological family.
Lamott chronicles a network of friends and relatives who help sustain her and
her son, referring to them as her "tribe" (117), while Moraga explains her use
of the term comadres to signify "a Mexican term denoting an intimacy similar
to that of a family member" (np). Lamott also represents her religious community as a part of her tribe, calling the members of her church her son's "new
family" and describing her sense of God as a presence of "something that is big
and real and protective," a description that encapsulates the functions implied
in her missing "armed husband" discussed earlier (27, 130, 157). She also relies
especially on her best friend Pammy, as Moraga does on her lover Ella.[28]

These various recastings of motherhood and family echo Rich's process of
attempting to dismantle universals of the institution of motherhood while also
remaining caught within them. Moraga, for instance, struggles to define,
within the specifics of her cultural context, "what blood and bones had to do
with this business of making queer familia. But we're Mexican. Blood matters"
(119). This question of blood's relation to a reconfigured family haunts Moraga's text, leaving her facing the same dilemma as Rich: even in a text

grounded in the specifics of difference, it remains difficult to escape the universalizing models of motherhood.[29] Moraga opens her memoir by pointing out the obvious: that "lesbians don't make babies with our lovers" (15), then goes on to query the relationships among the biological lesbian mother, her lover, and her child. She notes that in her case, she asked her lover "not to be a mother, but only a lover of my child, a lover to me" and explains that she "didn't know how much [. . . she] wanted to share motherhood" (15, 16). Moraga here dramatically reconfigures the family unit, rejecting a model of self-sacrificing and asexual maternity and insisting instead on maintaining an autonomous sexuality that allows her to position herself as simultaneously mother and lover. By not naming her lover as her son's mother, she also departs from a lesbian assimilationist model of the nuclear family with a twist.[30] At the same time, however, this move flirts dangerously with reinscribing motherhood in biology. A similar danger confronts Moraga in her decision to refer to her partner as "Ella," the Spanish word for "she." As Tatiana de la Tierra points out, "'She' implies that she could be anyone, but 'she' is a very specific someone" (22). Moraga's attempt to escape the roles of the conventional family by not defining Ella's position might, in homophobic circumstances like that of the hospital discussed earlier, allow for an erasure of a central figure in this "queer family." In the final entry of the memoir, Moraga concludes that "blood quantum does not determine parenthood any more than it determines culture. Still, I know blood matters. It just does not matter more than love," a comment that suggests the complexity of her struggle to reconfigure both maternity and family in ways that might retain the best inherent possibilities of these relationships while abandoning the oppressive institutional status of them (125).

Lamott articulates a similarly troubling relation to conventional family models even as she works to reconfigure them. She repeatedly records her regret that Sam doesn't "have his dad in his life" and describes as "my family portrait" a photo montage she's made of "me, Jesus, Sam, and the little seven-year-old-girl [a photo of herself as a child]. I'd say to myself, See? We are already a complete family unit. We don't need some guy. We are whole" (86, 141). This portrait serves as a metaphor for both her reconstructed sense of family and its debt to the conventional nuclear family. She also notes that in place of a father her son will have a "tribe" of men devoted to him, and comments, "I can't give him a dad, I can't give him a nuclear family. All I can do is give him what I have, some absolutely wonderful men in our lives who loved him before he was born [. . .] men who will be his uncles and brothers and friends, and I have to believe that this will be a great consolation" (86, 182–183). That her son, surrounded by a tribe of loving and supportive kin, still needs "consolation" for not having a biological father present suggests both the ongoing power of the nuclear family unit and the individual's limited ability to fully escape it.

To return to this essay's opening question, then, to what extent has the landscape—or feminist analyses of that landscape—changed since Rich's assessment of motherhood? Clearly, the conditions of class-privileged, privatized maternal isolation faced by Rich have in some degree shifted due to labor demands of a global economy, but as Gore demonstrates, working-class women continue to be castigated for both their poverty and their working outside the home. Meanwhile, a newly professionalized generation of class-privileged women struggle, but inevitably fail, to live up to the new model of "supermom," while simultaneously depending on the exploited labor of immigrant nannies.[31] The original racial and class blind spots of Rich's work remain unevenly present in contemporary texts. While many maternity guides (Pepper's among them) never even mention race and replicate the blindness of class privilege through assumptions of expendable income, insurance coverage, and professional perquisites like maternity leave, others, like Gore's, are more complex, also acknowledging the impact of racism and poverty on the lives of many mothers. Meanwhile, the self-consciousness with which mothers like Moraga and Lamott choose maternity positions them as more than simply the dupes of a benign version of a dangerous patriarchally controlled reproductive technology, although even with their best efforts both remain enmeshed—whether via resistance or compliance—in both the ideology and practice of patriarchal family structures.

Rich comments that "Ideally, of course, women would choose not only whether, when, and where to bear children, and the circumstances of labor, but also between biological and artificial reproduction. Ideally, the process of creating another life would be freely and intelligently undertaken" (174–175). She also understands, however, that for this to happen will be no small task: Her final exhortation is that "the institution of motherhood must be destroyed" (280). She sees this destruction, paradoxically, as a profoundly creative and freeing act, contending that, the "changes required to make this possible reverberate into every part of the patriarchal system. To destroy the institution is not to abolish motherhood. It is to release the creation and sustenance of life into the same realm of decision, struggle, surprise, imagination, and conscious intelligence, as any other difficult, but freely chosen work" (280). It's clear we're not there yet: Ultimately, Rich's critique has not yet had a socially significant impact. The structures of motherhood, the nation-state, and even contemporary icons (like the soccer mom) work jointly to reinforce a narrative of motherhood that remains deeply destructive for women. At the same time, however, texts like Gore's, Pepper's, Lamott's, and Moraga's suggest that the institution of motherhood continues to be attacked on the popular front, in varying ways and to varying degrees, and that Rich's critique, while still unfortunately timely in many respects, has also been heeded not simply by academic feminists, but also by myriad women who struggle, in the daily acts of their lives, to recast and reclaim motherhood.

NOTES

1. I would like to thank Frann Michel for first setting me on the path that led to this chapter and Teri Mae Rutlege for introducing me to Ariel Gore's work. Thanks also to Cybele Raver and Jackie Goldsby for many thought-provoking discussions on this topic (as well as the loan of various books and multiple forms of support in my own efforts to recast motherhood). Finally, thanks to Mary Pat Brady for her insightful comments on drafts of this piece and her collaboration in our own adventures in maternity.

2. Although Rich's impact on feminism is wide-ranging in both the United Kingdom and throughout North America, this chapter will focus specifically on the U.S. context. For while the U.S. context has been influenced by thinkers from other cultures/nations (the British Sheila Kitzinger, for instance, or the French Fernand Lamaze and Frederick Leboyer), both the histories of motherhood and feminist reworkings of it take on specific contours according to the specific culture/nation in which they occur. In order to avoid generalizing across cultures and nations, I will therefore confine myself to a discussion of the United States.

3. Rich notes that "[t]he 'childless woman' and the 'mother' are a false polarity, which has served the institutions both of motherhood and heterosexuality" (250). For a discussion of the link between motherhood and U.S. citizenship, see Linda Kerber's *Women of the Republic: Intellect and Ideology in Revolutionary America* (Chapel Hill: U of North Carolina P, 1980). See also Claire Buck's "Engendering the Political for Feminism: Citizenship and American Motherhood." Paragraph 21:3 (1998):290–307.

4. Perhaps the most eloquent statement of this later recognition on Rich's part of the intertwined nature of sexual oppression and racial and economic oppressions appears when she comments:

> I would not end this book today, as I did in 1976, with the statement "The repossession by women of our bodies will bring far more essential change to human society than the seizing of the means of production by workers." If indeed the free exercise by all women of sexual and procreative choice will catalyze enormous social transformations (and I believe this), I also believe that this can only happen hand in hand with, neither before nor after other claims which women and certain men have been denied for centuries: the claim to personhood; the claim to share justly in the products of our labor [. . .] ; to participate fully in the decisions of our workplace, our community; to speak for ourselves, in our own right. (xvii–xviii)

References to this new introduction will be cited in the body of this article as "Introduction." All other references to Rich are taken from the earlier edition of *Of Woman Born* entered in the works cited.

5. "In the American hospital delivery [. . .]" Rich notes, "birth is frequently treated as an operation, and always as a medical event" (163). Her scathing critique has sparked feminist analyses ranging from Mary Poovey's historical work to Jessica Mitford's more contemporary analysis, but can also be seen more broadly as part of the historical context out of which the feminist health care movement itself emerged.

6. Henci Goer notes that in the United States, "By the mid-1920s, half of all urban births took place" in hospitals, "and by 1939, half of all women and three-quarters of urban women gave birth in hospitals." Anthony Reading furthers this U.S. timeline by pointing out that "by 1973, 91 percent of babies were born in the hospital." See Goer's *The Thinking Woman's Guide to a Better Birth* (New York: Perigee Books, 1999:202) and Reading's *Psychological Aspects of Pregnancy*" (New York: Longman, 1983:8).

7. Feminist health care collectives and the homebirth movement must also be seen, of course, as parts of a broader spectrum of political activism on the part of second-wave feminists, a spectrum that also produced, for instance, rape crisis centers and battered women's shelters.

8. Gaskin's text might be seen as a radical feminist text both in its claim to the authority of women's knowledge and its linking of that knowledge to power. It articulates another form of feminism (closer to cultural feminism) in its claim to women's spiritual authority, as when Gaskin argues that birthing women, "under the right circumstances," have access to a level of insight and power that emerges from "a deeper level of meditation [. . . that produces] a consciousness of what is universal in humanity" (9).

9. Gaskin notes that the group who constituted the original collective at "The Farm" formed in the late 1960s in San Francisco (17). Judging by the extensive photographic evidence in *Spiritual Midwifery*, one might assume that the group evolved within the context of the hippies, a middle-class youth reaction to postwar U.S. culture. Whatever their class origins, the group (at least as represented in these photographs) was nearly exclusively white.

10. My focus here, as should become clear, is on maternity/childcare books aimed at women. A parallel, although much smaller, line of books has been developed for fathers (or, in the case of more enlightened authors, "partners"). Although space precludes a discussion of these texts, I would note that they are exclusively aimed at men: there is no guidebook aimed at the nonbiological lesbian co-mother. Also, the content of these texts is itself gendered in ways that reinforce maternity's location within a highly conventionally gendered heterosexual marriage. Books aimed at women, for example, focus on physical and emotional issues. In contrast, the only text that I have found that discusses the financial aspect of having a child is one aimed at men. See Armin A. Brott and Jennifer Ash, *The Expectant Father: Facts, Tips, and Advice for Dads-to-Be* (New York: Abbeville Press, 1995).

11. *What to Expect* implicitly reinforces the idea that even the "wife's" body belongs to the husband and exists to meet his needs. The chapter responds to the husband's complaint that his wife might get and stay "fat and flabby" as a result of her pregnancy, for example, by supporting his right to determine her body size (it advocates monitoring her diet). When the father reports feeling "turned off sexually" after watching his wife deliver, the authors reply sympathetically that some fathers "do come out of it [birth] feeling that their 'territory' [i.e., the vagina] has been 'violated,'" but assure him that this feeling will pass because he will come to realize that "the vagina is a vehicle of childbirth only briefly, while it is a source of pleasure for himself and his wife for a lifetime" (329, 330, 330). They respond to a similar complaint by dad that breast feed-

ing has de-eroticized his wife's breast for him by advising him "not to harbor any resentment against the baby for using 'your' breasts; try to think of nursing as a temporary 'loan' instead" (330). While the authors do use scare quotes for some of these terms, the text never contests the implication that maternity and sexuality are contradictory opposites, nor does it ever suggest that the deployment of the women's body or eroticism might be her, rather than her husband's, prerogative. Finally, that the mother might be experiencing her sexuality with a man other than a husband or even with a woman is never considered at all.

12. It should also be noted that the impact of this book is extended, for it prompted follow-up texts from the same authors. See, for instance, Arlene Eisenberg, Heidi E. Murkoff, and Sandee E. Hathaway, *What to Expect the First Year* (New York: Workman, 1989).

13. Pepper contends at her book's opening "[t]he more you learn now, the smoother it will all go later" (15), while Gore states in her introduction that she didn't want to write a "traditional" advice book: "I knew we didn't need any more 'my-way-is-best' tips on parenting [. . .] we need support. We need information so that we can choose our own ways to parent. We need options" (7).

14. A professional labor assistant, a doula is intended to provide guidance and support for any laboring woman. Pepper similarly suggests that a woman change doctors if she doesn't feel she is being "dealt with in an open and nondiscriminatory way" (68).

15. For an extensive discussion of the current politics of birth practices in the U.S. medical system, see Henci Goer.

16. One might think here of medical technology in the form of, for instance, ultrasounds, amniocentesis, drugs given during labor, and cesarean section deliveries, to name but a few of the most obvious.

17. Raising a related set of overlaps, Pepper, in a discussion of insurance coverage, warns her readers "To avoid being denied coverage, you may need to claim that you have been previously unable to conceive, rather than saying you are a lesbian" (51), a comment that reminds us of the degree to which the medical industry, to use Rich's terms, buttresses the heterosexual family.

18. Pepper comments that "Just as there are many of us who seek a lesbian family relationship typical in structure to the stereotypical nuclear family, there are also many who are looking for ways to build a new family dynamic. This could include a family with two moms and two gay dads, a lesbian and a gay man coparenting together, a single lesbian coparenting with a gay male couple . . ." (40).

19. Interestingly, Rich, Pepper, and Gore all comment upon motherhood's imbrication in the policing of female sexuality by patriarchal forces. Rich notes that although the physical relationship between mother and infant is intensely sensual, the eroticism of that relationship has been elided in a dichotomous structure that defines motherhood as nonsexual and in opposition to the erotic sexuality of the youthful non-mother. She points out that "Women are permitted to be sexual only at a certain time of life, and the sensuality of mature—and certainly of aging [and, we might add, lesbian]—women has been perceived as grotesque, threatening, and inappropriate" (183).

We might recall here *What to Expect*'s horrified father, who, recognizing the erotics of either the pregnant body or the mother-child relationship, responds with a disavowal articulated as repulsion. Rich makes the ramifications of this system explicit, arguing that "If motherhood and sexuality were not wedged resolutely apart by male culture, if we could *choose* both the forms of our sexuality and the terms of our motherhood or nonmotherhood freely, women might achieve genuine sexual autonomy" (184). Pepper contributes a specifically lesbian perspective to this discussion, noting that in mainstream pregnancy books, "References to lesbian sex during pregnancy are basically nonexistent" and cautioning her reader that her doctor is unlikely to offer information on the subject unless directly asked (126, 135). Given that mainstream pregnancy books do now contain information on heterosexual sex, Pepper's comment suggests that if the dichotomy of mother/sexual woman has broken down somewhat since Rich's day, it has done so only in relation to a heterosexual woman. But Pepper herself reinforces this dichotomy in terms of lesbians, noting "while some [lesbian] partners may find your new body luscious, some lovers turn off completely just when you start to feel comfortable with your larger size" (128). Pepper never challenges the ground of this response, simply suggesting instead that the pregnant woman get support from friends, a tacit acceptance of a coding of the pregnant body, as Rich puts it, as "grotesque, threatening, and inappropriate" (183). Contrast this to Ariel Gore's direct attack on the notion of mother-as-asexual: she opens her section on the second trimester with "What can I say? The sex is great. Not only can you expect to be totally horny, but the sex itself is awesome" (25). Like Pepper, she registers the cultural resistance to the idea of coterminous pregnancy and eroticism, but unlike Pepper she recognizes this as a manipulative strategy to control women. Gore confides, "Now I've heard a few stories about men who didn't think pregnant women were sexy. Please don't listen to any of this bullshit. If your man doesn't think you look awesome, he needs therapy, or maybe he should just go fuck himself in another state and leave you alone" (25).

20. Her deconstruction of the institution of motherhood and of the nuclear family begins in her book's prefatory pages, where she defines "mama" as, in part: "n. Mother, informal. . . . One who has a maternal relationship to . . . and/or generally makes it her (his) business to take care of the next generation . . . n. One who loves her children fiercely and herself unconditionally" (np). Notable here is the fact that Gore detaches the maternal relationship from the sex of the caretaker, understanding the act of nurturing as not innately a female act ("her his"). Also notable is the way her final definition flatly contradicts Rich's description in her journals decades ago of maternal love as "literally selfless" (23): Gore's mother simultaneously loves her children and herself.

21. As a young, single mom, Gore started the zine *(Hip Mama)* from which this book emerged out of the realization that according to the dominant representations of parenting that she found in books and on TV, she was, "perhaps, a total freak of nature" (3). Gore's text sets out to contest this ideological status quo, and does so both by offering information and support to her readers, and also by repeatedly contesting naturalized versions of motherhood and the family. She not only deromanticizes "family" life by noting the presence of poverty, violence, and divorce within it, but also interrupts the narrative that would automatically hold the mother responsible for these or any

other ills that befall the family unit. She blames postpartum depression and anger, for instance, on the system that isolates mothers and expects them to cope alone. And in a section on poverty, for instance, Gore flatly asserts, "It is the economy, not your character, that is fundamentally flawed. I don't care how you got into this situation; in a decent society, it would be *impossible*," while in a discussion of the family court system she reminds mothers, "Remember: You are not crazy. You are stuck in a crazy system" (199, 221).

22. Lamott's book appeared on the list on June 6 and 13, 1993.

23. Lamott recounts in an interview that the book got a big response from mothers who wrote to say her narrative was "what it's like for me—I'm glad someone finally said it" (Holt E5).

24. And there is an increasing amount of punitive rhetoric to resist in the wake of Clinton's "Welfare Reform" and the Republican party's emphasis on "Family Values" in recent years.

25. See, in particular, Chapter 8, "Mother and Son, Woman and Man."

26. For more on the issues confronting lesbians with sons, see Jess Wells's "Born on Foreign Soil." *Lesbians Raising Sons*. Ed. Jess Wells (Los Angeles: Alyson Books, 1997:20–30). Wells, for instance, comments that the news that the fetus she was carrying was male "brought up in me a frightening rage at the patriarchy" and that "It felt like a patriarchal setup at the most basic level—not just laboring for the patriarchy but actually creating its members" (20, 22).

27. Moraga notes, "I am afraid of the power of men and their gods over our lives. [. . .] I have constructed my daily life, to the degree to which I am able, outside the prison of patriarchy. This is not a rhetorical statement. This is the fact of my existence and the home-world in which I will raise my son. I am not fooled. They are not fooled. Even motherhood does not make me loyal to them" (108).

28. Lamott says of Pammy, "It feels good to say 'we,' even if that means my best friend, instead of me and a man. I could not have gone through with this, could not be doing it now, without Pammy. [. . .] She's my partner. In twenty-five years of friendship we've never even kissed on the lips, but in certain ways it feels like she's my lover and she's helping me raise my baby" (34), while Moraga observes of her relationship with her lover Ella, "'No more this is what 'a couple' is supposed to look like. We are what a couple looks like.' We are what a family looks like" (125).

On a broader level, both memoirs devote considerable narrative energy to death as an ironic means of constructing family: Lamott's best friend Pammy is diagnosed with terminal breast cancer half way through the memoir, while Moraga's story not only chronicles her son's near death as a result of his premature birth and consequent medical complications; it also takes place, as Moraga puts it, "in the age of death/the age of AIDS" (22). Throughout her narrative Moraga records the deaths of friends and acquaintances within her queer community, mainly men dying of AIDS, and asks, "Is there a kind of queer balance to this birthing and dying . . . lesbians giving life to sons, our brothers passing? He is the child of queers, our queer and blessed family, laughing with Pablo [her gay donor friend] and Ella after the insemination, sitting on the bed next to me" (62). Penelope Rowlands, in a review of *Operating Instructions*, echoes this invocation of a balanced relationship between life and death, contending that after Pammy's diagnosis with cancer, Lamott's book "assumes a kind of grotesque elegance, with the fates of Sam and Pammy each counterbalancing the other" (1). In each of these cases, a tragic but crucial means of defining family/community emerges from death, from a line of people linked to each other through a process of birth, death, and continuity. See Rowlands's "White-Knuckle Motherhood." *The San Francisco Chronicle* 2 May 1993, 1.

29. The question of the status of "blood" also raises further questions about blood's relation to nation and race, questions long at issue for Chicana lesbians, women often accused of abandoning their culture and especially their culture's imperative to make family through motherhood. See Moraga's discussion of this in *Loving in the War Years* (Boston: South End Press, 1983); see also Carla Trujillo, ed., *Chicana Lesbians: The Girls Our Mothers Warned Us About* (Berkeley: Third Woman Press, 1991).

30. This model offers a stable monogamous lesbian couple who raises their children in a family that is patterned after the heterosexual nuclear family, the twist being that the child has two mothers rather than a mother and a father.

31. The degree to which the labor needs of the nation-state influence the production of motherhood in general and the availability of child care more specifically is not lost on Rich, who explicitly notes that *Of Woman Born* is not "a call for a mass system of state-controlled child-care. Mass child-care in patriarchy has had but two purposes: to introduce large numbers of women into the labor force, in developing economies or during a war, and to indoctrinate future citizens" (14).

WORKS CITED

Boston Women's Health Book Collective. *Our Bodies, Ourselves for the New Century*. New York: Simon & Schuster, 1998; rvsd. rpt. of 1970.

de la Tierra, Tatiana. "Birth Smell." *Lesbian Review of Books* IV.4 (Summer 1998):22.

Eisenberg, Arlene, Heidi E. Murkoff, and Sandee E. Hathaway. *What to Expect When You're Expecting*. New York: Workman, 1984.

Faderman, Lillian. "Outside the Inside." *Lesbians Raising Sons*. Ed. Jess Wells. Los Angeles: Alyson, 1997:62–64.

Friedan, Betty. *The Feminine Mystique*. New York: Norton, 1963.

Gaskin, Ina May. *Spiritual Midwifery*, 3rd ed. Summertown, TN: The Book Publishing Company, 1990, rpt. of 1977.

Gore, Ariel. *The Hip Mama Survival Guide*. New York: Hyperion, 1998.

Holt, Patricia. "Taboo Emotions Are Laid Bare." *The San Francisco Chronicle* 28 June 1994, E5.

Jiménez, Karleen Pendleton. "Portrait of a Queer Motherhood." *Gay and Lesbian Times*, San Diego. 24 December 1997:8.

Lamott, Anne. *Operating Instructions: A Journal of My Son's First Year*. New York: Fawcett Columbine, 1993.

Mitford, Jessica. *The American Way of Birth*. New York: Dutton, 1992.

Moraga, Cherríe. *Waiting in the Wings: Portrait of a Queer Motherhood*. Ithaca: Firebrand, 1997.

Morgan, Robin. "Every Mother's Son." *Lesbians Raising Sons*. Ed. Jess Wells. Los Angeles: Alyson, 1997:38–50.

Pepper, Rachel. *The Ultimate Guide to Pregnancy for Lesbians: Tips and Techniques from Conceptions through Birth*. San Francisco: Cleis, 1999.

Poovey, Mary. *Uneven Developments: The Ideological Work of Gender in Mid-Victorian England*. Chicago: U of Chicago P, 1988.

Rich, Adrienne. "Compulsory Heterosexuality and Lesbian Existence." *The Lesbian and Gay Studies Reader*. Eds. Henry Abelove, Michele Aina Barale, and David Halperin. New York: Routledge, 1993; rpt. of 1980:227–254.

———. "Introduction: 1986." *Of Woman Born: Motherhood as Experience and Institution*. New York: Norton, 1995; rpt. of 1986:ix–xxxv.

———. *Of Woman Born: Motherhood as Experience and Institution*. London: Virago, 1984, rpt. of 1976.

SEVEN

Feminist Mothers

Successfully Negotiating the Tension between Motherhood as "Institution" and "Experience"

FIONA JOY GREEN

Throughout this book I try to distinguish between two meanings of motherhood, one superimposed on the other: the *potential relationship* of any woman to her powers of reproduction and to children; and the *institution*, which aims to ensure that that potential—and all women—remain under male control.
—Adrienne Rich, *Of Woman Born* (emphasis in original)

ADRIENNE RICH IS THE first person to have acknowledged that motherhood is a complex site of women's oppression and a potential location for women's creativity and joy. In *Of Woman Born*, Rich provides a detailed discussion of the social construction of motherhood and a critical analysis of how motherhood functions within patriarchy. Since its publication, over twenty-five years ago, feminists have been inspired to research many aspects of motherhood outlined by Rich. Early scholarship explored the ways social definitions and restrictions make motherhood an institution and examined various ways in which women are constrained by the socially accepted ideology of mothering. More recent discourse continues to unravel the complexities of motherhood by focusing on the multiple issues and experiences related to class, ethnicity, sexuality, and ability. Yet, still largely missing from the increasing dialogue and publication around motherhood is discussion of Rich's monumental contention that even when restrained by patriarchy, motherhood can be a site of empowerment and political activism for women.[1]

This assertion, that motherhood is simultaneously oppressive and potentially liberating, is reflected in my own experience as a feminist mother. Since giving birth to my son in 1988, I have consciously lived with, and managed, the tension between the oppressive and the emancipating components of motherhood. I continue to experience social pressure to conform to a standard of motherhood that feels restrictive and at times damaging. In particular, I find the expectation that I will, without question, follow and replicate "conventional" standards of motherhood and raise a son who will comply with the patriarchal expectations of masculinity offensive and harmful to my child, to myself, and to our family.[2] At the same time, however, I revel in the personal connection and relationship I have with my son. This unique relationship, one that I have yet to share with another person, offers moments when I experience my full potential as a human being. I believe this is partly because I try to be open to our mother/son relationship and I continually analyze the power dynamics within it. In addition to nurturing both my son's and my own growth within the arena of motherhood, I am able to actively undermine the institution of motherhood and challenge patriarchy. Rich's theory rings true for me; I can and do negotiate the tension between societal expectations of motherhood and my personal experiences of mothering.

While conducting research in Winnipeg during the mid-1990s for my PhD, I interviewed sixteen self-identified feminist mothers about their realities of being feminist mothers. Without exception, these women identify and experience both restrictive and liberating elements of motherhood. They also unanimously view their mothering as feminist because they actively challenge patriarchal assumptions about motherhood while parenting. Motherhood for these women is, as Rich proposes, certainly empowering and liberating.

THE INSTITUTION OF MOTHERHOOD

Before addressing the ways in which some of these feminist mothers manage the tension between the onerous and the emancipating elements of motherhood, I want to first explore the meaning of the institution of motherhood according to Rich and how this is understood by the feminist mothers in my research. Rich describes the institution of motherhood in this way:

> When we think of the institution of motherhood, no symbolic architecture comes to mind, no visible embodiment of authority, power, or of potential or

actual violence. Motherhood calls to mind the home, and we like to believe that the home is a private palace. . . . We do not think of the laws which determine how we got to these places, the penalties imposed on those of us who have tried to live our lives according to a different plan, the art which depicts us in an unnatural serenity or resignation, the medical establishment which has robbed so many women of the act of giving birth, the experts— almost all male—who have told us how, as mothers, we should behave and feel. We do not think of the Marxist intellectuals arguing as to whether we produce "surplus value" in a day of washing clothes, cooking food, and caring for children, or the psychoanalysts who are certain that the work of motherhood suits us by nature. We do not think of the power stolen from us and the power withheld from us, in the name of the institution of motherhood. (274–275)

Like Rich, the feminist mothers I spoke with understand that motherhood is part of our patriarchal society and, conversely, that patriarchy is highly incorporated within motherhood. While respondents do not specifically use the term "institution" when they speak about motherhood, they illustrate an understanding of this concept in their interviews. For instance, they speak of how motherhood is restrictive, and at times, oppressive because of the expectations placed on them to conform to and replicate an ideal of motherhood that prescribes particular behaviors.[3] They note the widespread use of messages about the virtues of the stereotypical "good" mother and warnings about the dangers of "bad" mothers. Television and radio talk shows, newspaper and magazine articles, and popular movies illustrate commonplace standards for both the exemplary and incompetent mother.[4]

We can all picture the ideal mother. She is a heterosexual woman who stays at home with her children while her husband (the father of their children) works in the labor force to support them financially. Because of her "innate" ability to parent and her "unconditional love" for her husband and children, the idealized mother selflessly adopts their wants, needs, and happiness as her own. Her willingness to participate in her children's schooling or in community activities is an extension of her maternal love. The perfect mother always has a connection with her children, never has an ill feeling toward them, and is completely responsible for caring for and nurturing all of her family members. The ideal mother never gets angry because she finds parenting to be the most meaningful aspect of her life. Providing love and care for her family fills her with boundless happiness and self-fulfillment.[5]

While this ideal is far removed from the reality of many women's lives,[6] the presentation of the "ideal mother" seen in mainstream media, advertising, and entertainment is nevertheless held out for mothers to strive for and is considered, to some degree, as the "legitimate" standard to which mothers are compared. The "perfect mother" is there for all to see; she becomes an ideal to believe in and one that people both expect and internalize. The participants in my research often hear comments from social workers, law and justice officials, teachers, medical professionals, and clergy about the legitimacy and predominance of the ideal mother and the righteous downfall of the "bad" mother. Peers, co-workers, family and friends also perpetuate concepts and expectations of motherhood that uphold patriarchal notions and expectations through commentary, free advice, or personal judgment. The message is clear; there is a correct way to be a mother and those women who do not meet this standard are "bad."

Being labeled "bad" or "deviant" for not adopting the idealized standard of motherhood means living with very real consequences. The feminist mothers I interviewed know from personal experience how women are subjected to external pressure to conform to the dominant image of the ideal mother and are punished when they do not. They spoke of suffering from feelings of inadequacy and guilt for not being "good" or "real" mothers when they have been unable to replicate, or find happiness in, the idolized stereotypical role of mother. Many verbalized feeling personally responsible for not obtaining the ideal, even though they are fully aware that it is socially constructed and unrealistic. To illustrate how they sometimes feel that they have fallen short of the impossible standard, participants cite examples of raising their voices to their children, of not providing homemade baking for a social gathering, of not meeting teachers when requested to do so, and of not being able to attend a child's sporting event due to study or work commitments.

These feminist mothers also spoke of how characteristics and expectations associated with the ideal mother set them up to fail. The patriarchal definition of motherhood places women in a no-win situation; the standard of motherhood is impractical and unreasonable and punishes those who fail to meet its criteria. Since their lives do not fit the prescribed mold of mother, many women experience painful consequences. For instance, mothers who are not partnered with men, who are financially impoverished, or who work for a living are often judged by others to be "unfit" mothers.

Neire, a forty-one-year-old lesbian of European and Jewish heritage, understands the realities of patriarchal motherhood. Recently divorced from her husband, the father of their teenage daughter and their ten- and six-year-old sons, Neire provides a critique of how patriarchal notions of motherhood set mothers up to lose:

> I think that society still sees mothers as being women who totally devote themselves to their kids. If the kid has a problem, you are completely tuned into that kid. And I mean, any variation on that is still seen as not being acceptable. In other words, the mother is still very much responsible for her kids and their actions and their behaviors and their whole being. And when your kid does something wrong, the mother is still blamed. That's still very prevalent.

I think it boils down to this whole ideology surrounding the family; that the family has two people, opposite sexes, and the children. And they're fully enclosed, a supposedly fully functioning family unit. And our society is still predicated on that. So if a woman finds herself in a position where she's not within that structure, the society only pays lip service to supports and that kind of thing.

But I think, given that this patriarchal model is still very much in existence, there are still a lot of women who are falling into this trap, and it just creates a hell of a lot of conflict and a hell of a lot of guilt, you know? I think it's very damaging. It's definitely damaging to mothers because it erodes our self-esteem and our self-confidence in our ability to be good mothers.

Like Rich and the other participants, Neire understands how the weight and "legitimacy" of patriarchy is able to dictate a standard of motherhood and to punish those who do not conform to its narrow definition and practice. Punishment is often devastating: the self-esteem and self-confidence of women and children can be shattered. Women often devalue themselves in order to put their children and families first. They may also profoundly limit their options due to abnegation. Many women endure isolation because they are unable to speak of the shame and guilt they experience for not living up to these unreasonable standards. Consequently, at times they suffer depression and, in extreme circumstances, complete mental breakdowns and suicide attempts. As we know, children are often removed from mothers who are considered "bad" or "unfit" by government and other agencies.[7]

LIBERATING EXPERIENCES OF MOTHERHOOD

The pressure to conform to the dominant model of motherhood and the consequences for noncompliance are very real. However, as Rich posits, patriarchal motherhood is not completely oppressive; there is room for women to practice agency, resistance, invention, and renewal within this institution:

What is astonishing, what can give us enormous hope and belief in a future in which the lives of women and children shall be mended and re-woven by women's hands, is all that we have managed to salvage, of ourselves, for our children, even within the destructiveness of the institution: the tenderness, the passion, the trust in our instincts, the evocation of a courage we did not know we owned, the detailed apprehension of another human existence, the full realization of the cost and precariousness of life. The mother's battle for her child—with sickness, with poverty, with war, with all the forces of exploitation and callousness that cheapen life—needs to become a common

human battle, waged in love and in the passion for survival. But for this to
happen, the institution of motherhood must be destroyed.

The changes required to make this possible reverberate into every part
of the patriarchal system. To destroy the institution is not to abolish motherhood. It is to release the creation and sustenance of life into the same realm
of decision, struggle, surprise, imagination, and conscious intelligence, as any
other difficult, but freely chosen work. (280)

Feminist mothers live Rich's emancipatory vision of motherhood. Driven
by their feminist consciousness, by their intense love for their children, and by
their need to be true to themselves, to their families, and to their parenting,
they choose to mother in ways that challenge the status quo. By consciously
resisting the restrictions placed on them by patriarchal motherhood, these
feminist mothers put Rich's theory into practice. Some women, for example,
openly reject the pressures and expectations placed upon them to reproduce
the ideal of motherhood by parenting in ways that openly challenge conventional standards of motherhood. Others consciously use their socially sanctioned position as mothers in subversive ways to teach their children to be
critically conscious of and to challenge various forms of oppression that support patriarchy. Regardless of the strategies invented and utilized by these
women as they live with the tension between the "institution" and "experience"
of motherhood, they successfully challenge and bring about social change as
Rich advocated more than a quarter century ago.

Overt Strategies of Resistance

Willow, a thirty-seven-year-old lesbian and lone parent of a ten-year-old
girl, provides an example of how feminist mothers use strategies that openly
and boldly challenge patriarchal motherhood. For Willow, mothering has
meant making "conscious decisions and actions of dissidence." The act of
birthing and solely raising a child, without any connection to a man, is a
deliberate act of resistance to dominant conceptions and practices of mothering. Willow explains:

> I mean basically, in order to do this, I broke all the rules and I went about
> this in the most conscious manner that I knew at that time. Although, to be
> honest with you, because my consciousness has changed, I'd probably go
> about it differently now. But back ten years ago, I broke all the rules by mak-
> ing a choice to be a mother. Nobody told me I had to be a mother because I
> was married or that I had to get married in order to do this. I made choices
> for myself. So in the late '80s and '90s there are particular ways that you're
> supposed to be a mother and they include either: be married to somebody
> who is relatively wealthy and can allow you to stay home, or put the kid in

day care at the age of six weeks or as soon as your maternity leave runs out, and pay attention to the money issue more than to anything else and run out to work. And I did not do that.

I did not let myself be subjugated, as it were, by men. I'm not married now, and I never have been and no man ever called the shots in my home, nor did a man ever support me in any way. So that is really breaking the rules in the patriarchy. It is clearly the most holistic act of resistance that I have ever done and the most difficult.

By consciously choosing to become a mother and raise her daughter alone, Willow has experienced hardship, as well as great pleasure. Because she wanted to raise her child without the interference of others and was without the financial means to do so, Willow lived on social assistance for a few years. She often bartered with others, exchanging child care or reading or singing lessons for goods and services. When her daughter reached school age, Willow chose to educate her at home, partly because she believed homeschooling was the best option for her daughter at the time and partly because, as a certified teacher, she was qualified to do so. Willow returned to work part-time in the labor force when her daughter, at the age of eight, entered the public school system after expressing a desire and demonstrating a need to do so.

When I last spoke with Willow in 1998, she was still openly challenging patriarchal notions of the motherhood. Finding it difficult to deal with some of her preteenaged daughter's behavior, she decided to call upon her network of friends for support. With the help of a close friend, who is also a feminist mother, Willow was able to effectively deal with the unwanted behavior of her daughter. For a few months the two women shared mothering responsibilities, allowing Willow and her daughter to remain strongly and positively connected but also providing the space for them to deal with the issue at hand. For a few days, or even a couple of weeks at a time, Willow's daughter would live with her social mother. Since both households were in the same neighborhood and the lines of communication were open, all three were in touch with each other on a regular basis. "Family meetings" were frequently held to discuss the situation and to work through difficulties as they arose. Within four months the disruptive behavior had been dealt with in a loving and effective manner, and Willow and her daughter were living together full-time.

Through successfully creating her own solution to what Willow believed would most likely have been considered a major concern by others, she has kept herself from being labeled an "unfit" mother and from possibly losing her daughter to the state. Willow not only addresses the needs of her daughter while keeping her family intact when she creates an alternative model of motherhood by expanding her family to include another woman/mother when necessary, she also challenges the patriarchal model of motherhood that is made up of the heterosexual nuclear family. Continually inventing ways to parent outside of the patriarchal standard also means that Willow enjoys a level of "freedom and strength" that she says she would not have experienced had she conformed to patriarchal methods of dealing with a "problem" daughter.[8]

Bringing down patriarchy is clearly a tricky and lengthy endeavor that requires numerous strategies and actions in various locations. For many participants, using their socially sanctioned position as mother is an effective tactic to challenge patriarchal constructs and notions of motherhood. The feminist mothers I spoke with see mothering, as does Rich, as a significant site of resistance to patriarchy. Under the cover of the institution of motherhood, they use the energy, focus, and dedication that women have always used in going to battle for their children to destroy the institution of motherhood. In doing so, their effective and subversive activity both challenges patriarchy and often goes unnoticed.

SUBVERSIVE STRATEGIES OF RESISTANCE

Deb, a thirty-five-year-old heterosexual mother of a seven-year-old boy, speaks openly about her strategy of using subversive strategies to contest patriarchy when she says:

> Someone can look at me on the surface and go, "O.K. There's a woman who's chosen to be a mother. Good, patriarchy likes that. Good, good." They don't have a clue! I have the ability to transform what I perceive the role to be, to take it on, to claim it, and to just create it. I'm a mother in my own image in the absence of a role model, or someone who's telling me how to do it. I guess the thing that I was amazed at was just how wonderful I find my experience of mothering to be in a nonpatriarchal way.

Deb knows she is considered a "good mother" because she fits, to some degree, the conventional notions of mothers being in monogamous, long-term relationships with the father of their children. She uses this belief in who she is as a mother to her own advantage; she quietly raises a son who is consciously aware of social injustice caused by patriarchy, racism, homophobia, agism, class bias, and capitalism. Deb recognizes that to be able to subvert motherhood she needs to be aware of what patriarchy expects from her as a mother and to have an understanding of how she can effectively manipulate and challenge those same expectations to her advantage.

Carol, aged forty-five, understands patriarchal motherhood and chooses to challenge it in her mothering. While she is the lone parent of her ten-year-old biological son and her thirteen-year-old adopted niece, she is also actively involved in mothering three adult children of her previous male partner. Carol speaks candidly about her understanding about the social expectations placed on her as a mother that she developed from her experience of mothering five children:

What they would have me do is raise my girl children and my boy children in a specific way, so that when they're adults, that's the way they are. That, to them, is truth. Patriarchal society dictates me to beat their spirit out of them.

Rather than follow the patriarchal dictate of beating the spirit out of her children, Carol chooses to help her children develop without forcing gender stereotypes upon them. She actively encourages the nurturing and noncompetitive tendencies of her son, while supporting her daughter in her pursuits of maths and science, which are often considered to be "male" subjects. By showing her children how to follow their own interests and by treating them with respect, Carol supports their development of autonomy and individuality. Carol tells me:

> I have always shown a great amount of respect for my children because they've always been human beings to me. Feminism has given me the freedom to talk to my children as if they were human beings, instead of "I'm superior."
>
> The patriarchal society is very competitive. Because I'm a feminist, I have absolutely no desire to compete with my children. So, consequently, I can tell them the secret recipe to the rhubarb pie, because hopefully they will end up making it better than I do.
>
> I created a world where competition doesn't go on in my house. They didn't have to fall into that machismo/feminine world, you know. They have to struggle through it, and it is a struggle, yes. But there's a different way.

Providing a noncompetitive, loving, and respectful environment is the strategy Carol uses to teach her children that there are different models and ways of being male and female in the world. By using her power and responsibility as a mother, Carol provides a milieu that is supportive of her children's personal development and teaches them alternative ways of being than those demonstrated in the media, popular culture, or in various social institutions. Like Carol, Beverly rejects the socially prescribed standards of motherhood and chooses to raise her children in ways that develop their self-confidence and self-governance. Beverly, a forty-four-year-old bi-sexual, is the lone parent of two daughters in their late teens. She speaks of how she tries to live out her principles of fairness, equality, and openness in her parenting. Rather than replicate hierarchical power structures presumed to be the basis of parent and child relationships, Beverly consciously shares the power she has as an adult and a mother with her two daughters. She notes:

> Because of my principles that I hold, I've had to treat my children in a equal fashion from the beginning so that they have always known that they have the right to express themselves, that they have the right to say no, and that we could engage in a dialogue about the issue as opposed to me wielding power over them, and that's still very important to me.

Not only does Beverly share her authority as an adult with her children, she also encourages her daughters to see how all people, including themselves, are accountable for their own choices and personal conduct. This has been most difficult at times, especially when one daughter, who was underage, began to drink alcohol. This action triggered a number of issues for Beverly because her father was an alcoholic and it raised concerns about the illegal behavior of her child. Through many hours of talking, often late at night and into the early hours of the morning, Beverly and her daughter came to understand why the drinking had begun and what it meant to each one of them. Within a few months, and much to Beverly's relief, her daughter freely chose to stop drinking.

Beverly believes her daughter's decision came about from the open, honest, and nonthreatening communication she continues to have with her children. Rather than using threats and punishment to try to curb or stop the drinking behavior, Beverly chose to talk with her daughter until they came to a place of deep understanding. Holding her daughter accountable for her behavior, both when she drank and chose to stop drinking, was tough and scary. Beverly believes showing respect for her daughter's autonomy throughout the entire process of dealing with the situation, even when Beverly disagreed with the choices her daughter was making, helped to resolve the problem and allowed her daughter to become fully responsible for herself.

Carol and Beverly are not alone. All interviewees, including Neira, Willow, and Deb, speak of the importance of teaching children to take responsibility for their own conduct, as well as respecting their choices and decisions. In doing so, power within the family is shared and people are held accountable for their own actions. This practice directly challenges patriarchal family structures that assume a hierarchical formation where women and children have less power, voice, and autonomy than men. By sharing power and exercising personal accountability within the family, the patriarchal familial structure is no longer present or effective, and respect for individuals, both within and outside the family, is developed and practiced.

Within the domain of motherhood, feminists actively engage their children in critical thinking. For example, they use watching television, going to movies, and seeing plays as forums to look at and discuss the power dynamics of the larger world. They also use situations in the media and in the lives of friends and acquaintances to discuss the ways in which people are oppressed by racism, class bias, sexism, homophobia, and notions of ability. Bringing issues of poverty, consumerism, and environmental devastation to the attention of children is another way of explaining the complex way in which oppression works. Shopping for groceries brings about conversations on the politics of boycotting products from particular countries because of environmental destruction, the exploitation of migrant labor or oppressive political regimes. These teachable moments are used by feminist mothers whenever and wherever they arise.

Equally important in the work of challenging patriarchy while within the sanctity of motherhood is taking risks in more overt ways and exposing children to public and communal political activism. It is not unusual for feminist mothers to take their children to marches organized around "Take Back the Night," "Gay Pride," or "Reproductive Choice." Visiting protest villages at the provincial legislative grounds, being part of collective student action against increasing tuition costs, participating in play-for-peace workshops and other antiwar protests, or showing support for child care workers and universal day care by joining marches are public demonstrations that feminist mothers have ensured their children have been a part of. They believe that because they are feminist mothers they must participate and take their children to these public and collective events.

Regardless of the ways in which feminist mothers parent, they use their positions within motherhood to both overtly and covertly challenge patriarchy by teaching their children to be critical of the power structures and to be aware of the damage social injustice does to the lives of people. By doing so, they raise the consciousness of their children and challenge patriarchy.

CONCLUSION

Feminist mothers recognize, as Rich theorizes, how motherhood is both an institution and an experience. In honoring their commitment to feminism and to raising their children from that perspective, they successfully negotiate the tension between the two. Whether like Willow, who calls upon others in her community to help her when she is unable to effectively parent by herself, or like the other women who use the cover of motherhood to connect with and to consciously educate their children, these feminist mothers, as Rich suggests, are actively destroying the institution of motherhood with their "conscious intelligence" and feminist praxis.

NOTES

1. Some writers, such as Patricia Hill Collins, Marjorie Hill, and Sandra Pollack do address how those women who are marginalized due to racism and heterosexism find empowerment in mothering.

2. These restrictions also influence my partner and the father of our child. For the purpose of this chapter, however, I restrict my discussion to the influence of motherhood on mothers and children.

3. Ann Dally notes that the concept of motherhood first originated in the Victorian era and has since developed to include the doctrine of the idealized mother, wife, and woman. Shari Thurer and Betsy Wearing also address the social construction of motherhood in their discussion of the ideology of motherhood.

4. Ray Richmond profiles over fifty TV moms, both good and bad.

5. Marlee Kline provides a good description and analysis of the "ideal mother."

6. For example, in Canada (1996) 19 percent of all families with children were female-headed, one-parent families (Statistics Canada).

7. This is especially true of lesbian mothers, racialized mothers, and impoverished mothers. See, for example, Katherine Arnup, Patricia Hill Collins, and Shari Thurer.

8. The term "patriarchy" and words ending in "ism" are used by some mothers to explain various forms of oppression to their children, while other mothers choose to speak about the concepts and realities of social injustices without using feminist language.

WORKS CITED

Arnup, Katherine. "Lesbian Mothers and Child Custody." *Gender and Society: Creating a Canadian Women's Sociology.* Ed. A. Tigar McLaren. Toronto: Copp Clark Pitnam, 1988:245–256.

Collins, Patricia Hill. *Black Feminist Thought: Knowledge, Consciousness and the Politics of Empowerment.* New York: Routledge, 1991.

Dally, Ann. *Inventing Motherhood: The Consequence of an Ideal.* London: Burnett, 1982.

Hill, Marjorie. "Child-Rearing Attitudes of Black Lesbian Mothers." *Lesbian Psychologies: Explorations and Challenges.* Eds. Boston Lesbian Psychologies Collective. Chicago: U of Illinois P, 1987:215–226.

Kline, Marlee. "Complicating the Ideology of Motherhood: Child Welfare Law and First Nation Women." *Open Boundaries: A Canadian Women's Studies Reader.* Eds. B. Crow and L. Gotell. Toronto: Prentice Hall and Bacon Canada, 2000:194–204.

Pollack, Sandra. "Lesbian Parents: Claiming Our Visibility." *Women-Defined Motherhood.* Eds. J. Knowles and E. Cole. London: Hawarth, 1990:181–194.

Rich, Adrienne. *Of Woman Born: Motherhood as Experience and Institution.* New York: Norton, 1976.

Richmond, Ray. *TV Moms: An Illustrated Guide.* New York: TV Books, 2002.

Statistics Canada. Women in Canada 2000, Catalogue No. 89–503–XPE:2000.

Thurer, Shari. *The Myths of Motherhood: How Culture Reinvents the Good Mother.* New York: Penguin, 1994.

Wearing, Betsy. *The Ideology of Motherhood: A Study of Sydney Suburban Mothers.* Sydney: George Allen and Unwin, 1984.

EIGHT

Immortality and Morality in Contemporary Reworkings of the Demeter/Persephone Myth

KARIN VOTH HARMAN

This cathexis between mother and daughter—essential, distorted, misused—is the great unwritten story.

Each daughter, even in the millennia before Christ, must have longed for a mother whose love for her and whose power were so great as to undo rape and bring her back from the dead. And every mother must have longed for the power of Demeter, the efficacy of her anger, the reconciliation with her lost self.

—Adrienne Rich, *Of Woman Born*

NEARLY THIRTY YEARS ON, it is possible to interpret Adrienne Rich's *Of Woman Born* as a bugle call that released packs of hounds, chasing pen in hand to "write" (and often to "right") the great unwritten cathexis. In 1981, just five years after *Of Woman Born*, Marianne Hirsch attributed an influx of scholarly work on mothers and daughters to Rich's challenge (1981, 200–222). Ten years after Hirsch, Virginia Smith credited Adrienne Rich with "channell[ing] both popular and academic American feminist scholarship into what has proven to be one of its most productive and profitable directions" (283). It is now impossible to overlook the number of texts on the mother/daughter relationship. Writers of fiction, poetry, psychology, sociology, literary theory, and all forms of popular self-help genres, have flooded this previously empty terrain with so many words that the stories of mother/son, or mother/children, now appear thoroughly underwritten in comparison.[1]

In her review of the first five years of this "surge," Marianne Hirsch provides a sense of the excitement with which Feminism "discovered" the mother/daughter dyad: "The study of mother-daughter relationships situates itself at the point where various disciplines become feminist studies, as well as at the point where the feminist areas of a number of disciplines intersect" (202). Hirsch's essay (and her full-length study of mothers and daughters, *The Mother/Daughter Plot* [1989]) map the three primary theoretical directions (all rooted in psychoanalysis) from which the mother/daughter relationship was initially approached. The most influential strand, led by Nancy Chodorow, and including Dorothy Dinnerstein, Jane Flax, and Jean Baker Miller, drew from the Freudian oedipal paradigm and object relations psychology. A second strand derived from Jungian studies, and the third, represented by Luce Irigaray as well as by Julia Kristeva and Hélène Cixous, were based on reactions to the work of Jacques Lacan.[2]

Hirsch points out the remarkable points of intersection between these various (male-dominated and usually antagonistic) theoretical strands when they consider the mother-daughter relationship. All, in various ways, stress the continuity between mother and daughter, insisting on "an ultimate lack of separation between daughter and mother and an emphasis on multiplicity, plurality, and continuity of being" (209). Interestingly, notes Hirsch, "although American psychoanalysis is essentially based on ego psychology and French psychoanalysis insists on the explosion of the unified ego, they intersect where female identity is concerned. . . . Women's being, because of the quality of the pre-oedipal mother-daughter relationship, is, according to both traditions, continuous, plural, in-process" (211).

Hirsch's essay of 1981 and her full-length study of 1989 paint, respectively, the theoretical frameworks, and details, that underpin feminist scholarship on mothers and daughters. What emerges is a relatively unified theoretical backdrop against which writers of fiction and poetry sketch out their understandings of mothers and daughters. In the decade following Hirsch, however, writers have, increasingly, challenged any unified reading of mothers and daughters. Indeed, even in her 1986 introduction to the updated *Of Woman Born*, Rich notes that her reliance on Greek mythological paradigms does not necessarily illuminate the variety of maternal writing coming from nonwhite, Western and middle-class perspectives. However, while writing on mothers and daughters has indeed become more diverse, adventurous, and representative of a variety of cultural perspectives, it is nevertheless fascinating to observe that even very recent writing on the subject often follows Rich in hovering, both explicitly or implicitly, around the most powerful of mother/daughter stories—the myth of Demeter and Persephone. In this chapter I hope to provide insight into what just a few writers are now doing with this myth and to look at two concepts—immorality and immortality—which begin, in these writings, to unsettle the relative theoretical unity that Hirsch observes.

For the very myth itself is not unified. The extant versions of this ancient story differ, primarily in two key respects: they disagree about the extent to which Demeter, Persephone, and the crone/grandmother figures Hecate or Rheia are indeed one (trinitarian) personality, and they argue about issues of agency and morality surrounding the rape of Persephone. Like attorneys at a modern-day rape trial, the Ancients differed as to whether Persephone's rape was a terrible tragedy, a timely and necessary occurrence, or indeed, an event that Persephone was actively (or passively) seeking.

Disagreement about these two fundamentals: the identity of the mother/daughter duo or triad and the evaluation of the rape continue to exercise reworkings of the myth in modern times. These are also precisely the issues that trouble psychoanalytic interpretations of mother/daughter relations. To what extent are mothers and daughters necessarily enmeshed and incapable of forming strong, individuating ego boundaries? And what is the impact of sexual activity upon the mother/daughter relationship? Can we envision separation, particularly sexually driven separation between mother and daughter that does not sever that "first love"? That these are questions debated not only by psychoanalysts, or the ancient versions of the Demeter myth, is evidenced in Mickey Pearlman's introduction to *Mother Puzzles,* a collection of essays on the mother/daughter relationship in contemporary literature. In her summary of what the literary texts have in common, Pearlman (unwittingly?) evokes the ancient myth:

> The reality of the mother/daughter experience (at least in the writing examined here) is that mothers are often more disabling than enabling, that daughters are often both attached to (or detached from) their mothers in ways that are disturbing and disheartening, and that both of these insights are a natural prelude to a vision of mothers, and especially daughters, as victims, sometimes sexual, of their male relatives. (6)

I have chosen to consider the questions of mother/daughter enmeshment and heterosexual activity[3] under the headings of "immortality" and "immorality" in four very different contemporary mother/daughter texts that follow Adrienne Rich in making use of the Demeter/Persephone paradigm. Jenny Joseph, (the British poet immortalized by her ubiquitous "When I grow old I shall wear purple"), offers in *Persephone* (1986) a "collage" of variations on the myth in poetry, in a variety of prose styles, and even in cartoon. Joseph's primary voices are those emanating from working-class England in the seventies and eighties. Rita Dove's *Mother Love* (1995), a volume of poems written during her time as U.S. poet laureate, muses on the Demeter story in a wide range of cultural settings reflective of Dove's own position as an African American poet and academic. Finally, we will consider two novels—Maggie Gee's *Lost Children* (1994), set in London during the late-eighties, and Barbara Kingsolver's

Pigs in Heaven (1993), set in the southwestern United States during the late-eighties—which do not explicitly refer to the Demeter story. Yet each incorporates elements of the myth in their stories of mothers and lost daughters.

In these texts we will find that "maternal omnipotence"—or the temptation within psychoanalysis and contemporary culture to see the mother as a godlike ground of being—is challenged by the mother/daughter relationship. The Mother's historical link to religious or quasi-religious ideas of transcendence or immortality is also interrogated by reworkings of the Goddess Mother myth. Closely allied to the intimations of immortality in these texts is the question of how men both prevent and are necessary to a maternal "immortality" between mother, daughter, and granddaughter. The question of the behavior of the fathers, and the uncles, is one that Rich also raises in her chapter on "motherhood and daughterhood" in *Of Woman Born*. I would push the connection even further to suggest that sexual morality or immorality is a mother/daughter issue, an arena in which the power of the mother is tested, the critical test that the mother/daughter bond must face.

JENNY JOSEPH'S *PERSEPHONE*

> "No, don't stop, Uncle Harry. I'm not frigh-tened. Go on. Don't
> stop. Higher, Uncle Harry; swing me higher. *High*er."
> —*Persephone*, final sentence (emphasis in original)

Jenny Joseph's 1986 version of the Demeter/Persephone myth is narrated through a verse line interrupted by fragments of letters, dialogue, story, poetry, and cartoon that explode the themes of the myth into contemporary, largely British settings.[4] Joseph seems to completely secularize the myth; she never invokes a "goddess" status for her merely mortal "Demeters" and "Persephones," nor does she envision the threat to time and death that an ongoing generational line of women can pose (neither Demeter's mother, nor Persephone's child are mentioned). The interesting bid for "immortality" in Joseph's *Persephone* is made through the authorial activities of Joseph herself. As Joseph explodes the age-old myth into a huge variety of voices, she provides a plethora of "literary offspring" for Demeter and Persephone. The focus in this text is on the literary immortality of the mother/daughter pair.

The question of morality, however, features very prominently. In an authorial note, Joseph draws attention to her role as author in placing "diminishment against gain, good against evil." She is explicitly trying to show the balance and naturalness of the story of a young girl's sexual awakening and separation from her mother. So she places the dire tales of the "Autumn" and "Winter" sections of her book against the more hopeful stories of "Spring" and "Summer." The central story of the text that seems its fulcrum, and its "ars poetica," is presented as a speech in which an ageing diplomat recalls two wartime memories. The first is of a distraught Jewish mother in eastern Germany at the beginning of World War II, tearfully bidding her daughter farewell as the child boards a train with a group of refugee children. The second memory is of watching an acquaintance on a train, a young woman who had been captured, raped, hidden, fed, and cared for during the war by a German soldier, alight from the train to reunite with her ecstatic mother. The gentleman concludes his powerful descriptions of these two events with the suggestion that memory does the work of redemption: it puts these two stories of loss and restoration together in order to prevent the (ultimate) triumph of evil.

Can Jenny Joseph do the same? Her bid to do so is often quite disturbing. For instance the text abounds with "Uncle Harry" figures, rapists and molesters, but these men are inevitably portrayed as less threatening to the daughters than the mother (or mother-reader) imagines. The rapist in Persephone's first tale thrusts a "somewhat limp bundle of flesh" at his victim: the girls "ask for it," and inevitably eventually become attached to their older abusers. Persephone "consoles" mothers with the thought that their darkest fears are not always realized, that the daughter's loss of virginity, even through rape, is not necessarily an unmitigated evil.

In Joseph's text we are in a recognizably oedipal, sexually charged world; fathers, however, (like Persephone's father, Zeus) are largely absent. The girl's sexual desire is awakened not by the father, who, as one sexually involved with the mother may be a safer object for her libido, but by the uncle who is only too happy to inform her desire for knowledge. Thus "the rape" both occasions the necessary separation from the mother and releases the daughter from the static power of the mother into a deep, more mysterious realm. Joseph is at pains to present this process as natural and necessary. The last lines of poetry in *Persephone* are spoken by a "black male bird," an authoritative figure who "marks the time":

> Mourn, he calls, mourn for Demeter, mourn
> For your poor cold hearth, your loss, your diminishment
> But as for Persephone, as for Hades' bride
> Why, she goes down to riches. (285)

Joseph's reflections upon the morality of the rape speak into fiercely controversial debates within feminism about sexuality. Bravely, and I think wisely, Joseph frames questions about the loss of virginity (how? when? why? who?) within the context of the (also problematic) mother/daughter relationship. However, what is left-over from these fragments of reflection troubles rather than soothes. Because Joseph transplants the myth onto thoroughly secular territory, what remains at the story's end is not a celebration of intergenerational female power, nor Demeter's and Persephone's work as powerful goddesses as they together establish the Eleusinian Mysteries. In fact what remains in Joseph's text is a clutch of images and stories that do not fit into her pattern of balancing out sad and happy stories simply by placing them together under one cover.

Joseph profoundly unsettles her own project, not only by seeming to provide apologias for pedophiles, but by including, at the nadir of her text, a string of stories of absolute abject misery. She interrupts her loose pattern of weaving together poetry and prose at this point in order to present a relentless series of nine prose pieces. In these stories a girl is crushed, screaming, by a lorry; women miscarry in horrendous and excruciatingly painful circumstances; a soldier describes finding a room (gas chamber?) full of skeletons; a woman gives birth to a baby with no head. These stories are prefaced by Persephone's call to:

> Come down with me
> Whom I would call my followers
> (But following suggests that you could move)
> Come down,
> You who turn from things,
> Into my blank domain where the silence would suit you. (47)

These are the stories of hell: the nine rungs of the inferno. And yet they are prefaced by Persephone's passivity and they are concluded by Hades's words to Demeter as he stills her anger and horror by whispering:

> Hush, sister, not down here. We have no horrors
> As you up on earth. Here all is quiet
> And orderly and unhysterical. Here is no pain
> No desperate striving. (85)

I find Hades's attempt to dissolve pain into nothingness totally unconvincing. The nine stories of hell are too vivid, too well told, to be digested by mere assertions that good and evil are part of the same thing, that they are naturally balanced, that we should not overreact. These stories sit uneasily at the moral black hole of the text created, I would suggest, by Joseph's reluctance to let concepts like pain, exploitation, maternal anger, and justice attach themselves to her "Uncle Harrys." In ancient Greek versions of Demeter and Persephone, what is left over, or famously unexplained are the Eleusinian Mysteries. In Joseph's contemporary setting what is left over, or unexplained, is this inferno of stories that seem to insist, against the thrust of the rest of the text, that the world initiated by Uncle Harry is more, not less, dangerous than we (and Joseph?) wish to think. Both in tone and style, Joseph's 1986 text is reminiscent of *Of Woman Born*. Like Rich, Joseph produces a rather unwieldy, passionate, and troubled account of motherhood. There's a sense in which, in these "early days" of writing on the subject, there is just so much to say—and the focus is very much on the "sins of the fathers." In contrast to Joseph, and to Rich, the texts of the 1990s will tend to be both more optimistic, and more measured.

RITA DOVE'S *MOTHER LOVE*

> Motherhood—I've always known this—is a profound distraction from philosophy, and all philosophy is rooted in suffering over the passage of time. I mean the *fact* of motherhood, the physiological fact. To have the power to create another human being is to be the instrument of such a mystery—is thus to triumph over death.
> —Cynthia Ozick, *The Shawl*

> There's a way to study freedom but few have found it;
> you must talk yourself to death and then beyond,
> destroy time, then refashion it. Even Demeter keeps digging
>   towards that darkest miracle,
> the hope of finding her child unmolested.
> —"Political" in *Mother Love*

Rita Dove's *Mother Love,*[5] like Joseph's *Persephone*, transplants the myth into a variety of contemporary settings and voices: both follow the trajectory from loss to (partial) resolution. Dove, too, offers an authorial commentary to her verse in a prologue. Her observations, however, reflect more upon the form of her poetry than its content, for in this volume, Dove, traditionally a free verse poet, claims to be writing "sonnets." Her introduction claims:

> Sonnets seemed the proper mode for most of this work. . . . I like how the sonnet comforts even while its prim borders (but what a pretty fence!) are stultifying; one is constantly bumping up against Order. The Demeter/Persephone cycle of betrayal and regeneration is ideally suited for this form since all three—mother-goddess, daughter-consort and poet—are struggling to sing in their chains. (ii)

Critics of *Mother Love* differ in their reading of the many liberties that Dove takes with the sonnet form. Lotta Lofgren reads the "bent sonnet" as emblematic of Persephone's struggle to escape the "pretty fences" of her mother's world: "The freedom Dove takes with the sonnet parallels Persephone's struggle for freedom and her ambivalence towards the security with the mother, who wants her relationship with Persephone to be fixed and immutable" (140).

Reading more playfully, Stephen Cushman suggests that the "fourteen-ers" of *Mother Love* ("the key to Dove's sonnets lies not in accentual-syllabic meter or regular rhyming but in their various arrangements based on the number fourteen" [132]) are appropriate to the Demeter myth, not because they represent the chains of the mother/daughter relationship but because they retell the ancient myth of "the nearly perfect sonnetness of the seasons":

> When Dove moves from free verse to free verse with irregular rhyming, occasional metrical lines, and various arrangements based on the number fourteen, she chains herself a little too loosely to make Houdini jealous. . . . In other words, Dove's self imposed limits do not function as chains that she sings in spite of but rather as talismans she is able to sing because of. . . . [The Demeter myth] is a story that marks time, that counts and by counting tells us what we can count on. Imagine the depression and panic of not knowing that the dwindling of the light each December is a phenomenon whose days are numbered. Because we can count, we take heart. Because we can take heart, we sing. (133)

Counting, as Cushman explains it, and as countless sonneteers have employed it, is a form of resistance to death. It is a form of "immortality" akin to the mother. Cushman points out the etymological connections between mater, meter, Demeter, menstrual, and menopause. What we find in *Mother Love*, he suggests, is reflections on maternal resistance to mortality expressed both in the content (the story of Demeter) and the sonnetlike form of the poetry. The verse on one hand resists "patriarchal" rigid timekeeping: the sonnets are not regular; a key poem in the volume tellingly lambastes the cycle-regulating birth control pill as "man's invention to numb us so we/ can't tell which way the next wind's blowing" (46). On the other hand, as Cushman argues, the verse, especially as it reflects a maternal voice, maintains a heavy investment in meter. Cushman finds only two poems, the long series "Persephone in Hell" and "Lost Brilliance," that bear no "family resemblance to the sonnet." He doesn't mention that these are precisely the poems from which a Demeter-voice is exorcised: they are, in fact, the celebrations of the power of Hades. It is Hades who breaks "de-meter," who expels the mother, who ruins her timing.

The "rapes" in Dove's poems do not, in fact, seem quite as untimely as those in Joseph's version. Dove's daughters tend to be older than Joseph's: her central "Persephone" is a somewhat sexually experienced young woman spending time studying in Paris. She goes willingly to the bed of her seducer. Yet though it might be easier for Dove, therefore, to adopt the "it's only natural, get over it mum" approach of Joseph's text, Dove seems to be more sympathetic to maternal grief and maternal schemes to turn back, or redeem, the time. Indeed, Dove's collection, in marked contrast to, but also in development from Rich's treatment of the mother/daughter relationship, focuses almost entirely upon the subjectivity of the mother.

Dove's final three sonnets relate a quest to discover the ancient site of Persephone's abduction on the island of Sicily. Having trailed past one shabby, weed and litter infested ruin after another, the poet and her husband travel counterclockwise around the island:

> We circle the island, trailing the sun
> on his daily rounds, turning time back
> to one infernal story: a girl
> pulled into a lake, one perfect oval (74)

The "perfect oval" that they finally locate is now surrounded by a racetrack:

> Bleachers. Pit stops. A ten-foot fence
> plastered with ads—Castrol, Campari—
> and looped barbed wire; no way to get near.
> We drive the circumference
> with binoculars: no cave, no reeds.
> We drive it twice, first one way, then back,
> to cancel our rage at the human need
> to make a sport of death. (75)

The final sonnet of this series returns directly to Persephone's story:

> Through sunlight into flowers
> she walked, and was pulled down.
> A simple story, a mother's deepest
> dread—that her child could drown
> in sweetness.
>
>   Where the chariot went under
> no one can fathom. Water keeps its horrors
> while Sky proclaims his, hangs them
> in stars. Only Earth—wild
> mother we can never leave (even now
> we've leaned against her, heads bowed
> against the heart)—knows
> no story's ever finished; it just goes
> on, unnoticed in the dark that's all
> around us: blazed stones, the ground closed. (77)

These final poems, with their authoritative tone, affirm a place for rage, a place for dread, a place for the time bending activities that Demeters through the ages have attempted. There are, in addition, chords of consolation struck at the very end. Dove invokes a capitalized "Earth," a wild mother figure whom we "can never leave." This "mother" offers at last, a defence against mortality, against the masculine death games all around, for she knows that "no story's ever finished; it just goes / on" underneath, or despite, the funereal landscape. This subtle evocation of (Eleusinian?) mystery with which Mother Love resolves some of its terrors is not altogether dissimilar, we shall see, from the vision with which Maggie Gee both begins and concludes her novel, *Lost Children*.

MAGGIE GEE'S *LOST CHILDREN*

WHAT IF NOTHING IS LOST, nor can ever be lost? What if all of time is still happening? What if we are the kind of creature we dream of being, finding the grey defeated sister (so badly married, so beaten down) a child again, straight and slim, doing handstands in the dandelions down the green back garden? If only we could slip from the room for a second. Maybe we could wake with the French windows flung wide and walk out into the landscape we have just dreamed, stretching away in every direction, perspectiveless, dazzling, unbounded, peopled. What if the children are there already? Millions of them. The uncountable lost ones. Loud as life, running, laughing. Sun on the black, the ash-blonde, the auburn. Myself, yourself, my mother, my father. Still young, still potential. All the lost children.

—Maggie Gee, *Lost Children*

This vision of a sunlit place in which children of all colors frolic, where time is suspended so that all are immortalized as children, is the epiphany that both begins and concludes Maggie Gee's *Lost Children*. Utopian, time-bending moments, glimpsed in *Mother Love,* and fleshed out by Gee, are surprisingly typical of contemporary mother-writers. There are increasing numbers of examples of maternal figures in literature who lean on such visions of immortality where Something Else holds the children in a haven/heaven of vitality, joy, and, interestingly, multicultural harmony:

I see them showering like stars onto the world—
On India, Africa, America, these miraculous ones,
these pure, small images. They smell of milk.
Their footsoles are untouched.
They are walkers of air.

—Sylvia Plath, "Three Women,"
Collected Poems

Barbara Kingsolver's *Pigs in Heaven*, which explores this vision even further, actually revolves around a place called "Heaven, Oklahoma"—an impoverished Cherokee town that embodies an ideal of child raising based upon shared responsibility.

Why are so many maternal voices fantasizing about a sort of multiracial day care center in the sky? Starting with this uncanny congruence of vision I wish, in this section, to examine the streams of story and ideology that feed the move away from a "maternal immortality" based upon the mother/daughter relationship toward more traditional religious and communal "immortalities."

Though Demeter is never mentioned in Gee's *Lost Children*, the novel is clearly a take on the ancient story.[7] The story begins in autumn as Alma, a middle-aged mother ("Alma Mater"?), discovers one morning that her teenage daughter Zoe (Greek for "life") has disappeared. It ends with Zoe's return midwinter, which (somewhat unseasonably) coincides with a regeneration of nature: Alma sees "all down the road . . . leaves moving, the dark camellias beginning to shine . . . the brown hydrangeas with their long-dead flowers all waking" (319).

One of the notable features of Adrienne Rich's chapter "Motherhood and Daughterhood" is the way in which a heavy sense of disappointment in her own mother, and other mothers of that generation, seems to disallow any discussion of what, in mythology, is the very positive portrayal of the relationship between Demeter and Persephone. By the 1990s, however, it is possible for Maggie Gee to create Alma and Zoe, who like Demeter and Persephone, are presented as a relatively unconflicted mother/teenaged daughter pair. Despite what seems a Chodorowian closeness, Alma has enjoyed, in fact, not so much her daughter's dependence, but her daughter's growing independence. Alma never hearkens back, in her obsessive remembering of Zoe, to the pre-oedipal period—a stage at which Alma was working too hard to spend much time with her children. Instead Alma's favorite memory is of teaching Zoe to float, withdrawing her hands from beneath her, appreciating the little body that was differentiating itself from Alma's. Floating side by side is the vision of mother/daughter relations that both Alma and Zoe hold most dear (15). It is worthwhile noting that, in the Demeter story as well, the mother's grief is not so much in having lost "her baby" (that is a different kind of event) as in having lost her companion. One way in which the Demeter story, and particularly this novel, challenge contemporary mother/daughter theory is in their depiction of maternal desires to find in the daughter a companion or an equal: these are the less discussed desires that can exist alongside (traditional) desires to control or subsume the daughter. And these are desires that Rich's rather daughter-centric readings fail to recognize.

Lost Children further challenges mother/daughter theory by exploring the possibilities for the mother when the daughter leaves. As Elaine Tuttle Hansen has noted in an essay on contemporary mother/daughter fiction, mothers so often must be separated from their daughters before they can reignite an aspect of their subjectivity (even their "maternal" subjectivity) that has died during the flamboyant assertion of the teenage daughter's subjectiv-ity.[8] The journey Alma makes during her daughter's absence is a journey in which the mother relives her own "daughterhood." The act of mourning the lost daughter ironically frees Alma (as it had once freed Demeter) from "maternal" behavior: Alma ejects her husband and son from the family home; she restricts her friendships to childless women and repels their attempts to look to her for mothering. She takes a job—lets housework and routine go. She is, classically, a middle-aged woman trying to find not only her lost daughter, but (primarily) her own lost self. It transpires, however, (somewhat disappointingly) that motherhood is not the main culprit for her lack of secure ego boundaries. The novel becomes ever more insistent in its hints of childhood incest and Alma's journey becomes a search for the truth about that abuse.

Although we eventually discover that sexuality was indeed behind the disappearance of the (pregnant) daughter, it is Alma, the mother, who in this case grapples with predatory male sexuality. The climactic (or, as it happens, unclimactic) sexual seduction scene is the crucible in which the two identities of Alma—the mother and the daughter—come face to face: "Alma has one hand upon her thigh, her narrow thigh in its lean black skirt. Alma is laugh-ing, and licking her lips. Alma doesn't look at all like a mother" (304). How-ever it is precisely because Alma resembles the dead mother of her seducer, Simon, that he is pursuing her. Simon's initial ploy is to evoke the "little girl" in Alma: "You're my little girl. Let's get undressed. Here, I'll undo these but-tons for you" (306). This arouses not sexual passion in Alma, but repressed memories of early childhood abuse at the hands of her "Daddy." As the seduc-tion progresses, Simon ceases to play "Daddy" and becomes the insatiable child looking for satisfaction from the mother: "[he was] licking at her face like a plate of food, gorging like a child who could never be satisfied, tearing at her blouse, eating her breasts" (307). Because Simon calls forth both the boundariless daughter and the boundariless mother in this scene, Alma's "sud-den twist and lift of her body"—her repulsion of his sexual advances—enables her suddenly to find a "core of self" which can direct and delimit both her daughterly and motherly subjectivity: "She became her anger, her lost clear self. She knew she was no longer smaller than him" (307). The crucial part of the healing process for Alma involves expressing her anger: "'I will not be abused, I will not be abused!' She was screaming at [Simon], her voice was hoarse" (307). Having got this (as well as him) off her chest, Alma is able to dust herself off and return home to care for her suicidal son, her distraught husband, and finally her returning prodigal daughter.

> And every mother must have longed for the power of Demeter, the efficacy of her anger, the reconciliation with her lost self.
> —Rich, *Of Woman Born*

What Maggie Gee seems to suggest is a parallel between the difficulty of a daughter's maintaining bodily and psychic integrity in the face of powerful abusive adults and the difficulty of a mother's maintaining bodily and psychic integrity when the limits of her body have been broken in pregnancy and childbirth and her ego boundaries have been stretched, changed, perhaps even broken by the demands of raising children. This (surely taboo) similarity between the psychic effects of sexual abuse and motherhood is not one that Gee develops. However it is particularly interesting in the context of the Demeter/Persephone myth. Perhaps the mother does see predatory males as threats to the mother's own power over her daughter. But perhaps she also sees these men (and the maternity they may eventually "plant" in their daughters) as threats to the daughter's power that the mother has worked to nurture. In some versions of the Demeter myth, and several of its contemporary reworkings (such as Rita Dove's *Mother Love* and Anne Roiphe's *Lovingkindness* [1987]), the mother resigns herself to the loss of the daughter only when there is a promise, or the actuality, of a granddaughter: a new chance to nurture a strong, secure woman who might be unharmed by the onslaughts to self posed both by male relatives and the institution of motherhood. There are strong suggestions in *Lost Children*, as well as in many other texts, such as a passionate essay by Rose Stone that insists, on the basis of her own experience of sexual abuse at the hands of her mother, that fluid ego boundaries are nothing to be celebrated,[9] that the mother/daughter relationship—its intricate dance between continuity and difference—is formed within the minefield of sexual morality (i.e., sexual activity plus the ideology that governs it).

Strangely, *Lost Children* does not end with its restoration of the nuclear family, but with an epilogue that, repeating the opening of the novel, makes a bid for transcendent immortality. Gee's novel is haunted by a "remainder" of lost children, who cannot fit within the middle-class, white, working mother's purview. In the visions of a multiracial "heaven" that frame this novel, the desires of all these "children" for mothering are directed upward in an uncanny inverse of the movement by which Jenny Joseph thrusts her remainder of pain into the depths of Hades.

BARBARA KINGSOLVER'S *PIGS IN HEAVEN*

The ultimate question for all of these "neo-Demeter" texts is whether there will be a heaven or a Hades in the gap between mother and daughter. Barbara Kingsolver's novel, *Pigs in Heaven*, features a close-knit, three-generational mother/daughter triad: Taylor Greer, her six-year-old adopted daughter, Turtle, and her mother Alice.[10] One of the outstanding characteristics of this novel is its delight in the portrayal of good mother/daughter relationships,

relationships that are depicted in the novel primarily through dialogue. In a conversation between Taylor and live-in boyfriend, Jax, for example, the detailed ways in which Taylor knows her mother are highlighted:

> "[Your mother] wants a new picture of Turtle. Her theory is that in the one you sent, Santa Claus looks like Sirhan Sirhan."
> "No, like Lee Harvey Oswald."
> He looks at her, takes off his glasses and throws the notepad on the floor.
> "How did you know that?"
> "I lived with her twenty years. I know what she'd say."
> "You two ought to be in the *National Enquirer.* TELEPATHIC MOTHER-DAUGHTER DUO RECEIVE MESSAGES THROUGH FILLINGS."
> "We're just close." (39)

Though *Pigs in Heaven* colludes in a Chodorowian idealization of harmonious mother/daughter bonds, its understanding of how those bonds work owes more to Sara Ruddick than to any form of psychoanalytic emphasis on the early physical, intuitive, pre-oedipal mother/child. Kingsolver's primary understanding of the mother/daughter bond is rooted in, and fleshed out through, speech and a quality of reflective thinking very reminiscent of Ruddick's emphasis on a maternal voice and logic. The pre-oedipal is never presented as a beckoning lost paradise: in fact, in contrast to the original Persephone, it was during her pre-oedipal stage that Turtle had been sexually abused by an uncle.

This is not a textbook mother/daughter relationship. The daughter has been separated from her Cherokee tribe and adopted by a racially different (white) mother.[11] Despite the presence of boyfriend Jax, there is no father figure in Turtle's life, nor was there one in Taylor's. "Women on their own run in Alice's family," reads the opening sentence of the novel. Nothing comes between Taylor and Turtle.

Enter Annawake Fourkiller, unlikely parallel to Hades, God of the Underworld. Annawake, a brilliant, young Cherokee lawyer who hails from Heaven, Oklahoma, presents Taylor with the illegality of Turtle's adoption and claims that she may need to be returned to her Cherokee tribe. Annawake invokes not only the legal right of the tribe to decide Turtle's fate, but the racial difference that makes Turtle more "other" than Taylor is prepared to acknowledge. Thus a debate opens up in the novel between the value of a child's belonging to an individual mother and the value of tribal belonging, between the parenting structures of "white" America and the parenting structures of certain racial-ethnic groups. This conflict is set against the historical battle of Native Americans to keep their children.

> "I'm trying to see both sides" [claims Annawake].
> "You can't, " Jax says. "And Taylor can't. It's impossible. Your definitions of 'good' are not in the same dictionary. There is no point of intersection in this dialogue." (89)

Kingsolver polarizes these points of view even more sharply as Taylor leaves the close-knit circle of family friends she has enjoyed in Tucson and sets off with Turtle in that great symbol of American individuality, the car, on a journey to evade "The Indians."

Scenes of Taylor struggling against the odds are interspersed in the novel with scenes from Heaven, Oklahoma where Taylor's mother, Alice, has gone, ostensibly to visit a cousin, primarily to bargain with Annawake. As Alice discovers the rich community behind the ramshackle walls of Heaven's houses, the reader joins her in shifting at least some sympathy from Taylor's point of view toward the Cherokees. Desire is refocused from the nearly ideal mother figures of Taylor and Alice, to the nearly ideal community of Heaven, Oklahoma, in a way somewhat analogous to the shifting of desire away from Alma toward a nonspecific heaven/haven in *Lost Children*.

The custody compromise decided by the Cherokee office of child welfare is, in many ways, excruciating for Taylor: she is stripped of legal guardianship of Turtle, which goes to Turtle's grandfather, Cash. She is nevertheless able to keep Turtle for nine months of the year provided she cooperates with the Cherokees in the child's upbringing. The pain Taylor feels at this loss of possession, or ultimate responsibility, is mitigated by the comic ending of the novel. As the elders announce their decision, Cash stands and publicly asks Alice to marry him. She refuses on the grounds that he owns a TV (she has had bad experiences with men who watch too much TV). He then leads the assembled group over to his house where he publicly executes his television. Taylor admits to her mother that she intends to marry the besotted Jax. Alice decides to marry too: both believe that extending the family would be the best thing for all concerned. "The family of women is about to open its doors to men," thinks Alice in the novel's final sentence, "Men, women, children, cowboys and Indians. It's all over now but the shouting" (343).

The traditional Shakespearian comic ending of this novel—Turtle's grandmother's new boyfriend is Turtle's grandfather, intimations of not one but two weddings—may seem incongruous in the late twentieth century. However, *Pigs in Heaven* poignantly articulates the desire to rework a concept of motherhood that has left America reeling from a string of highly publicized, emotionally searing custody cases: Baby M, Baby Jessica, Baby Richard, and others. The solution offered in the novel can not be universalized: it is firmly set within the context of the Cherokee Nation and the circumstances of Taylor's mothering of Turtle. Nevertheless, as a portrayal of the desires and fears that most mothers feel about the prospect of being forced to share ultimate responsibility for their children, Kingsolver's novel is quite significant, offering, as it does, a much greater fleshing out of the "heaven" only glimpsed by Maggie Gee and others. Into the gap between mother and daughter in this novel is projected a community that allows mother and daughter to separate, to recognize and encourage difference, and then to come together again. As in the Homeric version of the Demeter story, *Pigs in Heaven* is a story in which the loss of "immortality" through unbroken communion between mother and daughter is mitigated by a sense of worlds opening up for mother, daughter, and grandmother as the story ends. This "happy ending" however may only be possible because Kingsolver has not had to address the sexuality of the pre-adolescent daughter.

THE UNWRITTEN CATHEXIS
NEARLY THIRTY YEARS ON

In her celebrated chapter, "Motherhood and Daughterhood," which Rich, interestingly, calls the "core" of her interdisciplinary exploration of mother-hood, contemporary examples of the Demeter myth involve mothers seeking to shed their role, or daughters searching for mothers. Over twenty-five years on, we can hear, and read, the voices of mothers looking for their daughters. Indeed, we can even afford to consider subsets of this literature. In my subset of writers who evoke the Demeter myth as they grapple with issues of immor-tality and morality within the mother/daughter relationship, we can trace the effect of contemporary cultural concerns. First and foremost, these texts reach for a vision of maternity in which the mother is not solely responsible for her daughter. In an age in which children are increasingly constructed as the per-sonal possessions of their parents, a Demeter-style compromise will seem tragic—at very least "unnatural." What is important to glean from these texts is that in each case the Hades who threatens to overwhelm the mother with unbearable loss becomes less threatening. In Barbara Kingsolver's novel, "Hadesis," renamed "Heaven." In Jenny Joseph's *Persephone*, the Uncle Harry figures are somewhat emasculated. In Rita Dove's *Mother Love*, the central "Hades" figure is also softened and recurrent images of various Demeters: sad-dened, bowed—but still speaking and journeying—lift the text. In Maggie Gee's *Lost Children*, the daughter's disappearance actually occasions the opportunity for her mother's rebirth. Though permanent loss of the daughter would destroy the mother, temporary loss of the daughter actually strengthens the mother. What each of these (women) writers in fact fantasize is maternity with a sizable chunk of time off. Whereas Adrienne Rich writes in her fore-word to *Of Woman Born*, "I could not begin to think of writing a book on motherhood until I began to feel strong enough, and unambivalent enough in my love for my children," today's writers write, to a great extent, out of just such an ambivalence.

Unlike the victimized mothers of Rich's analysis in 1976, who remain helpless at male exploitation of their daughters, the mothers of these contem-porary stories begin with total power, and have to come to terms with some sort of power sharing. They go some way toward fleshing out the desires of daughters for a mother whose "love . . . and power is so great as to undo rape and bring [the daughter] back to life" (240). Additionally, however, at some point in each of these contemporary texts, the reader is encouraged to shift desire away from the mother onto Something Else a Bit More Mysterious, a reflection, both of contemporary spiritual hankering, particularly after maternal icons, and of our growing awareness that the mother cannot serve as Ground of Being. The original Demeter myth, of course, culminated in the Mysteries, encouraging its devotees to transfer desires for earthly motherly consolation onto the Goddess Mother, Demeter.[12] Jenny Joseph's *Persephone*, despite its efforts to remain rooted in a secular vernacular, ultimately encourages us, I feel, to shift desire away from the mother toward the deep, mysterious sexuality personified by various Hades figures. It is in Hades that we are to find both a revivifying Knowledge and a numbness that comforts by annulling pain. Dove's *Mother Love* ends with a quiet epiphany of rest in the immortality of Mother Earth. *Lost Children* frames its narrative in a vision of eternal youth that also shifts responsibility and desire away from the mother. *Pigs in Heaven* most obviously refocuses desire away from the mother onto the myths, ritual, stories, and personalities of the tribe.

Both the Demeter myth and the contemporary texts examined in this chapter challenge traditional psychoanalytic paradigms because they banish fathers from the equation. They look to other figures in the effort to prise apart the mother/daughter dyad. In our world of absent fathers, these stories can be read as offering both hope and warning. For male morality is as much a part of the story of psychosexual development as are the hopes of immortality that the Demeters invest in their Persephones. One solution to the overenmeshment of the mother/daughter relationship, presented by early theorists such as Nancy Chodorow, was more active parenting from fathers. Current feminism has tended to eschew that model, hoping, instead, as indeed Rich does, for models of child development that do not depend upon a male presence. It will be interesting to see where the Demeter story, or the story of mother/daughter separation, goes next. Now that writers have looked at the effects of Hades, Heaven, and a tribal community in the gap between mother and daughter, it is perhaps inevitable that fantasies of a "good enough" nonpatriarchal father will creep into this space. The stories envisioned by Chodorow, in which men and women parent together, are still to be written. Perhaps it is these stories that will help to tempt fathers down from Mount Olympus.

NOTES

1. Much of the important theoretical work on mothers and daughters was written in the decade following Rich. This can be found listed in Abbey Werlock's "Nonfiction About Mothers and Daughters: A Selected Bibliography," *Mother Puzzles:*

Daughters and Mothers in Contemporary American Literature, ed. Mickey Pearlman (Westport, Conn.: Greenwood, 1989:185–193). More recent work includes Pearlman's *Mother Puzzles,* Hirsch (1989), Phillips (1996), Suzanna Walters (1992), Elizabeth Brown-Guillory, ed. (1996).

2. The American Psychoanalytic strand begins with: Dorothy Dinnerstein, *The Mermaid and the Minotaur* (NY: Harper, 1976); Nancy Chodorow, *The Reproduction of Mothering* (Berkeley: California UP, 1978); Jane Flax, "The Conflict Between Nurturance and Autonomy in Mother/Daughter Relationships and within Feminism," *Feminist Studies* 4 (1978) 171–189; Jane Flax, "Mother-Daughter Relationships: Psychodynamics, Politics and Philosophy," *The Future of Difference,* eds. H. Eisenstein and A. Jardine (Boston: G. K. Hall, 1980); Jean Baker Miller, *Towards a New Psychology of Women* (Boston: Beacon, 1976). For Jungian work see Erich Neumann, *The Great Mother: An Analysis of the Archetype,* trans. Ralph Manheim (Princeton: Princeton UP, 1955); Carl Kerényi, *Eleusis: Archetypal Image of Mother and Daughter,* trans. Ralph Manheim (NY: Schocken, 1976); Nor Hall, *The Moon and the Virgin: Reflections on the Archetypal Feminine* (NY: Harper, 1980); Marjorie McCormick, *Mothers in the English Novel: From Stereotype to Archetype* (NY: Garland, 1991). The most important French feminist work on the mother/daughter relationship is Luce Irigaray's "And the One Doesn't Stir without the Other" (1979), which appears in English in *Signs* 7 (1981) 60–67. For work on maternal subjectivity that builds heavily upon Irigaray, see Janet Campbell, "The Mother as Subject within the Writings of Psychoanalysis and Women's Literature," (diss.) U of Sussex, 1994.

3. For discussions of how lesbian sexuality might affect mother/daughter relationships, see Judith Roof, "'This is Not for You': The Sexuality of Mothering," in Daly and Reddy (1991) 157–174; Rosemary Curb, "Core of the Apple: Mother-Daughter Fusion/Separation in Three Recent Lesbian Plays," *Lesbian Texts and Contexts,* eds. K. Jay and J. Glasgow (NY: New York UP, 1990) 355–376.

4. Critical reception was scant. See Jo-Ann Goodwin, "A Myth Kitty," *TLS,* 29 August 1986:932.

5. Dove, a recent poet laureate, is well known in the United States where *Mother Love* attracted much critical attention. See Helen Vendler, "Twentieth Century Demeter—*Mother Love,*" *New Yorker,* 15 May 1995:90–92; Sarah Maguire, "Sailing around Sicily—*Mother Love,*" *TLS,* 17 November 1995:29; Alison Booth, "Abduction and Other Severe Pleasures: Rita Dove's *Mother Love,*" *Callaloo* 19:1 (1996) 125–130; Stephen Cushman, "And the Dove Returned," *Callaloo* 19:1 (1996) 131–134; Lotta Lofgren, "Partial Horror: Fragmentation and Healing in Rita Dove's *Mother Love,*" *Callaloo* 19:1 (1996) 135–142; Ben Howard, "Forms and Discoveries: *Mother Love* and *The Darker Face of Earth* by Rita Dove," *Poetry* 167:6 (1996) 349–353.

6. See for example, Perri Klass's *Other Women's Children* (London: Lime Tree, 1991) and Mary Gordon's *Men and Angels* (London: Cape, 1985).

7. For a sample of the critical reception of *Lost Children,* see Mary Scott, "Crisis Talks: *Lost Children* by Maggie Gee/*Closing the Book* by Stevie Davis," *New Statesman* Ap. 22, 1994:48; Isobel Armstrong, "Bloody Parents: Lost Children" *TLS,* 29 April 1994; Barry Unsworth, "The Child Within" (rev. of *Lost Children* by Maggie Gee), *The Sunday Times,* 24 April 1994:10.

8. Elaine Tuttle Hansen, "Mothers Tomorrow and Mothers Yesterday, but Never Mothers Today," in Daly and Reddy (1991) 21–43.

9. Rose Stone, "Night Song for the Journey: A Self-Critical Prelude to Feminist Mothering," in Reddy, Roth, and Sheldon, 229–242.

10. *Pigs* came out to much popular acclaim. See: Karen Darbo, "And Baby Makes Two" (rev. of *Pigs in Heaven* by Barbara Kingsolver), *NYTBR,* 27 June 1993; Angela Johnson, "The Return of Taylor and Turtle—*Pigs in Heaven," Off Our Backs* 23:7 (1993) 12; R. Z. Sheppard, "Little Big Girl—*Pigs in Heaven," Time,* 39 August 1993:65; Travis Silcox, "Welcome to Heaven—*Pigs in Heaven," Belles Lettres: A Review of Books by Women* 19:1 (1993) 4, 42; Mary Scott, "Solomon's Wisdom—*Pigs in Heaven," New Statesman,* 10 December 1993:40.

11. The novels of Louise Erdrich also explore the history of adoption and Native American children. See Hertha D. Wong's essay, "Adoptive Mothers and Thrown-Away Children in the Novels of Louise Erdrich," in Daly and Reddy (1991) 174–196. See also Beth Brant's anthology of Native American women's writing, *A Gathering of Spirit* (Ithaca, NY: Firebrand, 1988). Jane Lazarre's memoir, *Beyond the Whiteness of Whiteness: Memoir of a White Mother of Black Sons* (Durham: Duke UP, 1996), is also interesting in this context.

12. Julia Kristeva's classic text, "Stabat Mater," spells out what she feels is lost in a culture that no longer maintains a representation of the "Holy Mother," for example, The Blessed Virgin Mary. Moi (1986) 180–181.

WORKS CITED

Bassin, Donna, Margaret Honey, and Meryle Mahrer Kaplan, eds. *Representations of Motherhood.* London: Yale UP, 1994.

Bell-Scott, Patricia, et al., eds. *Double Stitch: Black Women Write About Mothers and Daughters.* New York: Harper, 1993.

Benjamin, Jessica. *The Bonds of Love: Psychoanalysis, Feminism and the Problem of Domination.* New York: Pantheon, 1988.

———. *Like Subjects, Love Objects: Essays on Recognition and Sexual Difference.* London: Yale UP, 1995.

Brown-Guillory, Elizabeth, ed. *Women of Color: Mother-Daughter Relationships in Twentieth Century Literature.* Austin: U of Texas P, 1996.

Chodorow, Nancy. *Femininities, Masculinities, Sexualities: Freud and Beyond.* Lexington: U of Kentucky P, 1994.

———. *The Reproduction of Mothering: Psychoanalysis and the Sociology of Gender.* Berkeley: U of California P, 1978.

Daly, Brenda O. and Maureen T. Reddy, eds. *Narrating Mothers: Theorizing Maternal Subjectivity.* Knoxville: U of Tennessee P, 1991.

Davison, Cathy and E. M. Broner, eds. *The Lost Tradition: Mothers and Daughters in Literature.* New York: Ungar, 1980.

Dove, Rita. *Mother Love*. 1995. New York: Norton, 1996.

Foley, Helene P., ed. *The Homeric Hymn to Demeter: Translation, Commentary and Interpretive Essays*. Princeton: Princeton UP, 1994.

Gee, Maggie. *Lost Children*. London: Flamingo, 1994.

Hansen, Elaine Tuttle. *Mother Without Child: Contemporary Fiction and the Crisis of Motherhood*. London: U of California P, 1997.

Herman, Nini. *Too Long a Child: The Mother-Daughter Dyad*. London: Free Association, 1989.

Hirsch, Marianne. "Feminism at the Maternal Divide: A Diary." *The Politics of Motherhood: Activist Voices from Left to Right*. Eds. Annelise Orleck, Diana Taylor, Alexis Jetter. Hanover: UP New England, 1996.

———. "Review Essay: Mothers and Daughters," *Signs* (1981):200–222.

———. *The Mother/Daughter Plot: Narrative, Psychoanalysis, Feminism*. Bloomington: U of Indiana P, 1989.

Hirsch, Marianne and Evelyn Keller, eds. *Conflicts in Feminism*. London: Routledge, 1990.

Jackson, Rosemary. *Mothers Who Leave*. London: Pandora, 1994.

Joseph, Jenny. *Persephone*. Newcastle: Bloodaxe, 1986.

Kingsolver, Barbara. *Pigs in Heaven*. London: Faber, 1993.

Koppelman, Susan, ed. *Between Mothers and Daughters—Stories Across a Generation*. New York: Feminist Press, 1985.

Mens-Verhulst, Janneke, Karlein Schreurs, and Liesbeth Woertman, eds. *Daughtering and Mothering: Female Subjectivity Reanalysed*. London: Routledge, 1993.

Ozick, Cynthia. *The Shawl*. New York: Summit, 1987.

Park, Christine and Caroline Heaton, eds. *Close Company: Stories of Mothers and Daughters*. London: Virago, 1987.

Pearlman, Mickey, ed. *American Women Writing Fiction*. Lexington: U of Kentucky P, 1989.

———, ed. *Mother Puzzles: Daughters and Mothers in Contemporary American Literature*. Westport, Conn.: Greenwood, 1989.

Phillips, Shelley, *Beyond the Myths: Mother-Daughter Relationships in Psychology, History, Literature and Everyday Life*. Harmnondsworth: Penguin, 1996.

Plath, Sylvia. *Three Women: A Monologue for Three Voices*. London: Turret Books, 1968.

Reddy, Maureen T., Martha Roth, and Amy Sheldon, eds. *Mother Journeys: Feminists Write about Mothering*. Minneapolis: Spinsters Ink, 1994.

Rich, Adrienne. *Of Woman Born: Motherhood as Experience and Institution*. London: Virago, 1976.

Roiphe, Anne Richardson. *Lovingkindness*. New York: Warner Books, 1987.

Ruddick, Sara. *Maternal Thinking: Towards a Politics of Peace*. Boston: Beacon, 1989.

——. "Thinking About Fathers." Hirsch and Keller 222–233.

Smith, Virginia A. "Unspeakable Plots and Unamazing Puzzles." *Review* 13, U of Virginia P (1991):283–297.

Snitow, Ann. "Feminism and Motherhood: An American Reading." *Feminist Review* 40 (1992):32–51.

Walker, Alice. *In Search of Our Mother's Gardens*. London: Women's Press, 1984.

Walters, Suzanna Danuta. *Lives Together, Worlds Apart: Mothers and Daughters in Popular Culture*. Berkeley: U of California P, 1992.

NINE

Mothering against Motherhood and the Possibility of Empowered Maternity for Mothers and Their Children

ANDREA O'REILLY

We were conspirators, outlaws from the institution of motherhood.
—Adrienne Rich

A CENTRAL THEME of *Of Woman Born* and arguably the most significant and enduring insight of this landmark book is the crucial distinction Rich made between motherhood as an institution and a nonpatriarchal experience of mothering. In the foreword to the book, Rich distinguishes "between two meanings of motherhood, one superimposed on the other: the potential relationship of any woman to her powers of reproduction—and to children; and the institution—which aims at ensuring that that potential—and all women—shall remain under male control" (13). In other words, while motherhood as an institution is a male-defined site of oppression, women's own experiences of mothering can nonetheless be a source of power. The oppressive and the empowering aspects of maternity, as well as the complex relationship between the two, has been the focus of feminist research on motherhood over the last twenty-eight years.[1] More specifically, many of the themes of contemporary feminist thought on motherhood originate from and have developed in reference to concerns raised by Rich more than twenty-eight years ago. Elsewhere I have argued that feminist thought on motherhood, particularly over the last fifteen years, may be characterized by three interrelated themes.[2] The first theme is concerned with uncovering and challenging the oppressive patriarchal institution of motherhood. The second focuses upon the formulation and articulation of a counter discourse of mothering, one that redefines mothering as a female-defined or, more specifically, a feminist, enterprise. This new perspective, in emphasizing maternal power and ascribing agency to mothers and value to motherwork, gives rise to the third theme: the view that mothers can affect social change through the socialization of children, particularly, in terms of challenging traditional patterns of gender acculturation. While numerous feminists have located these themes in Rich, none have returned to *Of Woman Born* to consider how these themes were first developed or to review how Rich's initial insights may aid contemporary theory in its formulation of these three central concerns.

This chapter will focus upon the second and third themes—the formulation of a female-defined and centered experience of mothering and the development of a feminist practice of gender socialization. While the two aims seem similar, the first is concerned with mothering in terms of the mother herself—her experiences of mothering, the meanings she attaches to it—while the second theme focuses upon the relation she has with her children and in particular the manner in which she raises them. It has been long recognized that Rich was one of the first feminist writers to call for antisexist child rearing and women-centered practices of mothering. What has been less acknowledged, and what will be the focus of this chapter, is how the two, in Rich's view, are intrinsically linked in so far as the goal of antisexist child rearing depends upon the abolition of patriarchal motherhood and the achievement of feminist mothering. Antisexist child rearing—a challenge to traditional practices of gender socialization for both daughters and sons— Rich argues, depends upon motherhood itself being changed; it must become, to use Rich's terminology, mothering. In other words, only in mothering becoming a site, role, and identity of power for women is feminist child rearing made possible.

The chapter will first revisit Rich's vision of new modes of child rearing for both sons and daughters. Next it will explore Rich's argument that these new feminist practices of relating with and raising sons and daughters become actualized only through the eradication of patriarchal motherhood and the emergence of feminist mothering. Though more than twenty-eight years have passed since the publication of *Of Woman Born*, Rich remains the only feminist critic, to my knowledge, to recognize and argue that the changes we pursue in child rearing are made possible only through changes in mothering. While feminist mothers today seek to raise empowered daughters and antisexist sons, Rich understood some twenty-eight years ago, that this is achievable only *outside* the patriarchal institution of motherhood. Women must, to use Rich's terminology, mother against motherhood to raise a new generation of feminist children. It is this insight, I argue, that makes *Of Woman Born* the truly visionary, indeed prophetic, book that it is.

MOTHERS AND DAUGHTERS
"As daughters we need mothers who want their own freedom and ours."
                                                    —Rich (247)

Rich was one of the first feminist theorists on motherhood to define mothering as a socially engaged enterprise particularly as it seeks to effect cultural change through new feminist modes of gender socialization and interactions with daughters and sons. Two of her chapters in *Of Woman Born* examine the mother's relationships with her children and consider how mothers may challenge traditional gender socialization through feminist child rearing. Chapter 9 on motherhood and daughterhood is described by Rich as the "core of [her] book" and is the chapter most referenced by maternal scholars. "The cathexis between mother and daughter, essential, distorted, misused," wrote Adrienne Rich in her oft-cited quote, "is the great unwritten story" (225).

MOTHER AND DAUGHTER ESTRANGEMENT UNDER PATRIARCHY

However, as Rich noted the absence of mother-daughter stories, she simultaneously argued that patriarchal culture scripts the roles mothers and daughters are expected to play. The patriarchal view of mothers and daughters, according to Rich, is that this relationship, particularly in the daughter's adolescent years, is to be experienced as antagonism and animosity. The daughter must differentiate herself from the mother if she is to assume an autonomous identity as an adult. The mother, in turn, is perceived and understood only in terms of her maternal identity. The mother represents for the daughter, according to the received narrative, the epitome of patriarchal oppression that she seeks to transcend as she comes to womanhood. This is the patriarchal narrative of the mother-daughter relationship as it is enacted in the patriarchal institution of motherhood.

Across cultures and throughout history most women, as noted in the introduction, mother in the institution of motherhood; that is, women's mothering is defined and controlled by the larger patriarchal society in which they live. Mothers do not make the rules, Rich emphasizes, they simply enforce them. Whether it is in the form of parenting books, a physician's advice, or the father's rules, a mother raises her children in accordance with the values and expectations of the dominant patriarchal culture. Mothers are policed by what theorist Sara Ruddick calls "the gaze of others"; "Under the gaze of others, Mothers relinquish authority to others [and] lose confidence in their own values" (111). "Teachers, grandparents,

mates, friends, employers, even an anonymous passerby," continues Ruddick, "can judge a mother by her child's behavior and find her wanting"
(111–112). Inauthentic mothering and the abdication of maternal authority
is at the heart of patriarchal motherhood and is what gives rise to the dis-
empowerment of mothers and the estrangement of mothers and daughters.

Daughters, Rich argues, perceive their mothers' inauthenticity and
understand the powerlessness that underpins their mothers' compliance and
complicity. "Many daughters," Rich writes, "live in rage at their mothers for
having accepted too readily and passively 'whatever comes.' A mother's victimization does not merely humiliate her, it mutilates the daughter who
watches for clues as to what it means to be a woman. Like the traditional
foot-bound Chinese woman, she passes on her own affliction. The mother's
self-hatred and low expectations are the binding-rags of the psyche of the
daughter" (243). However, as the daughter experiences this rage toward her
mother, she is expected to identify with her because as a woman it is assumed
the daughter will become a mother/wife as her mother did. The daughter
resists this identification because she does not want to live a life like that of
her mother's, nor does she wish to be affiliated with someone who is
oppressed and whose work is devalued. "Thousands of daughters," writes
Rich, "see their mothers as having taught a compromise and self-hatred they
are struggling to win free of, the one through whom the restrictions and
degradations of a female existence were perforce transmitted" (235). Rich
defines this viewpoint as matrophobia: "the fear not of one's mother or of
motherhood but of *becoming one's mother*" (236, emphasis in original). Matrophobia, Rich continues:

> can be seen as a womanly splitting of the self, in the desire to become purged
> once and for all of our mothers' bondage, to become individuated and free.
> The mother stands for the victim in ourselves, the unfree woman, the mar-
> tyr. Our personalities seem dangerously to blur and overlap with our moth-
> ers'; and, in a desperate attempt to know where mother ends and daughter
> begins, we perform radical surgery. (236)

The devaluation of motherhood, the mother's abdication of maternal
authority, maternal inauthenticity and so on, give rise to matrophobia; this in
turn frustrates and thwarts understanding and intimacy, empathy and connection between mothers and daughters. "The loss of the daughter to the
mother, the mother to the daughter," writes Rich, "is the essential female
tragedy. We acknowledge Lear (father-daughter split), Hamlet (son and
mother), and Oedipus (son and mother) as great embodiments of the human
tragedy, but there is no presently enduring recognition of mother-daughter
passion and rapture" (237). Building upon Rich's insights on mother-daughter estrangement, feminist theorists, particularly since the mid-1980s, have

focused upon the importance of mother-daughter connection and closeness to argue that such are essential for female empowerment, particularly in the daughter's adolescent years.

FEMINIST NARRATIVES OF MOTHER-DAUGHTER CONNECTION

Writers as diverse as Paula Caplan, Elizabeth deBold, Miriam Johnson, Carol Gilligan, Virginia Beane Rutter, and Mary Pipher argue that a strong mother-daughter connection is what makes possible a strong female self. Rutter, in her book *Celebrating Girls,* argues that high self-esteem in girls is made possible through close relationships with mothers. "Mothers," writes Rutter, "can raise girls with a vital, intact feminine spirit. [. . . The] mother-daughter relationship is the ground for teaching, talking, and sharing the feminine experience and the more we empower that experience, the healthier our girls will be. We need to secure our daughters' sense of self-worth, in their mind and their bodies, so that they will not turn away from us and from themselves" (2, 9–10). These writers maintain that the daughter's empowerment through the valuation of the feminine depends upon a close and vital mother-daughter relationship.

However, Western culture mandates separation from parents in adolescence to enable the emerging adult to achieve an autonomous sense of self. Recent feminist writers call into question this "sacred cow" of developmental theory and argue that it constitutes a betrayal of both mothers and daughters. "Separation and autonomy are not equivalent," Elizabeth deBold explains, "[daughters] need not separate from mothers emotionally to be autonomous. [. . .] Early childhood and adolescence are the two stages of life where separation has been decreed as imperative to the independence and autonomy of children. To mother 'right' women disconnect from their daughters. [. . .] Rather than strengthen girls, this breach of trust leaves girls weakened and adrift" (36). What is most disturbing about this pattern of separation and betrayal is its timing. "In childhood," deBold writes, "girls have confidence in what they know, think and feel" (11). With the onset of adolescence, girls come up against what she calls the wall: "The wall is our patriarchal culture that values women less than men. [. . .] To get through the wall girls have to give up parts of themselves to be safe and accepted within society" (12). Daughters are thus abandoned by their mothers when they need them the most. Mothers can aid daughters in their resistance to the wall through sustained and sustaining mother-daughter connection. Drawing upon the ancient Elyeusis rites of Demeter and Persephone first discussed by Rich, recent feminist writings on the mother-daughter relation celebrate mother-daughter connection and explore how such is achieved and sustained through maternal narratives, the motherline, and feminist mothering.[3]

MOTHERING AGAINST MOTHERHOOD:
EMPOWERING DAUGHTERS THROUGH EMPOWERED MOTHERS

This recent feminist aim to fashion an alternative mother-daughter narrative modeled on mother-daughter connection has resulted in perceptive and useful literature on how to raise empowered girls. In addition, this counternarrative has gone a long way to destabilize the patriarchal view that positions mother and daughter disconnection as inevitable and necessary. However, I want to suggest that these achievements remain partial because of the failure of this new literature to fully comprehend the connection-empowerment trajectory as theorized by Rich. While Rich champions mother-daughter connection, she recognizes, as these writers do *not,* that connection gives rise to the daughter's empowerment *if and only if* the mother with whom the daughter is identifying is herself empowered. "What do mean by the nurture of daughters? What is it we wish we had, or could have, as daughters; could give, as mothers," asks Rich:

> Deeply and primally we need trust and tenderness; surely this will always be true of every human being, but women growing into a world so hostile to us need a very profound kind of loving in order to learn to love ourselves. But this loving is not simply the old, institutionalized, sacrificial, "mother-love" which men have demanded; we want courageous mothering. The most notable fact that culture imprints on women is the sense of our limits. The most important thing one woman can do for another is to illuminate and expand her sense of actual possibilities. For a mother, this means more than contending with reductive images of females in children's books, movies, television, the schoolroom. It means that the mother herself is trying to expand the limits of her life. *To refuse to be a victim:* and then to go on from there. (246, emphasis in original)

Karen Payne's *Between Ourselves: Letters Between Mothers and Daughters* provides a lived example of Rich's mutual empowerment thesis: "When Mum finally left Dad she was giving up female martyrdom; she was waving farewell to that womanly virtue of self-sacrifice. And if she could escape that bondage then so could I. [. . .] In setting herself free, [my mother] set me free" (244). In the same collection, renowned sociologist Jesse Bernard wrote to her daughter: "For your sake as well as mine, I must not allow you to absorb me completely. I must learn to live my own life independently in order to be a better mother to you" (272). Or as Judith Arcana, an early feminist theorist whose work was greatly influenced by Rich advised: "We must live as if our dreams have been realized. We cannot simply prepare other, younger daughters for strength, pride, courage, beauty. It is worse than useless to tell young women and girls that we have done and been wrong, that we have chosen ill, that we hope they will be more lucky" (1979, 33). What daughters need, therefore, in Rich's words: "[are] mothers who want their own freedom and ours. [. . .] The quality of the mother's life—however, embattled and unprotected—is her primary bequest to her daughter, because a woman who can believe in herself, who is a fighter, and who continues to struggle to create livable space around her, is demonstrating to her daughter that these possibilities exist" (247).

Writing of lesbian mothering in *Politics of the Heart*, Baba Cooper describes radical mothers as "involving children in disloyalty to the culture the mother is expected to transmit at the expense of woman-bonding and female empowerment" (238). This radical mothering works *against* matrophobia that is at the heart of mother-daughter estrangement and is what makes possible reciprocal mother-daughter empowerment. Whether it be termed courageous mothering as Rich describes it, or radical mothering as defined by Cooper, this practice of mothering calls for the empowerment of daughters *and* mothers and recognizes that the former is only possible with the later. As Judith Arcana concluded: "If we want girls to grow into free women, brave and strong, we must be those women ourselves" (33, 1979). By mothering against motherhood, and becoming, in Rich's words, "outlaws from the institution of motherhood" (195), women obtain power in mothering and thereby are able to model the empowerment the daughter will acquire in and through mother-daughter connection.

MOTHERS AND SONS
"Discover[ing] new ways of being men [. . .]
as we are discovering new ways of being women."
—*Rich (211)*

As with the mother-daughter relationship, Rich emphasized the necessity of interrogating and dismantling the patriarchal institution of motherhood in the raising of sons. In the instance of daughters Rich argued that in order for mothers to instill agency, autonomy, and authenticity in their growing daughters, the mothers must model these same attributes in their own daily lives. With sons, Rich likewise argued that mothers must reject traditional motherhood in order to challenge and change normative practices of masculization because the institution of motherhood serves to foster in sons both sexism and patriarchal masculinity. Thus, while the teaching of antisexism and undermining of masculine socialization may be the explicit goals of feminist mothering of sons, such depends upon mothers dismantling the institution of patriarchal motherhood.

Contemporary feminist scholarship on mothers and sons may be organized under three interrelated aims or themes: a challenge to traditional masculine socialization, an emphasis upon mother-son connection, and, to a lesser degree, a critique of patriarchal motherhood.⁴ As with current mother-daughter literature, these mother-son themes may be traced back to *Of Woman Born*. And similar to her mother and daughter connection through mutual empowerment thesis, Rich argues that in order for sons to become caring and connected men they must likewise be mothered outside the patriarchal institution of motherhood.

Rich's chapter "Mother and Son, Woman and Man," while arguably not as developed as her mothers and daughters chapter and less cited by maternal scholars, is arguably the more radical chapter in so far as Rich was the first— and for the longest time—the only feminist theorist to confront head-on the thorny issue of being a feminist mother of sons, an issue that was, in Linda Forcey's words "a taboo topic" among feminists until quite recently (2). "Few subjects so provoke anxiety among feminists," Robin Morgan wrote in 1993, "as the four-letter word *sons*" (38). "We've talked about, written and read about, mothers and daughters," Morgan continues, "but with a few notable exceptions we've averted our eyes from The Other Touchy Subject. Yet that subject goes to the heart of practicing what we claim to believe, that 'the personal is political.' It goes to the crux of power and of patriarchy—even though it also grazes the living nerves of love" (38).

MOTHER AND SON CONNECTION

Central to contemporary feminist thought on the mother-son relationship is a celebration of mother-son connection and a challenge to the belief that mother-son separation is normal, inevitable, and good for our sons. While this concern is peripheral to the mother and son chapter in *Of Woman Born*, Rich nonetheless does consider the issue of mother-son separation and asks: "How does the male child differentiate himself from his mother, and does this mean inevitably that he must 'join the army,' that is, internalize patriarchal values? Can the mother, in patriarchy, represent culture, and if so, what does this require of her? Above all, what does separation from the mother mean for the son?" (198). "Across all cultures sons, at the onset of puberty," Rich goes on to observe, "experience a 'second birth' into patriarchal culture. [T]he child-with-a-penis is expected to bond himself with others who have penises. [. . .] He must still [. . .] come to terms with the Fathers, the representative of law and tradition, the wagers of aggression, the creators and purveyors of the dominant culture. And his mother, whatever her deepest instincts tells her, is expected to facilitate this" (200). Since the early 1990s feminist writers have taken up these questions to emphasize mother-son connection and position it as central to the reconfiguration of traditional masculinity.

The hegemonic narrative of mother and son attachment—as scripted in parenting books, psychoanalytical theory, and popular wisdom—assumes that sons must separate from their mothers in order to acquire a "normal" masculine identity. A close and caring relationship between a mother and her son is pathologized as aberrant, while a relationship structured upon separation is naturalized as the real and normal way to experience mother-son attachment. Olga Silverstein and Beth Rashbaum write in *The Courage to Raise Good Men:* "[O]ur culture believes that a male child must be removed from his mother's influence in order to escape the contamination of a close relationship with her. The love of a mother—both the son's for her, and hers for him—is believed to 'feminize' the boy, make him soft, weak, dependent, homebound [. . .] only through renunciation of the loving mother does the boy become a man" (11). Feminist theorists on the mother-son relation have begun to challenge this received narrative by calling into question the central and organizing premise of patriarchally mandated mother-son separation, namely that this process is both natural, hence inevitable, and that it is "good" for our sons. Feminist writers argue that while we may perceive mother and son separation to be a natural process, it is, in reality, a culturally scripted and orchestrated act. "By expecting our sons to cut off from us," Silverstein and Rashbaum write, "we make sure that they do" (159). Whether the son is fully cognizant of this sudden or subtle detachment, he nonetheless experiences it as a profound and inexplicable loss that leaves him feeling vulnerable and alone. To save our sons, who are destined to become detached and wounded men, and to change the patriarchal world in which they and we live, a mother must foreground her presence in the life of her son; furthermore, she must establish and maintain a close and caring connection with her son throughout his life. By way of this new relationship mothers will dismantle, destabilize, and deconstruct normative patterns of male socialization and traditional definitions of masculinity. These theorists, as with the feminist writers on daughters, seek cultural change through new feminist practices of mothering modelled on connection and concerned with the creation of new modes of masculinity.

CHALLENGING TRADITIONAL MASCULINITY

Feminist literature on masculinity, written by both men and women, argues that while men learn that they are beneficiaries of power and privilege, they pay a high price for this status. Michael Kaufman, for example, describes masculinity as "an idealized version of what it means to be male [. . .] a collective hallucination [. . .] a state of mind and a story of how to behave" (25, 32, 29). Having been socialized to repress and deny emotions associated with the feminine—empathy, vulnerability, compassion, gentleness—and taught to tough it out on their own through our culture's valorization of an independent, individualistic (and fully individuated) masculinity, men grow into manhood deeply wounded and isolated. Masculinity then becomes a facade or a place of refuge, where men seek to convince themselves and others that they are as brave and strong as the idealized version of masculinity purports them to be. Writers on masculinity agree that masculinity, as with femininity, is a cultural construct that exists in a constant state of flux, its meaning continually shifting in response to changing economic, political, and social times. Today, feminist mothers seek a new mode of manhood wherein feminine characteristics such as gentleness, vulnerability, and compassion are emphasized and the more harmful aspects of traditional macho masculinity are eliminated. However, the work of raising antisexist sons has proven to be more difficult and daunting than the task of rearing feminist daughters. Alison Thomas explains in her article "Swimming Against the Tide: Feminists' Accounts of Raising Sons":

> [T]here has been a general lack of antisexist men willing and able to act as unconventional role models for their sons (at least until recently), and this has again meant that mothers are the ones who are taking responsibility for directing their sons toward resisting traditional forms of masculinity. On top of that, it is clear that for young men "the costs" of challenging conventional masculine roles are much higher—given a society that still does attach considerable prestige to "masculinity"—and when this entails (for example) sharing domestic responsibilities with women, such "costs" are not compensated by tangible benefits. (125)

Numerous feminist writers and scholars have recognized the need to change traditional masculine socialization and have recommended various strategies for antisexist child rearing. However, few have acknowledged how truly arduous and contentious a task this is. Rich in *Of Woman Born* was the first to appreciate the ambivalence and anxiety mothers often feel in raising a boy feminist. "If we wish for our sons—as for our daughters—that they may grow up unmutilated by gender roles, sensitized to misogyny in all its forms, we also," Rich emphasizes, "have to face the fact that in the present stage of history our sons may feel profoundly alone in the masculine world, with few if any close relationships with other men" (207). "The fear of alienating a male child from 'his' culture seems to go deep," Rich writes, "even among women who reject that culture for themselves every day of their lives" (205). "What do we fear?," Rich asks, "That our sons will accuse us of making them into misfits and outsiders? That they will suffer as we have suffered from patriarchal reprisals? Do we fear they will somehow lose their male status and privilege, even as we are seeking to abolish that inequity?" (205). In identifying this ambivalence and this conflict, Rich was the first to emphasize that the task of rearing feminist sons demands formidable courage of mothers *and* sons; as well it requires that the institution of motherhood itself be eradicated.

MOTHERING AGAINST MOTHERHOOD:
CONNECTED AND CARING SONS AND COURAGEOUS MOTHERS

To truly free our sons, to move beyond a mere critique of traditional masculinity, mothers must become, in Rich's words, "outlaws from the institution to motherhood." In her oft-cited quote, Rich describes her brief exile from the institution of motherhood.

> I remember one summer, living in a friend's house in Vermont. My husband was working abroad for several weeks, and my three sons—nine, seven, five years old—and I dwelt for most of that time by ourselves. Without a male adult in the house, without any reason for schedules, naps, regular mealtimes, or early bedtimes [. . .] we fell into what I felt to be a delicious and sinful rhythm. [. . .] At night they fell asleep without a murmur and I stayed up reading and writing as I had when a student, till the early morning. I remember thinking: This is what living with children could be—without school hours, fixed routines, naps, the conflict of being both mother and wife with no room for being, simply myself. Driving home once after midnight from a late drive-in movie [. . .] I felt wide awake, elated; we had broken together all the rules of bedtime, the night rules, rules I myself thought I had to observe in the city or become a "bad mother." We were conspirators, outlaws from the institution of motherhood. (195)

"Of course the institution closed down on us again," writes Rich, "and my own mistrust of myself as 'good mother' returned" (195).

Rich was the first to recognize how traditional motherhood leads to traditional masculinity. Judith Arcana, a theorist greatly influenced by Rich and the first to write a book on mothers and sons, argues that mothering is about caring for and catering to the needs of children, and nurturing self-esteem so that children see themselves as special and deserving, what Sara Ruddick defines as the second demand of maternal practice, "to foster growth [. . .] sponsor or nurture a child's unfolding, expanding material spirit" (83). However, in the institution of motherhood this nurturance may be, in the instance of sons, according to Judith Arcana, interpreted as privilege and entitlement: "Though children of both sexes put their mothers in the position of servants [. . .] mothers of sons are, whether we feel it in the moment or not, inadvertently reinforcing the sexist premise that women exist to serve men. [. . .] Men learn from infancy to expect and solicit selfishness and cherishing care at the hands of women" (101, 102). While "[d]aughters learn from our mothers to *be mothers*, to give in [sic] that disastrously self-destructive way that has been honored by men as true motherhood; sons learn *to expect such treatment from women*" (102, emphasis in original). Women in patriarchal culture are expected to devote their time and attention to children and men; sons thus, as

Arcana identifies, derive double benefits from these patriarchal imperatives as both men and children (1983). Given that women's secondary status is enforced in both the gender arena, service to men, and in the maternal realm, service to children, mothers must, if they hope to raise antisexist men who reject traditional masculinity, challenge both patriarchal imperatives, that women are to serve both men and children. Women, Arcana writes, "need to live out of ourselves. We wrong ourselves and our children if we subordinate our lives to theirs" (235). Mothers must, Arcana continues, "[r]eject [the] traditional mother role [and . . .] accept [. . .] our sons into our daily lives" (247). In so doing the mother will enable her boy child to see her outside and beyond her maternal identity that positions her as secondary to, and in service to, children and men. Coming to know their mothers outside motherhood, sons learn to view and appreciate their mothers as, in Arcana's words "whole people."

Mothers must, therefore, according to Arcana reject traditional motherhood if they hope to raise nontraditional sons; that is, men who have renounced patriarchal masculinity and the entitlement and privilege that such accords. No longer can mothers be, or be seen as, "the primary source of praise, encouragement, and selfless service [for sons]" (1983, 280). However, as mothers reject this role of selfless service to sons, traditional male socialization, as Arcana explains, teaches boys "that they are to be the beneficiaries of a male culture: they will grow up to power, status, and the admiration and support of women. [. . . W]hen [a mother] moves to change that pattern with her son, he understands that she wants him to give up power. [. . . A] boy has to begin by *losing*" (280). In other words, to become more human, he must become less "male."

Mothers must dismantle the patriarchal institution of motherhood, Rich argues, in order to effect the gender transformations and new relations they wish for themselves and their sons. Audre Lorde once wrote: "The strongest lesson I can teach my son is the same lesson I teach my daughter: how to be who he wishes to be for himself. And the best way I can do this is to be who I am and hope that he will learn from this not how to be me, which is not possible, but how to be himself" (77). Feminist writers on the mother-daughter relationship argue that mothers must act and speak from truth and authenticity if they hope to achieve empowerment for themselves and their girl children. A mother of sons also must mother from a place of truth and authenticity and model for her son resistance so that he may, in Lorde's words, "move to that voice within himself, rather than to those raucous, persuasive or threatening voices from outside, pressuring him to be what the world wants him to be" (77). Therefore, as Mary Kay Blakey concludes, "[while] getting bounced from the game [of Let's Pretend, passing for perfect mothers, living in the traditional version of a perfect family] into actual life is invariably traumatic, it is better for us and our sons" (34). "What do we want for our sons?" asks Rich (211). "We want them to remain, in the deepest sense, sons of the mothers, yet also grow into themselves, to discover new ways of being men even as we are discovering new ways of being women" (211). And for Rich this only becomes possible by mothering against motherhood.

CONCLUSION

Feminist theorists on motherhood call for the eradication of the institution of motherhood so as to make mothering less oppressive to women. Feminist thinkers concerned specifically with the issue of child rearing seek feminist practices of gender socialization and 'in-connection' models of mother-child relations so as to raise a new generation of empowered daughters and empathetic sons. However, Rich was the first and, to my knowledge, the only feminist theorist to recognize that the former depends upon the latter: we can not effect changes in child rearing without first changing the conditions of motherhood. A review of feminist thought on motherhood reveals that a critique of the institution of motherhood and a concern with new modes of child rearing have developed independently of each other and that feminists committed to the abolition of motherhood and the achievement of mothering have seldom considered what this means for the mother *herself,* apart from the issue of child rearing.

In her chapter in this book, Fiona Green interviews feminist mothers who, in Green's words, "live Rich's emancipatory vision of motherhood." Driven by their feminist consciousness, their intense love for their children and the need to be true to themselves, their families and their parenting, [these] feminist mothers," Green writes, "choose to parent in a way that challenges the status quo." They do so, according to Green, by way of two different approaches: "overt strategies of resistance" and "subversive strategies of resistance." To illustrate the first strategy Green gives the example of a lesbian and lone parent of a ten-year-old girl who births and raises a child without any connection to man. "No man ever called the shots in my home," the woman explains, "nor did a man ever support me in any way. So that is really breaking the rules in the patriarchy." According to Green, this is "a deliberate act of resistance to dominant conceptions and practices of mothering." The second strategy is less overt; with this approach mothers "under the cover of the institution of motherhood effectively challenge patriarchy and their subversive activity often goes unnoticed." Green provides examples of two heterosexual married mothers to illustrate this strategy, one who raises a son to make him consciously aware of social injustices, while the second mother "actively encourages the nurturing and noncompetitive tendencies of her son, while supporting her daughter in her pursuits of math and science." The second subversive strategy thus seems to focus on child rearing undertaken by women in the institution of motherhood while the former, the overt strategy, involves a challenge to the institution itself and is concerned with the empowerment of the mother. Speaking of the first (the example of overt resistance) mother's choice to rear her daughter with another mother during a difficult time in her daughter's adolescence, Green comments that this mother "enjoy[ed] a level of freedom and strength that she would not have experienced had she conformed to patriarchal [motherhood]."

I refer to Green's research here because I think it illustrates well the argument I have been developing on what makes Rich's insights on mothering and motherhood significant and groundbreaking; namely, we must eradicate oppressive motherhood and achieve emancipatory mothering for mothers themselves so that they may be enriched and empowered by mothering. That is reason enough to abolish motherhood. However, in so doing we also invest mothers with the needed agency, authenticity, autonomy, and authority to effect the feminist child rearing they desire. Furthermore, daughters, in connecting with mothers who model and mentor empowered womanhood, will be empowered as advocated by writers who advance the connection and empowerment argument. A son with an empowered mother will similarly desire and seek connection with her and thus will be more likely to develop feminine characteristics as desired by masculinity writers. In the introduction to this volume, I discussed briefly how African American mothering is a site of empowerment for women because it accords mothers power alongside responsibility, as well as eschewing the patriarchal dictates of intensive mothering. In contrast, we find few examples in either Anglo-American feminist thought or practice of mothers or scholars on motherhood who advocate and position mothering as a site of empowerment for mothers themselves. Instead, we see feminists, in theory and practice, agitating for feminist child rearing within the institution of motherhood. Again, and as Rich realized more than a quarter-century ago, this is not enough. While we can never abolish motherhood as Rich wished, her belief that we must strive to do so for mothers is what makes *Of Woman Born* a truly radical and, for those who benefit from patriarchal motherhood, a truly subversive text. I also believe, as Rich did, that mothering that invests mothers with agency, authority, autonomy, authenticity, is better for children as well. In other words and to conclude, in being "bad" mothers—outlaws from the institution of motherhood—we become better mothers for ourselves and our children.

NOTES

1. Please visit *The Association for Research on Mothering* (ARM) website *www.yorku.ca/crm* for a listing of the various topics explored by maternal scholars. ARM, founded in 1998 and now with more than five hundred members worldwide, is the first international feminist organization devoted specifically to the topic of moth-

ering-motherhood. ARM hosts two international conferences a year and publishes *The Journal of the Association for Research on Mothering* biannually. For more information, please visit the ARM website.

2. Please see my chapter, "Feminist Perspectives on Mothering and Motherhood: Power and Oppression" in *Gendered Intersections: A Collection of Readings for Women and Gender Studies*, eds. Pamela Downe and Leslie Biggs, Ferwood Press, forthcoming. See also my book *Reconceiving Maternity: From Sacrificial Motherhood to Empowered Mothering*, forthcoming.

3. This is examined at length in my two recent articles, "Across the Divide: Contemporary Anglo-American Feminist Theory on the Mother-Daughter Relationship," in *Redefining Motherhood: Changing Identities and Patterns*, eds. Sharon Abbey and Andrea O'Reilly, Toronto: Second Story Press, 1998, 69–91; and "Mothers, Daughters and Feminism Today: Empowerment, Agency, Narrative," *Canadian Woman Studies* 18:2 & 3 (Summer/Fall 1998) 16–21. See also the introduction to *Mothers and Daughters: Connection, Empowerment, Transformation*, eds. Andrea O'Reilly and Sharon Abbey, New York: Rowman and Littlefield, 2000.

4. Contemporary feminist theory on Mothers and Sons may be organized under three interrelated themes: "Mothering and Motherhood," "Men and Masculinities," "Mother and Son Connections and Disconnections." Please see the following two articles for a detailed discussion of these themes and how they are featured in Anglo-American and African American Theory: my introduction to and chapter, entitled "In Black and White: Anglo-American and African-American Perspectives on Mothers and Sons," in *Mothers and Sons: Feminism, Masculinity and the Struggle to Raise Our Sons*, ed. Andrea O'Reilly (New York: Routledge, 2001) 1–21; 91–118.

WORKS CITED

Arcana, Judith. *Every Mother's Son*. New York: Anchor Press/Double Day, 1983.

———. *Our Mother's Daughters*. Shameless Hussy Press, 1979.

Blakey, Mary Kay. "Who Are We This Time?: An Excerpt from *American Mom*." *Mothers and Sons: Feminism, Masculinity and the Struggle to Raise Our Sons*. Ed. Andrea O'Reilly New York: Routledge, 2001:25–41.

Caplan, Paula. *The New Don't Blame Mother: Mending the Mother-Daughter Relationship*. Routledge, New York, 2000.

Cooper, Baba. "The Radical Potential in Lesbian Mothering of Daughters." *Politics of the Heart: A Lesbian Anthology*. Eds. Sandra Pollack and Jeanne Vaughn. Ithaca, NY: Firebrand Books, 1987:233–240.

deBold, Elizabeth, Marie Wilson, and Idelisse Malave. *Mother Daughter Revolution: From Good Girls to Great Women*. New York: Addison-Wesley, 1993.

Forcey, Linda. *Mothers of Sons: Toward an Understanding of Responsibility*. New York: Praeger, 1987.

Gilligan, Carol. *In a Different Voice: Psychological Theory and Women's Development*. Cambridge: Harvard UP, 1982.

Johnson, Miriam. *Strong Mothers, Weak Wives: The Search for Gender Equality*. Berkeley: U of California P, 1989.

Kaufman, Michael. *Theorizing Masculinities*. Thousand Oaks, CA: Sage, 1994.

Lorde, Audre. "Man Child: A Black Lesbian Feminist's Response." *Sister Outsider: Essays and Speeches*. New York: Quality Paperback Book Club, 1993:72–80.

Morgan, Robin. "Every Mother's Son." *Lesbians Raising Sons*. Ed. Jess Wells. Los Angeles: Alison Books, 1997:38–59.

O'Reilly, Andrea. "Across the Divide: Contemporary Anglo-American Feminist Theory on the Mother-Daughter Relationship." *Redefining Motherhood: Changing Identities and Patterns*. Eds. Sharon Abbey and Andrea O'Reilly, Toronto: Second Story Press, 1998:69–91.

———. "Mothers, Daughters and Feminism Today: Empowerment, Agency, Narrative." *Canadian Woman Studies* 18:2 & 3 (Summer/Fall 1998):16–21.

———. Introduction. *Mothers and Daughters: Connection, Empowerment, Transformation*. Eds. Andrea O'Reilly and Sharon Abbey. New York: Rowman and Littlefield, 2000:1–18.

———. Introduction. *Mothers and Sons: Feminism, Masculinity and the Struggle to Raise Our Sons*. Ed. Andrea O'Reilly (New York: Routledge, 2001):1–21.

———. "In Black and White: Anglo-American and African-American Perspectives on Mothers and Sons." *Mothers and Sons: Feminism, Masculinity and the Struggle to Raise Our Sons*. Ed. Andrea O'Reilly. New York: Routledge, 2001:91–118.

———. "Feminist Perspectives on Mothering and Motherhood: Power and Oppression." *Gendered Intersections: A Collection of Readings for Women and Gender Studies*. Eds. Pamela Downe and Leslie Biggs, Fernwood Press, (in press).

———. *Reconceiving Maternity: From Sacrificial Motherhood to Empowered Mothering* (Forthcoming).

Payne, Karen, ed. *Between Ourselves: Letters Between Mothers and Daughters*. Boston: Houghton Mifflin, 1983.

Pipher, Mary. *Reviving Ophelia: Saving the Selves of Adolescent Girls*. New York: Ballantine, 1994.

Rich, Adrienne. *Of Woman Born: Motherhood as Experience and Institution*. New York: Norton, 1986.

Ruddick, Sara. *Maternal Thinking: Toward a Politics of Peace*. New York: Ballantine Books, 1989.

Rutter, Virginia Beane. *Celebrating Girls: Nurturing and Empowering Our Daughters*. Berkeley: Conari Press, 1996.

Silverstein, Olga and Beth Rashbaum. *The Courage to Raise Good Men*. New York: Viking, 1994.

Thomas, Alison, "Swimming Against the Tide: Feminists' Accounts of Mothering Sons." *Mothers and Sons: Feminism, Masculinity and the Struggle to Raise Our Sons*. Ed. Andrea O'Reilly, New York: Routledge, 2001:121–140.

TEN

The Broken Shovel

Looking Back from Postmaternity at Co-Parenting

MARGARET MORGANROTH GULLETTE

> Of course a mother's feelings are too deep for words. How sad it
> would be, if they were not!
> —Ivy Compton-Burnett, *A God and His Gifts*

PART ONE

BEFORE ADRIENNE RICH could write *Of Woman Born*, she had to become post-maternal.[1] In other words, she came to consider her children adults. (Her eldest was twenty-one, a canonical emancipation age.) The emotional prerequisite for her writing, however, as for others who have waited until their middle years to write about their early mothering, was to like her children better as adults.

> For a long time, I avoided this journey back [. . .] because it meant going
> back into pain and anger that I would have preferred to think of as long since
> resolved and put away. I could not begin to think of writing a book on moth-
> erhood until I began to feel strong enough, and unambivalent enough in my
> love of my children. (Rich, 15)

This kind of autobiographical retrospect restores real time to child rear-ing. It is not usually a lifetime of self-abnegation nor "an identity for all time" (as Rich had once despairingly felt) (Rich, 37). It's not static. Even a woman who mothers "ambivalently" may reach a point when she judges her chil-dren worthy of a new kind of relationship, because the children finally can offer her a new kind of affection and attention: adult recognition. I call this relationship *being (more or less equally) adults together.* Some women endure child rearing better because, unlike Rich, they consciously anticipate that the two-decade process will bring them to this happy point.

It may or may not. What has turned out best for the postmaternal me ought to figure in my judgment of the past and any advice or warning I might have to give on earlier mothering. At the personal level, the process can be unearthed by asking a specifically postmaternal question: "What inhibited or developed my child's ability to recognize me as an independent, valuable human being as well as her/his mother?" With such a question firmly in mind, every aspect of child rearing can be remembered afresh, in startling detail.[2]

THE BROKEN SHOVEL

We were a family, a threesome. We bought a little cabin on a lake in the country, just Jason and I and our son, Peter. We bought our first little boat to row on the lake. One foggy summer day, we drove down with our brand new little boat tied on top of our battered little car, Mommy and Daddy in front, oars stretched backward between us, and Son in back to one side. The three of us sang, "We all live in a yellow submarine. . . ." It was launch day, time for a ritual.

Peter was just twelve, slender and fine-boned but strong for his age and build. In a pinch he could have slid the light aluminum skiff from the car to the shore all by himself, without Jason. But on launch day the Boy helped the Father carry the boat to the water, while I put the groceries away. In off-key glee, I was belting out the elegiac love lament "O dolci baci, languide carrezze . . ." that Jason and I sometimes sang to each other from *Tosca.*

But when I strolled down to the lake for the inaugural ride, the boat was gone and my husband was gone and my son was gone. I scanned the thick layer of gray mist from side to side, scarcely believing that this had happened, that I could have been left behind. The thick scrims swam from right to left in front of my eyes, driven by the warm wind. I couldn't see them. They weren't there. An air balloon could have carried them away. Swiftly, expertly, helplessly bundled by men in black into the gondola, they hadn't had time to call out for me. Or they had called out, frantically, but I hadn't heard them, crooning full-voiced into the refrigerator's cave. No, I couldn't find them because I didn't believe they were out there. But methodically I kept peering, because the only rational hypothesis was that the sonuvabitch had arrogated this trip to himself. He—the male feminist!—had forgotten me or disdained me. Holding that hypothesis, eventually my eyes locked through the veils onto the butt-shape of boat and the two sticks Jason wielded with his back to me, rowing deliberately away. Better if an eagle had plucked him up.

I started to shout into the wall of vapor. COME BACK. COME BACK. My words struck on the wall and blew back on me; they clanged in my ears louder than when they left my mouth.

I doubled my outcry, shrieking upwind. GET BACK HERE. Tautened and exposed, my vocal cords dried in the humid air. Jason didn't hear, even Peter didn't hear. The sticks twitched through the water. The boat insolently distanced itself from the trembling shore. I was left on the last spit of land before the immensity of lake, unable to walk on water.

In search of a flag, a sky-signal, a pillar of fire, I grabbed a shovel that was lying in the shrubbery and started shaking it in the air over my head, screaming in outrage. I shook it from side to side, rocking like Cyclops. I thought there came an instant of cessation in the motion of that receding back. With the moisture driving into my face, it was hard to descry whether the boat was still relentlessly traveling down its vanishing points or striving to return. I dashed the shovel up and down on the earth, yelling hoarsely, HOW DARE YOU? The boat seemed to be approaching. Peter's narrow back now partly covered the hulking rower, but gradually Jason's shoulders came into view heaving up and down. He was straining to make guilty speed. Guilty. I was out of my head with fury, his desperation justified my wrath. That titanic helpless fiend who was me took a step forward and pounded the shovel through the spongy grass onto the hidden granite ledge under her feet. Her head jerked back, her teeth were smashed together by the impact. The tip of the shovel broke off and flew into the air as the boat broke out of the mist and they could see her distorted sneer and demented brows and she could see Peter's astonished sorrowful eyes and Jason's foolish, remorseful, and frightened face. Remorseful. *Dayyenu.* As the Israelites said when the first plague struck the Egyptians: Let there be more of that.

Only a being with a continuously rational, flexible record—as a sensitive mother, a considerate wife, a tender daughter—can inflict an episode like that on herself and loved ones and have it read as "extraordinary" and a lesson. In my defense, I'll add: I think women-as-mothers are not as likely to do what Jason did: usurp the child and the ritual while her husband was momentarily preoccupied. Or not the way a man who does it, does it. Heedlessly, narcissistically. "I didn't think you'd care. I didn't think you'd even want to go." That was what Jason explained, into the clenched teeth of my silent outrage, when Peter was out of hearing.

Very well: I was not insane but an unjustly treated woman. Woman. With Peter almost thirteen, Jason was inducting him into the Men's House reflexively. Boating had been coded male. The wife and the mother—one entire third of our threesome—could be excluded unthinkingly as a *woman.* In late twentieth-century America, even in a feminist family, the separation of the boy-child from his mother could begin with no warning given.

Yet only a repentant male feminist, loving husband, and sensitive father could have striven as hard as Jason to show remorse. He wanted the three of us to go out in the boat together immediately. I suggested waiting until the rain let up. It never cleared entirely; it was a dampened day. When I finally took the oars, I gave us a tour of one end of the lake. But the occasion had lost its high-hearted festive aura, its sense of being a definitional ceremony. The ride felt like a doom that we were sentenced to carry out. I had been innocent, but somehow I felt guilty.

I thought often about what the effect had been on Peter. I could only guess, intensely guess. . . . He must surely have been terrified. Parents are warned about the long-lasting effects of their "outbursts of violence." It wasn't aimed at him, that violence, but the broken shovel must have folded into a sense on his part that women have power to harm. And of course, nothing I might dream up to *say* could efface that fear, if he had it. So I said nothing. After that day, normal days and normal years passed and nothing like that happened again. Trust healed over the jagged edges. But doubtless, none of us forgot that blunt distorted iron shape. I slowly became another person—less quick to anger, less willing to act out—but I certainly didn't forget.

THE NEW FATHERRIGHT

I'm not insinuating that those were the right means, but I'm impressed by how consistently—and when the need was there, desperately—that earlier self willed my goals. I was clumsy, even reckless, but not passive. I'm still married to the man who repented so wholeheartedly that day and who struggles against his solipsism, which he too knows depends on a history of having privilege conferred on his male wantings, starting in childhood. It's then that men are taught, not "limitless self-confidence [but] limitless self-sympathy" as Jane Smiley says about a husband in an early novel, so that later, "he didn't know how not to be the center of his own attention" (216–217). And I am now post-maternal like Rich, able to look back with more equanimity.

My reflections may be useful to others because this whole subject of *recognizing the mother* is hard to notice, let alone measure. Useful too, I hope, because, following in Rich's pioneering footsteps, I will try to fit our experiences into the institutional history of child rearing. In progressive, middle-class U.S. households, the end of the twentieth century was a period of turmoil in mother-father-child relationships. "The Kingdom of the Fathers," as Rich called it, was shaken. Feminism stirred some women to overthrow the monarchy and block the straight path leading the sons to the Men's House. Democratic change in relationships created a heightened desire among many young mothers not to be obliterated by motherhood and introduced new kinds of gender trouble.

The context for me was co-parenting—a situation Rich could not envision because the system then "exonerate[d] men from fatherhood in any authentic sense" (13). Co-parenting in a tiny triad, not even of replacement size. One child. It is becoming a more frequent family form as economic pressures mount, divorce rates rise, marriage comes later. But even in large two-parent families, each child lives in a triangle.[3] A triad tends to break in two. Someone is left out. If the child is a boy, the excluded one can often be "the woman" and "the mother." But that was mostly fine with me, a person with a high need for solitude, particularly during the intensive early years of mothering, when I was also a preprofessional requiring absolute silence for work. The fact that Jason cared for Peter voluntarily was a relief; that they enjoyed each other's company, a pleasure. Years before I read *The Reproduction of Mothering*, I judged fathering a necessary and loving task. I was not jealous whenever child rearing became a fifty-fifty venture. I didn't regard their regular twosomes as my "exclusion." I might have, if Peter's father had promoted gendered behavior. But Jason was as hostile as I to the Rose Bowl syndrome, where men and boys abandon the clean-up of family gatherings to huddle together around licit vicarious violence. Given how many men evaporate in the face of parenting responsibility, I was most of the time at the lucky end of the historical spectrum.

That traditional father—call him "Harry"—may be indifferent until adolescence approaches and then suddenly proprietary. "Beget and forget" until adolescence;[4] then, FatherRight. A woman may not notice Harry's takeover at this time because she thinks this is "male bonding"; it must be "natural." Even though all that she loved and valued in this relationship with her child is being torn away. The son (who loved and admired her too) doesn't resist: he's flattered by the father's attention, distracted by male culture. No one tells him that he's losing his mother. She's still there on shore—somewhere, her head stuck in the refrigerator, doing something in the kitchen, something less interesting. She becomes vague; her life is vague. He loves her still; but soon she's an absence albeit so close by. Fathers can take over maturing daughters as well as sons, particularly now that girls do sports and become intellectuals. A father could sweep a *daughter* of twelve off on that boat alone.

Many more fathers since Rich's time are Jasons now, good dads from the beginning, men who share feminist, antimaterialist, and antiwar values. Economic history and feminism handed men these goodies. Hands-on child rearing has increasingly become a source of status and power as well as pleasure for such men. As the child becomes a future companion, her/his attention becomes more of a prize. Father competes with mother, may muscle in more. Thus he gives "largely covert parent-to-child [signals] undermining or conveying disparagement of the co-parent," in the words of psychologist James McHale.[5]

Co-parenting is the new paradigm. In the "new major category of two-working-parent families . . . collective child-rearing is an absolute necessity," Diane Ehrensaft argued (44–45). Women raising children welcomed it in the wake of Chodorow and Dinnerstein. Presumably young women who plan to mother, are looking out for men-who-will-share-childcare. Ten and twenty years ago, almost no feminist theorists anticipated male power within co-parenting as a problem and they have scarcely noticed it since.[6] Yet in co-parenting, interests are not always congruent; they may conflict. If a man wants "senior parent status," he's got a lot of cultural influence (a form of power) on his side.[7] The new FatherRight gives more, pays its dues—but the Jasons feel even more entitled. The "local variations" Rich warned us about, obscuring patriarchy's universality (58), include fathers' soft, invisible encroachment.

I'm sure mothers in this situation live their growing exclusion and invisibility with grief. But they can't figure out in the fog of newness what to do. There's no patriarchal image to attack, as in the past. The media have given them language for the overhyped "empty nest"[8] but not for this earlier vacuuming out at no particular sanctioned time. I for one hadn't then heard of "male separation/individuation," the old analytic justification for getting boys to detach from their moms. But even if the mother of a son denies this is a psychological need, deciding to resist more effectively just as a boy is becoming a teen seems futile. Try to organize a bigger share of time with him as he bonds with his buddies? Become more relational as heterosexuality looms, when the incest tabu kicks in? Expect sustained intimacy *then?*

Early and often, I reacted from my gut. Even ignorant, you can know when something is wrong; the blow teaches. Of course I didn't want to be excluded as a "girl." When Peter told me at the age of ten or eleven that he no longer wanted to invite girls to his birthday party, I decided that we would no longer hold birthday parties. We had loved those June festivities, with our friends chatting and flirting on the lawn, and the kids performing an impromptu play or hitting a piñata. But Jason must have agreed; we stopped giving them. After that, we treated Peter to a gourmet dinner on his birthday with a friend of his choice.

With hindsight, can I now state what my goals were? *I wanted to be a center of attention for my only child.* That's the simplest way to put it. By breaking the shovel, I wanted Peter to hear: *"You have a mother as well as a father. They are different. Mother has a self. Mother's is as important as father's. Pay equal attention."* I couldn't have explained why this was so grave.

Now I can. I speak primarily on behalf of our current adult relationship, those past fifteen years: dense, sweet; another new kind of "we," with decades more still to come of being adults together. Maybe thirty years. As early as toddlerdom, as they come to need less intense daily mothering, a woman who raises children must have her chance at beginning the long process of becoming equally adults together with them. For this to actually eventuate rather than remaining only a vivid dream of midlife happiness, she may need to break the paternal monolith early on, challenge any looming male monopoly, and present herself *continually* as a person in her own right. I did this instinctively. The broken shovel tells me how supremely important it was to me that Peter possess an uninterrupted history of cumulatively "recognizing" me as a self.

Jessica Benjamin says in *The Bonds of Love* (1999) that this is supposed to begin before children turn two. I am grateful to her for giving us the language of "recognition" and embedding it in a natural process that counters "separation/individuation." But that level of recognition within the first exclusive dyad is not a full-grown accomplishment at the age of two! It's the barest beginning of a process in which fathers and others and culture intervene. Theorists need to inquire, What next? My subject in this essay is what mothers do—or what they could do—between their child's second birthday and adulthood, through latency and adolescence, to become and stay recognized.

Twelve was not too late to make the point to Peter: he was still tender and open, not yet seared over with adolescent self-protectiveness and rudeness, nor warped away by socially sanctioned teen individuation. No doubt his adolescence was not as solipsistic or defensive as it might have been had I not let him know beforehand that I was a person capable of being hurt and capable of resenting it. Within a history of mothering that included consistent affection and attention, this mother/person felt freer to take him aside, tell a secret and keep one. Or be silly and impetuous: do a little dance in the kitchen. Talk up the loyalty parents can be trusted to maintain. Riffle his hair. I tried to convey that I was a person more like him than he might have thought. A person who had known him in all his stages and would appropriately honor or conceal our mutual histories. A female person more imposing than the culture wanted her to be. More and more a person different from his father, but above all an Other to reckon with.

PART TWO

The uprisings. My topic is heterosexual women with male partners, breaking the paternal monolith for the sake of their future relationship with their children, whether girls or boys. At this early phase of describing the unknown sides of postmaternity, the most illuminating genre for this effort (as Rich taught us) is a theorized memoir supplemented by other postmaternal recollections on the same themes.

Divorced or never-married hetero women who mother may have less of a monolith to tear down. The other authority is often absent. When it's present, the competition may be overt. If these women feel like lesser beings in their children's eyes, they readily spy the source: it has one man's name on it. We mothers living with men-who-father know that you don't marry only "Jason" or "Harry" but a whole culture; patriarchy sleeps in the bed with you. (Lesbian mothers with female partners were raised in patriarchy but probably don't have *this* problem.) Some mothers contribute to making the monolith strong, against our own interests. Even if we dream of something better, we may be unable to act. More is at stake than our personal future with our children, or even our postparental relationships with our partners. The stake is a different culture, where postmaternity would be honored, and, as a result, the prepost-maternal period would be lived and regarded differently.

The monolith is dangerous. For the woman/mother as well as the child.

It's the dangers to the woman that concern me most here. Women who raise children have to keep reminding ourselves, "Think (female) SELF, not always small child." Okay, start with ME, focus on ME. But at the same time, the sweetness that comes later from postmaternity, comes *through* the child: so how the child is formed, the influences on the to-be-adult-child, matters to the mother forever. "The best for the child" slides into "what is best for me." And vice versa. Let us try to banish the aspersion of "selfishness"—so quick to arise when a woman anticipates postmaternity from her own point of view—and let us boldly revise mothering-a-younger-child to establish values we can rely on in later life. It's not selfish to want to have a separate and equal self and to design one's own singular path to adult friendship with one's children. Long before their children's adolescence, still in deep childhood, mothers could *consciously* try to figure into their child rearing practices this value that hasn't been named, *our* value: being an equally important self.

The monolith is about power. As first experienced by a woman/new wife and new mother, this may seem like "parental" power: age, not gender, creates the hierarchy. Full monumentality rears over the small, weak child. "It's unfair," I thought once or twice, pitifully, when our son was old enough to have to hear his first combined "No." How he cocked his two-year-old head to the side, wavering, considering obedience, allured by folly and desire. "No," we said again, more sternly, "No no, sweetie." And then the little hesitating one wavered and desisted. It was startling. Who had expected that child rearing had this lordly side? Our power was so magnificent, so imperial—we needed to release only the tiniest, mildest voice of it to command. Long used to stubbornly negotiating power *between* us, Jason and I experienced the pleasurable shock of ascending the throne together. The relief of the common front.

We became a new "we"—parents: "we" not only over the clean diaper, the warm bath, the aromatic sleeping bundle, but over the wavering, testing, merry, naughty, challenging little cocked head. "No," we said, practicing, savoring. They name those toddler years "the terrible twos" because the child, learning to speak, sometimes practices the grammatical negative. They don't realize that the parents got to "NO" earlier. Call it the Scene of the Constitution of the Parental Dyad. The first stony blocks of the monolith.

Our "we" exemplified the reign of NO in its turn-taking, egalitarian mode. The monolith at its best: gentle, minimal, necessary. "No, that will hurt you." The dangerous joy of exercising power benignly faded in and out of anxious watchfulness and its attendant irritability. I trusted Jason to exercise the saving, dominating NO sparingly; he trusted me—the same. Discipline—time to call it by its proper name—was yet another outcome of the complex love that had united us in bed and at board. Thus, at best, is the monolith formed.

Where is the danger to the woman? I didn't see inequality: not consciously. I couldn't have said how in our triad Jason dominated the monolith through the maleness conferred on him. Who does, at the time? As parents we seemed instead rivals in charm, contriving delicious alternatives to the forbidden or the boring, bringing comfort to childhood's frequent miseries. Well, that was good mutual parenting. Lively Jason offered more by way of physical distractions—tickling, games where balls were thrown and fetched. I offered reading aloud, child tucked up within the curve of mother's left arm, head over heart, the warm beat underneath the narrative; also card games, chess, drawing. Children learn their parents have different personalities from the division of the distractions too. Sometimes they also learn sexist stereotyping that way, but not in our house, not too much. If both play chess, if both read aloud, the child learns "personality" instead: one parent is impatient when reading the same book twice, the other needs a long pause before moving a pawn. There was difference but not much gender difference. After babyhood, Peter sought either when he stubbed his toe, wanted to learn to fry an egg, was snubbed by a friend. Those with a single child know this parental alertness to being preferred. ("Come to Mamma!" "Come to Daddy!" Which will it be?) I didn't disparage Jason; I invoked and affirmed him: "Daddy will love this drawing too!" When it turned out I wasn't the one who taught Peter street hockey, a few years later I summoned up my father's long-neglected teaching and became the one who taught tennis.

Underneath, beneath consciousness, beneath my love for Jason, I was in fact running and striving and competing all the time. For what? Not to seem "different": that's ridiculously easy to come by in a sexist society. I fought, though I would have shied away from the words, for equal importance. "Striving for equality is humiliating!" some writer said. That adjective demeans the oppressed because they resist. But striving for a right is humiliating. I fought not to be irrelevant on important occasions. I fought not be be excluded—excluded unconsciously, without malice, in such a way that no self-respecting woman could invent words to expostulate against. More positively, I fought for my time to be reckoned quality time, for my values to win Peter's heart, for my share of his mind. Except for that day at the lake, I was alert to danger, swift into action.

Gun control. In the early 1970s, unisex child rearing sometimes meant giving girls toy guns as well as boys. I took the peace option, the hardest to control. "No guns." An absolute ban: no water pistols, no drawings of guns, no holsterlike paraphernalia or stuffed pockets, no quick draws, no pointed fingers. None from you, none from your little friends who come to the house. If pint-sized American males-in-training came packing, I said, "In this house we confiscate the guns at the door, just like in the Westerns," with my hand out, to teach the word "confiscate."

This stance provoked the most appalling opposition from other adults (in the midst of the Vietnam War!). "He'll be ostracized," they worried. "He'll shoot and die in other people's yards," they liked to remind me, "behind your back." They believed every parent had to yield to the status quo. American kids have guns, period. Nobody even said, "It's impossible, but you're right to try." Jason said, "If you don't let him have a toy gun, he'll find a stick; if you take away the stick, he still has the finger." No one said girls would automatically do this. Freudian/ evolutionary phallic essentialism, that's what we could call it now: It's the essence of males to want to threaten to kill. It was then uncontested, unrestrained, rampant, and triumphalist.

The baby's gun lobby only made me obstinate. For the first time in my young life I found myself in charge of an issue on which I had no doubts. Jason went on about boys' phallic fingers in public conversations where we were competing for the attention of our friends, but in practice, he didn't oppose me. He didn't buy Peter guns clandestinely, he didn't debate it in front of him.

I won that one. But Jason probably won more. We are still, I feel I must make occasion to repeat, married to each other; we like each other. We probably began the process during the Equality Wars. Conflict sharpened our liking, by bringing the other into clearer focus. For me in the 1970s, a new mother in graduate school with a little feminist backing, the imperative was to not fail to assert myself. Overall I tried for balance. We argued—often in front of Peter—about books, ideas, people, etymologies, politics. A child too makes an audience, and every marital conversation becomes a kind of performance. "The denial of women's cognitive authority begins at home," philosopher Hilde Nelson has said (92). Not my home. I already knew from college that women have to represent themselves as intellectuals, "moral deliberators" (Nelson, 97). Okay, I didn't buckle just because I anticipated his disagreement,[9] I didn't yield "gracefully." I made sure that "the Woman" won even more than 50 percent of the time, because as long as patriarchy lasts, 50 percent will create no conviction of woman's importance in any observant child's mind. Our occasional vehemence may have scared Peter at times but the conversation included him and solicited his opinion: he grew up talkative and lively. Probably we disputed in front of him more as he got older and realized that intellectual difference, even raised voices, didn't mean hatred. Marriages too would benefit from arguing more, if more women knew how to argue. (I didn't argue well at first, but I got better with practice.)

It was probably crucial that Jason relinquished to me some early important difference. Jason had his cuddle at goodnight time. But from the daycare years on, I was usually the one who sat on the bed last and stroked Peter's hair and wound down his day on the long, fat skein of days. It seemed to require a whispery croon. "You had a gooooood day today. You brought home a lovely drawing. Sally pulled your hair, but she said she was sorry, and you . . . aren't . . . angry . . . with her . . . anymore. You helped Daddy put the silverware away. This was a pretty happy day." Putting him to sleep on the good news he had told me, coloring the bad a little more rosily, I constructed him to himself as a moral being familiar with his emotions, an optimist of the will, a good profeminist man-to-be. A person I would like to spend time with and have on my side.

Of many findings in Carol D. Ryff and Marsha M. Seltzer's collection, *The Parental Experience at Midlife,* the one that seems to me most significant here is that women think they have been successful as mothers if their sons as well as their daughters handle affective life well (415). Mothers now want that particular "competence" in their futures, for themselves as well as their children. I imagine this is true whether they are feminists or conservatives, readers of mothering manuals or winging it on traditions. For most women, having a lovable and loving child is more precious than having one who makes lots of money. Mothers might well want all their children to be "daughters" in this sense. When I recall the sweetness of those bedtime chats, which must have lasted into his early teens, I see that doing what I could to those nurturing ends must have felt deeply necessary.

In sum, on behalf of the unknown future, I got the record I designed, with or without my conscious design.

POSTMATERNAL AGE AUTOBIOGRAPHY

Often it is only in postmaternity that a woman can see, belatedly and regretfully but with clarity, what she has sacrificed to maintain the male-dominated monolith. In a course I taught on "Postmaternal Women in Fiction, Film, Media, and Their Own Words" at the Radcliffe Seminars, I encouraged the participants to write "age autobiography," a form in which age and aging (in history and culture) become a more conscious aspect of memoir.[10] The task was to write specifically about the mothering each had done, if any, that prepared her (and her partner) for her postmaternal freedom and autonomy, and for her becoming equally adults together with her children. Five weeks into the course, one woman—she's chosen the pseudonym Carol Egan—announced that she had made discoveries that had been hidden from her by three decades of habit. In her memoir, Carol wrote,

> When I look back at the way my husband and I confronted our sons, it was always as a team. We agreed *[sic]* even when I did not necessarily agree with what my husband said or did: we could not be divided. Maybe this is necessary for teaching values—two voices may be too confusing to a child—

and for forestalling a child pitching one parent against the other hoping somehow to get an advantage. However, the cost of this approach is to leave the child out there alone—two against one. And the child does not see each parent as a separate person having his or her own thoughts, words, beliefs, soul, and voice.

Unity that is only apparent is open to being called a lie. But falsity is not the worst thing about it. There can be wise emotional reasons for a woman sometimes to act a togetherness she doesn't feel. First for temporary relief, if she's striving for equality on all the other days. Or to help preserve her love for her partner, without which there's no reason to stay close enough to grapple. But once there are children, this trivial feigning becomes far more serious. Not necessarily for the child, "out there alone."

In many a woman's marriage there's a tension between asserting herself and recognizing her male partner's needs.[11] One feminist/mother married to a male feminist told me she'd had *no* problems of this kind. Wonderful. But for most of us, maintaining that balance is difficult. Some women give up fighting. Out of multiple motives and blessed by traditional child rearing manuals, as Carol learned, many a mother practices "unity." Deferring to her husband stops being an occasional, generous gift of love. It can become habitual self-suppression.

It's the unequal, antiwoman side of enacting "unity" that needs to be made salient. The monolith the children see has been constructed by burying the husband's opinion inside the wife. Like tiny, wooden Charlie McCarthy on Edgar Bergen's lap, she only *seems* to talk out of her own mouth. Despite the appearance of unity, the children effectively recognize their father as a "separate person." Do they believe their mother is a dummy, without seeing that he is a ventriloquist? Precisely at times of stress, when her thoughts, words, beliefs, soul, feelings, values, opinions, and "voice" could matter most, she yields.

"In therapy, the woman cries, Why should *I* put aside my unhappiness? Why should *I* be the one not to fight because of the children? Why should *I* be the angel in the house who makes peace and a creative milieu? The man, she cries, can go scot free." This is feminist psychoanalyst Ruth-Jean Eisenbud, writing in a book from 1986 (281). Well, I know—excuse a remnant of bitterness that postmaternity hasn't quite conquered—*why* she puts herself aside and lets the man be boss. Because it's so exhausting not to. Because being an audible, visible center of self takes vigilance, energy, and effort. Because your children believe that their parents "argue too much," rather than observing that equality, true love, and recognizing the mother are all at stake. It isn't enough just to "fight," wildly and spontaneously, one round; as I did that one time. This is about conversation: daily, getting-up-in-the-morning to last-word-at-night speech. It may involve a *long* fight, starting early on, against a person you love, a good father, a feminist husband, who cannot (yet) stop being a man who wields the social power of maleness and the traditions of patriarchy he imbibed when young.

Maybe what I had to do will slowly become less necessary for women. In the meantime, while their children are still young, women must demonstrate their importance consistently, go to the mat on some issues, be prepared to be obdurate precisely at terrifying moments. Ugliness, disinhibition, the humiliation of your partner's looking as if you were *not* an equal—these are risks. High risks. *Of course* it is easier not to struggle and, later, in postmaternity, to cry out to a therapist.

And because, beneath all that, you may have had no other models, you may have been intellectually critical of the verbal models you saw, growing up—your mother as dummy, your father as bully. You may not recognize elements of this in your own more feminist life, or you may see them and still be unable to avoid them as an adult.

The participants in the postmaternal seminar had been asked not only to describe their feelings and behavior, but to investigate the cultural pressures to which they had been subjected. Carol Egan wrote:

> I am wondering where this concept of seeing my husband and myself as a "team" when the children were younger came from. My parents were always fighting in front of my sister and me as we grew up. But my mother was not able to speak on her own with any authority. My father gave out the rules with no discussion from my mother so I [still] do not know whether or not she agreed with them. In some ways, this was a "couple" approach although it was always very clear that my father was in charge. And he was formidable.
>
> I know that a TV program that we watched avidly each week, *Father Knows Best*, also influenced me. Somehow that became my ideal family. The ideal family was one that got along, made joint decisions, cared for each other and lived in peace and harmony. The mother and father never disagreed, never put forward two conflicting viewpoints or ideals to the children. I guess I thought if my husband and I acted like that then we would have a peaceful, loving family unlike the one that I grew up in. That TV family became my role model. How else did I know how to behave? I certainly did not see any thing better around me.

Parenting is a school of moral reasoning and self-development every single day. Attendance is mandatory: parents clock in daily just as the child does. Parents with young children are inventing and modeling morality for their child as they go along. Even mostly absent men wind up present for discipline. Along the way, in hundreds and thousands of decisions and practices, mother may help father stack the monolith higher. Like many women, Carol feared that "two voices may be too confusing. " But women may want to decide that "confusion" is not the worst danger or "peaceful" families the highest good. The dangers of the monolith to the children include learning depreciation, abuse, or cruelty toward a female authority; learning sexism. The danger to women is patriarchal possessiveness and expropriation. The woman loses not just her rightful, nonexclusive claim on her children, but the selfhood she would *develop* by representing herself to her children as she is.

Since mothers must construct for themselves importance in the eyes of their children, they need to develop new behaviors and practice them early. Recently, I have been asking midlife mothers a preliminary consciousness-raising question, "How did you distinguish yourself from your husband vis-à-vis your child?" I hope younger mothers too will meditate on how they do this, not waiting for a hypothetical future in which they'll have more cultural support.

This self-suppression, this failure of development, may go on. Not necessarily forever, but for twenty or thirty years—until the moment we claim postmaternal status and relations. The woman/mother is now in her middle years, the "child" an adult. That makes a great difference, involves a double psychic change. Carol's sons were by now twenty-six and twenty-nine:

> Now that my sons are adults, one of the major changes that I have made is to not approach them as [part of] a couple. Rather, I make an effort to have my voice heard as one single person, not as part of a team. If I think that something needs to be said, I say it. I resist the temptation to have my husband do the "dirty" work. If I want to see them, then I go to New York to spend time with them on my own. I do not wait to see if my husband will accompany me. [. . .] I relate to [each of] my sons one on one. I do not mean to suggest that I am antagonistic toward what my husband does or says to our sons. I simply state what I think and feel when asked for an opinion. It is the same respect that I give to a friend that I do not always agree with during a conversation. My sons are then allowed to relate to me as a person. A person with my own set of values, experience, feelings, and needs that are separate from any other person.
>
> This is not always an easy task, especially since I am breaking many years of habit when the boys were young. However, I know that it is extremely beneficial to me and to all four of us. It has allowed me to discover who this person really is now that I am seeing my self as separate from my husband and my sons. In our family, there are three very strong males, two of whom are successful salesmen and very persuasive. To be able to say what I think is a challenge, but worth the effort.

Being equally adult with your children is precious indeed. What did Carol lose through waiting? Only women who walked her road have the right to say.

An Ending of Sorts

I wrote the scene on the lake in November of 1998, and writing did what it usually does: it raised questions. So I took a great risk on Peter's next visit home. I asked him, in essence, to judge my behavior. I was standing, ironing a tablecloth (shades of Tillie Olsen!), and he was sitting nearby, basting up the legs of some new trousers. Such domesticity made an atypical moment for us, but it was peaceful. As nonchalantly as I could—not to bring all the terror back in a rush—I asked whether he had any recollection of an episode from when he was about eleven or twelve, in which we were launching our first boat and his father had taken him out alone and I got so furious that I broke a shovel. That sketchy outline was all I could bring myself to provide. In answer, he just looked incredulous—as incredulous as if I'd just told him (perhaps as a stab at making myself interesting in a innovative and preposterous way), that I'd once had a fling at robbing banks.

He obviously remembered none of it. I had simply been wrong about what he observed. I had guessed with "a mother's" exaggerated sense of the immensity of her powers. What must have happened is that I smoothed my face out for him when they closed in to the dock; Jason had done the same, and while Peter was with us we refrained from acrimony or even discussion. . . . The likelihood was that Peter had not even seen my face that day. Because he was facing his father rowing, he must have had his back to me as the boat came in. That "memory" of seeing his face looking sorrowful and perplexed must have been a guilt-driven invention.

Jason came hurrying in just as I finished speaking, and must have overheard some key words. *"Yes,"* he said, looking slightly shamefaced but also slightly nostalgic, and added with relish (as if remembering with applause a fine performance of a fierce role, say Irene Pappas as Clytemnestra in *Iphigenia*), "yes, your mother broke a shovel. We still have that shovel."

That was all. Time had done its cleanest healing as far as Jason was concerned. Since then, he had renounced the early self that could blindly exclude the female other from a moment of ritual family unity. He may still demand more than his share of Peter's attention, but he couldn't act that proprietorial "Father"—that nonhusband—again.

So. In fact, Peter had attended a family ceremony that had mysteriously lacked his mother, and all he had seen when he returned from male bonding on the foggy sea—at his lovely unsuspicious age—was familiar parental harmony. The normal exclusion of Woman and Mother.

But it could have been much worse. Suppose—horrified by his having seen me frantic and violent, as I thought he had, with a broken shovel in my hand—I had depended on that one symbolic moment to do a life's work of differentiation, and at that crucial moment in a son's development had fearfully desisted from my regular, persistent campaign to represent my own being and remain important in his life? That would have been the real disaster.

NOTES

1. "Postmaternity" is my own coinage. My other essays on the postmaternal phenomenon include "'Postmaternity' as a Revolutionary Feminist Concept"; "Wicked Powerful: The Postmaternal in Contemporary Film and Psychoanalytic Theory"; and "Inventing the 'Postmaternal' Woman, 1898–1927: Idle, Unwanted, and Out of a Job."

2. Although what follows is true, I have changed the names of everybody.

3. McHale and Fivaz-Depeursinge pointed out in 1999 that the triad has been neglected, until quite recently in psychology, by researchers biased toward thinking of families as dyads (mother-child or father-child) or as collections of individuals (107).

4. The expression comes from Susan Rae Peterson, "Against 'Parenting,'" p. 64.

5. James McHale, "Overt and covert parenting processes in the family," p. 183 et seq.

6. One exception is Iris Marion Young, who noted "a curious lack of reference to male power" in all theories that called for more fathering from men (137, 138–142).

7. See Pepper Schwartz. Schwartz finds no fault with co-parenting: It's better for a couple as a couple not to have such gendered, divergent lives; it's better for the woman that "no one parent is blamed with the outcomes of parenting" (167). Yet she uses the term "senior parent status" (162), which implies hierarchy. Her two paragraphs on female jealousy appear on page 169.

8. For the origins of the "empty nest" see Gullette, "Inventing the 'Postmaternal' Woman."

9. Marie Withers Osmond and Barrie Thorne have described women's deference as the result of men's "latent power": "anticipating negative reactions from husbands, wives do not express their desires" (603) or, I would add, their opinions.

10. There are two chapters in my book, *Aged by Culture*, that try to define age autobiography: "Age Identity Revisited" and "From Life Storytelling to Age Autobiography."

11. This language about "tension" in striving for the "mutual encounter" comes from Laura Lee Downs, page 425.

WORKS CITED

Benjamin, Jessica. *The Bonds of Love: Psychoanalysis, Feminism, and the Problem of Domination*. New York: Pantheon, 1999.

Downs, Laura Lee. "If 'Woman' Is Just an Empty Category, Then Why Am I Afraid to Walk Alone at Night? . . ." *Comparative Studies in Society and History* 35.2 (April 1993):414–443.

Ehrensaft, Diane. "When Women and Men Mother." *Mothering: Essays in Feminist Theory*. Ed. Joyce Trebilcot. Totowa: Rowman and Allanheld, 1983:41–61.

Eisenbud, Ruth-Jean. "Women Feminist Patients and a Feminist Woman Analyst." *The Psychology of Today's Woman: New Psychoanalytic Visions.* Eds. Toni Bernay and Dorothy W. Cantor. Hillsdale, N.J.: Analytic, 1986:273–290.

Ginott, Chaim. *Between Parent and Child: New Solutions to Old Problems.* New York: Macmillan, 1961.

Gullette, Margaret Morganroth. *Aged by Culture.* Chicago: U of Chicago P, 2004.

——. "'Postmaternity' as a Revolutionary Feminist Concept," *Feminist Studies* 28.3 (Fall 2002):553–572.

——. "Wicked Powerful: The Postmaternal in Contemporary Film and Psychoanalytic Theory," and "Response," *Gender and Psychoanalysis* 5 (Spring 2000): 107–139 and 149–154; with a comment by Carolyn Stack.

——. "Inventing the 'Postmaternal' Woman, 1898–1927: Idle, Unwanted, and Out of a Job," *Feminist Studies* 21.3 (Summer 1995):221–253.

McHale, James. "Overt and Covert Parenting Processes in the Family," *Family Process* 36.2 (June 1997):183–201.

McHale, James and Elizabeth Fivaz-Depeursinge. "Understanding Triadic and Family Group Interactions During Infancy and Toddlerhood," *Clinical Child and Family Psychology Review* 2.2 (1999):107–127.

Nelson, Hilde Lindemann. "Sophie Doesn't: Families and Counterstories of Self-Trust," *Hypatia* 11.1 (Winter 1996):91–104.

Osmond, Marie Withers and Barrie Thorne. "Feminist Theories: The Social Construction of Gender in Families and Societies." *Sourcebook of Family Theories and Methods.* Eds. Pauline G. Boss et al. New York: Plenum, 1993:591–622.

Peterson, Susan Rae. "Against 'Parenting.'" *Mothering: Essays in Feminist Theory.* Ed. Joyce Trebilcot. Totowa, N.J.: Rowman and Allanheld, 1983:62–69.

Rich, Adrienne. *Of Woman Born: Motherhood as Experience and Institution.* New York: Norton, 1986. Tenth Anniversary edition.

Ryff, Carol D. et al. "How Children Turn Out: Implications for Parental Self-Evaluation." *The Parental Experience at Midlife.* Eds. Carol D. Ryff and Marsha Mailick Seltzer. U of Chicago P, 1996:383–422.

Schwartz, Pepper. *Peer Marriage: How Love Between Equals Really Works.* New York: The Free Press, 1994.

Smiley, Jane. *At Paradise Gate.* New York: Simon and Schuster, 1981.

Young, Iris Marion. "Is Male Gender Identity the Cause of Male Domination?" *Mothering: Essays in Feminist Theory.* Ed. Joyce Trebilcot. Totowa, N.J.: Rowman and Allanheld, 1983:129–146.

PART THREE

Narrating Maternity

Writing as a Mother

ELEVEN

Adrienne Rich's
"Clearing in the Imagination"

Of Woman Born *as Literary Criticism*

D'ARCY RANDALL

BECAUSE *OF WOMAN BORN* has so profoundly influenced our cultural and social understanding of mothering, readers sometimes wonder why Adrienne Rich published so little poetry to or about her children, or about her own maternal experience. Rich anticipates such questions in her introduction, writing that "[f]or me, poetry was where I lived as no-one's mother, where I existed as myself"(31). Still, the questions persist, partly because of how *Of Woman Born* is situated in maternal literature's curious history. Although mother-poets like Sappho and Anne Bradstreet thrived in other times and places, by the middle of the twentieth century, Anglo-American literary culture seemed to have forgotten that mothers could write poetry at all.[1] Now, of course, when maternal poetry fills anthologies and individual collections, it is Rich's generation of poets—Sylvia Plath, Lucille Clifton, Judith Wright, among others—who are largely credited for (re)asserting maternal points of view in English language poetry (Ostriker, Friedman, Gilbert and Gubar). So why would Rich not participate in such a significant development? This chapter argues that whatever Rich's reasons may have been for avoiding the maternal in her poetry, *Of Woman Born* contributes substantially to the field if we read the text as literary criticism.[2] I show how Rich's visionary analysis of motherhood complements a variety of twentieth-century maternal poems.

This reading of Rich's text may appear eccentric, for *Of Woman Born* neither announces itself as literary criticism, nor does it generally foreground poetry. But I read *Of Woman Born* as the kind of literary criticism that elucidates not poems themselves, but the cultural and social expectations that western, educated readers commonly bring to them. Certainly Rich critiques the images of motherhood found in mid-twentieth-century canonical literature, particularly if we expand the term "literature" to include religious, medical, and Freudian psychoanalytic texts. Elsewhere Rich comments that "[t]he critic's task is not to try to deflate, shrink, and contain the scope of poetry, but rather, as John Haines has written, to provide 'a space in which creation can take place, a clearing in the imagination.'" (*A Clearing in the Imagination* 110). *Of Woman Born* works intertextually with maternal poetry by making "a clearing in the imagination" for readers.

For maternal poetry, this kind of reader-based literary criticism was, and remains, vitally important, because western, educated readers often bring to this poetry a thicket of preconceptions about "motherhood" and a historically masculinized notion of "creativity." Even now, some readers harbor doubts that mothers can be serious poets, or even "creative" artists.[3] In his psychoanalytic study of the creative personality published in 1996, John E. Gedo admits that "having babies does not eliminate creativity" (75). Still, his exemplary creative individuals are nearly all male, and his definition of creativity maintains a rigid boundary between maternal and artistic "work": "The most difficult and most essential of our tasks, the upbringing of our children, is almost never looked upon as a creative domain, probably because it is rightly regarded as an aspect of our narrow self-interest" (5). Such reductive distinctions obscure our apprehension of what maternal poets offer, the challenges and possibilities of what Susan Stanford Friedman calls the "genuine bond between creation and procreation" (94).

Rich's comment that she had separated her poetic from her maternal "self" indicates that, as a young poet and mother, she brought these unfortunate distinctions to her own work. Many of us still do. Yet *Of Woman Born*'s self-reflexive quality emphasizes Rich's awareness that the first imagination cleared must be her own. For Rich, "motherhood" was "a ground which seemed to me the most painful, incomprehensible, and ambiguous I had ever traveled, a ground hedged by taboos, mined with false-namings" (15).

Rich's subtitle, *Motherhood as Experience and Institution*, addresses the problem of "false-namings" directly. Quotations from Rich's notebooks from that period illustrate the "anger, weariness, demoralization" of contemporary "motherhood" (30). In retrospect, however, she argues that such negative consequences stem not from the biological "fact" of maternity, but from "motherhood" as "patriarchal institution" (33). She contrasts two meanings of motherhood, one superimposed on the other: "the *potential relationship* of any woman to her powers of reproduction and to children; and the *institution,* which aims at ensuring that that potential—and all women—shall remain under male control" (13). Far from reflecting a "natural" state of woman, the "institution of motherhood" is an artificial construct that was "invented" by "patriarchy." Patriarchy silences women, particularly mothers, as well as what both men and women define as "maternal" or "feminine" in themselves. This silence has been historically enforced through male-dominated professions, most notoriously monotheistic religious and Western medical professions. Patriarchy expects all of its high offices to be inhabited by males, or by women willing to sacrifice maternity (or maternal voices) for power, be it political, social, intellectual, artistic, or literary. For a mother to write and publish poetry foregrounding or acknowledging her maternal experience refuses both silence and sacrifice: maternal voices demand to be heard. Yet readers may still turn a deaf ear because there is no "clearing" in which to hear amid patriarchal definitions of "motherhood." *Of Woman Born* shows how such definitions interfere with our reception of maternal voices, in literature and within ourselves.

Since *Of Woman Born* was first published, the fields covered by its individual chapters have attracted extensive feminist scholarship, challenging, updating, and building on Rich and the sources she consulted. Rich acknowledges some of these in her new introduction of 1986. Nevertheless, many of Rich's general points remain valid, and *Of Woman Born* is valuable for uniting complex fields of study under a single, passionate vision.

For instance, in chapters 3, 4, and 5, Rich traces patriarchy's cultural silencing of mothers through the institutions of monotheistic religion, "the Kingdom of the Fathers." She reviews the literature and artifacts of anthropology and archaeology, seeking to expand the story of human origins to allow imaginative "space" for maternal power and influence in human development. In chapter 3, Rich considers the dominant male deity and meditates on a possible alternative, an ancient "Goddess" figurine, in which, she claims, "we encounter the female as primal power." In Rich's reading, such figurines:

> express an attitude toward the female charged with awareness of her intrinsic importance, her depth of meaning, her existence at the very center of what is necessary and sacred. [. . .] If, as very often, there is a child at her breast, or on her lap, she is not absorbed in contemplation of him. [. . .] She exists, not to cajole or reassure man, but to assert herself. (93–94)

When Rich was writing *Of Woman Born* in the 1970s, "Goddess" figurines had been a source of inspiration and controversy in academic and literary communities, and the fascination and arguments continue today. Some feminists use the figurines as evidence to support the idea that long before patriarchy, human societies worshiped a Great Mother Goddess (or goddesses) and held women in high regard. Others, like Cynthia Eller, question whether these claims derive from rigorous historical and archaeological research, or, rather, from "passionate hope and religious faith."[4] But Rich's hybrid text refuses false distinctions between "secular" and "sacred": she had read enough misogyny parading as "objective scholarship"(16). Rich engages the historical and archaeological debate, but in remarks like the following she foregrounds a spiritual quest: "The images of the prepatriarchal goddess-cults did one thing: they told women that power, awesomeness, and centrality were theirs by nature, not by privilege or miracle; the female was primary" (94). Rich's "goddess" meditation speaks to a need among contemporary women for a source of spiritual power, authority, and inspiration that is woman-centered. It is "a springboard into feminist desire" (93).

Of course, some maternal poets make more of the goddess than others. Many maternal poets are less concerned with arguing for "truths" about the past than they are with presenting sustainable myths for the present and future. Rich writes that maternal "power" is qualitatively different from the more familiar patriarchal forms that dominate: "not power *over others*, but *transforming* power, was the truly significant and essential power, and this, in prepatriarchal society, women knew for their own" (99). Such comments resonate in the works of maternal poets H. D., Denise Levertov, and Audre Lorde. Through the transformative power of the crucible in "Tribute to the Angels," H. D. delivers "mer, mere, mère, mater, Maia, Mary / Star of the Sea / Mother" (71).

We also find in such poets a rearticulation of the muse.[5] Most readers can accept poets evoking a muse, or some source of creative power, but for maternal poets, the image of that force needs to come from beyond the mainstream, masculinist poetic and religious traditions. The romantic figure of the passive, female muse does not suffice.

Denise Levertov conjures both male and female muses. In "The Goddess," she keeps the female muse, but transforms her conventional aspects: No "gentle muse," Levertov's "Goddess" ejects her disciple from "Lie Castle," which one could read as "patriarchy":

> There in cold air
> lying still where her hand had thrown me,
> I tasted the mud that splattered my lips:
> the seeds of a forest were in it,
> asleep and growing! I tasted
> her power! (12–17)

"The Goddess" inspires a forthright divine maternal voice in the speaker. The speaker tastes the "mud," a word etymologically related to "mother," and partakes of the Goddess's transformative power. "She"—the Goddess/poet—creates life and poetry at once.

Audre Lorde locates power in a transformed image of blackness, divinity, and maternity. In "Black Mother Woman":

> I Am   a dark temple
> where your true spirit rises
> beautiful   tough as chestnut
> stanchion against nightmares of weakness (19–22)

If, as Rich laments, "female [cultural] evolution was mutilated" under patriarchy, H. D., Levertov, Lorde, and other maternal poets "take it into female hands" (127).

Rich's image of "female hands" marks a transition from the topic of women's spiritual midwifery to childbirth itself. Rich follows her chapters of patriarchal monotheism and women's spirituality with two, "Hands of Flesh, Hands of Iron" and "Alienated Labor," focusing on midwifery and the obstetric profession. This organizational move emphasizes the commonalities between Western religion and medicine, as both promote "motherhood as institution." Just as patriarchal monotheism "buried" the goddess, the obstetrical profession demeaned and (in the United States) nearly destroyed the practice of midwifery, which has supported women in childbirth throughout human history.[6] Hospitals, as well as churches and temples, are sites of exaggerated patriarchal rituals that suppress maternal agency and leadership.

Rich defines American hospital birth as "alienated labor" because of her own experience and those of countless other twentieth-century women: "The loneliness, the sense of abandonment, of being imprisoned, powerless, and depersonalized is the chief collective memory of women who have given birth in American hospitals" (176). Rich's text, like others in the women's health movement, opens up a (more) public discussion of birth and its rituals as a first step in correcting this condition.

Rich cites Sylvia Plath's *The Bell Jar*, which critiques the obstetrical profession's dehumanization of mothers (170). Toi Derricotte's long poem *Natural Birth* is even more damning of U.S. birth rituals that promote "alienated labor." The mother-narrator hopes for a Lamaze delivery, but finds labor to be almost beyond her power to endure. Clearly unused to Lamaze, the nurses can offer nothing but "a shot." During the first stage of labor, the mother describes the doctor's internal exam as if it were a rape. Worse, the laboring mother is too outraged to communicate to the doctor her pain. Even if the doctor himself does not literally "silence" the mother, she is just as effectively silenced by her resentment when "he wants me to roll and beg like a dog": "i keep / my pain locked up inside. he'll never know how much / he hurts, i'll never let him know" (27).

Silent resistance remains an all-too-common response by women patients to the arrogance and failures of empathy among medical doctors (Todd). In "Unknown Girl in the Maternity Ward," Anne Sexton's unwed mother refuses to name the father of the child. Her "enamel" doctors "want to know / the facts" (12–13), but she insists that "our case history / stays blank" (15–16).

Few would argue that these unfortunate mothers' tactics are, in the long run, helpful or useful. Speaking out is surely a more effective strategy to secure authority. But one also needs to be heard, and for the profoundly disempowered at a time of crisis, silence may appear the only dignified option. Note that both mothers cling to precious "knowledge" withheld from the doctors. Rich does not deny the limited options faced by most real mothers, but *Of Woman Born* gives women space to imagine themselves reclaiming the institutional frameworks in which we give birth. Plath, Derricotte, and Sexton illustrate the consequences if we do not, at least, try.

Fortunately, much childbirth poetry *does* try to reclaim the institutional frameworks, and is invested, directly or indirectly, in claiming birth as a site of voice, power, and community support. In 1914, Mina Loy's "Parturition" shocked readers with an account of birth presented as an intellectual and a spiritual event. In *Natural Birth*, Derricotte's narrator moves beyond the unhappy labor to a delivery in which she locates a woman-centered source of power both spiritual and physical: "i felt something pulling me inside, a soft call, but I / could feel her power. [. . .] the more i gave / to her, the more she answered me" (33). Finally, Derricotte gives voice to an alternative vision of what giving birth could be like: "why wasn't the room bursting with lilies? [. . .] / why were they acting the same when, / suddenly, everything had changed?" (33).

No one expects nurses to deliver shoots of lilies as well as anesthesia, but the institutional imposition of obstetrical authority on childbirth, particularly in the 1950s and 1960s, led to absurdly obtuse behavior. Since the 1970s, hospitals have partially responded to demands of the women's health movement, easing restrictions against delivery by midwives, and allowing greater communal and familial support for childbirth. But, as Rich points out in her new introduction to the 1986 edition, childbirth reform has also been "subsumed into a new [conservative] idealism of the family"(xii).

Rich's vision of the power and authority of the obstetrical profession led to several deeply pessimistic statements about the "choices" offered Western women by reproductive technology. She is not convinced by Shulamith Firestone's claims that in vitro fertilization will liberate women. As Rich sees it, "the female generative organs, the matrix of human life, have become a prime target of patriarchal technology"(127). In this, she anticipates Gena Corea and other feminists suspicious of reproductive technology. In Stephanie Strickland's *True North*, a section entitled "Mother Lost World" echoes and elaborates on many of Rich's concerns. In "Lodged in the Nursery Glass," the in vitro embryo is, for the poet, a prophet of her culture's ideal human, which is gendered male. She wonders if women can afford to buy into

> A more expensive bargain
>   pact; a patented genomic sac,
> and stainless act, for unto an infant
>   TechnI.con,™ in fact,
> is born:
>   a real being, being re-
> hearsed for the real
>   [per] Son
>
>   to come. (7–15)

Rich's chapters on religion and medicine stress the way mothers have been disempowered through large, impersonal, patriarchal institutions. But Rich also points out the tragic irony that patriarchy is not simply imposed on women by men, but is taught and perpetuated by mothers themselves: "Patriarchy depends on the mother to act as a conservative influence" (61). Chapters 8 and 9 examine how patriarchy thwarts the relationships between mothers and sons, and mothers and daughters. Sanctioned for little but sacrifice to others, mothers in effect train their children not to listen to them.

In chapter 8, "Mother and Son, Woman and Man," Rich confronts the Monster Mother of Sons from patriarchal literature: "controlling, erotic, castrating, heart-suffering, guilt-ridden, and guilt-provoking; [. . .] on her lap a helpless infant or a martyred son. She exists for one purpose: to bear and nourish the son" (186). Rich also evokes this demon in one of her few published poems of maternal experience, "The Crib." The mother covers up her sleeping infant, but his "eyes / spring open, still filmed in dream" (5–6). Through the "dream" of the infant male, the mother loses control of her "self." She wonders if the infant sees her as "death's head, sphinx, medusa?" (8) and concludes: "Mother I no more am, / but woman, and nightmare" (12–13).

Perhaps "The Crib" is less about Rich's "maternal experience" than it is about her vision of motherhood in the Western, male literary tradition. In the twentieth century, the tradition had been "saturated with Freudian hostility— and sentimentality—toward the mother" (202). The poem begins portraying a tender maternal moment, then shows the mood interrupted by the static scream of an infantile male voice. Rich views much of Western literature as authored by "grown-up male children" who "have written of women out of the unexplored depths of their fears, guilt, centered on our relationship to them" (191). "The Crib" bears witness to the literary/Freudian "shadow" that hovers over her maternal experience. Chapter 8 endeavors to illuminate the source of such shadows, to clear them away.

Rich insists that mothers must cease to act in patriarchally sanctioned roles if the "motherhood as institution" is to be overthrown. In one passage much loved and quoted by her readers, she offers glimpses of her own sense of maternal alternatives. Rich recalls a holiday that she took with her young sons away from both her husband and the patriarchal "institution of motherhood":

> It was a spell of unusually hot, clear weather, and we ate nearly all our meals outdoors, hand-to-mouth; we lived half-naked, stayed up to watch bats and stars and fireflies, read and told stories, slept late [. . .] we lived like castaways on some island of mothers and children. [. . .] I remember thinking: This is what living with children could be—without school hours, fixed routines, naps, the conflict of being both mother and wife with no room for being, simply, myself. (194)

Rich asks: Why cannot the mother live her own life, fully? And allow her sons to live theirs, without carrying the burden of their mother's ambitions? She looks to contemporary poetry by Robin Morgan and Sue Silvermarie that protests conventional mother-son relationships or that imagines those relationships differently.[7] Rich poses the question, "What do we want from our sons?" Speaking for herself, she replies, "If I could have one wish for my own sons, it is that they should have the courage of women" (215).[8] Lucille Clifton, in "wishes for sons" also responds to this question, with comic relief:

> i wish them cramps
> i wish them a strange town
> and the last tampon
> i wish them no 7-11 (1–4)

In chapter 9, "Motherhood and Daughterhood," Rich had originally commented that "the cathexis between mother and daughter—essential, distorted, misused—is the great unwritten story" (225). This single remark both creates a "clearing" and challenges women writers to fill it. Borrowing a term from Lynn Sukenick, Rich observes in existing mother-daughter literature a pattern of "matrophobia," or "the fear [. . .] of *becoming* one's mother" (235). Anne Sexton had noticed the same thing, and lines from her poem "Housewife" still send middle-class women into fits of denial: "A woman *is* her mother. / That's the main thing" (9–10).

But this "cathexis" is by no means universal, and Rich's challenge now appears welcome but limited in scope. Rich's new introduction notes the chapter's oversight: its exclusive attention to white, middle-class, urban (or suburban) writers and terms of reference. Rich and her readers can recognize her oversight by virtue of the explosion, during the 1980s, of "mother-daughter" literature by African American, Hispanic, Asian, and Native American women. She lists plays, fiction, and poetry from women writers of color who, she writes, "have challenged and amplified my thinking"(xxx).

One major amplification in Rich's thinking is to see around the (white, middle-class, urban) "cathexis" to different literary models of mother-daughter relationships, which are inflected by racial, ethnic, and other cultural distinctions; she mentions such writers as Toni Morrison, Alice Childress, and Bea Medicine (xv–xxviii).

Lucille Clifton also reimagines the mother-daughter relationship. In "daughters" the poet does not fear "becoming" her maternal ancestors, but rather affirms her identity as a distinct woman connected to a radiant matrilineage:

> [. . .] woman, i am
> lucille, which stands for light,
> daughter of thelma, daughter
> of georgia, daughter of
> dazzling you. (19–23)

But despite Rich's disclaimers, chapter 9 remains useful as a partial introduction to mother-daughter poetry. The "cathexis" has certainly not disappeared, and while Rich herself may have moved beyond "ready-to-hand Greek mythology," chapter 9 nevertheless anticipates an important poetic strategy in contemporary literature and film: the recovery, exploration, and development of the Demeter and Kore myth. This myth, while certainly Western, speaks to the devastation of maternal loss that is common ground among women of vastly different cultures. Moreover, it lends itself well to stories of generational tension in families negotiating for position between two or more worlds: white, nonwhite; rural and urban; western and non-western. In Lee Tamahori's 1994 film *Once Were Warriors,* set in New Zealand, the Demeter/Kore myth combines with Maori legends to inform a story of an urban Maori mother and daughter torn among rural Maori, urban Maori, and urban *pakhea* (white) cultures.

For maternal poets, the Demeter/Kore myth is like a passport freeing them from the stasis of "motherhood"; they gain access to a dual identity as mother and as daughter. Rita Dove's book *Mother Love* (1995) revisits the Demeter/Kore story from multiple points of view. "The Bistro Styx" complicates Kore's tale by accounting for her attraction to Hades; "Missing" complicates Demeter's by allowing the mother to recall her own wayward youth: "I am the daughter who went out with the girls, / never checked back in and nothing marked my 'last / known whereabouts,' not a single glistening petal" (1–3). Irish poet Eavan Boland embraces the Demeter/Kore myth: "The only legend I have ever loved is / The story of a daughter lost in hell" (1–2). She continues, "And the best thing about the legend is / I can enter it anywhere. And have" (6–7). The story, with its inevitable track of pain and loss, is a part of the mother's legacy to the daughter: "If I defer the grief I will diminish the gift. / The legend must be hers as well as mine" (49–50). The "cathexis" is not resolved—how can it be?—but readers at last have the beginnings of the literature that Rich so sorely missed.

Rich's last chapter, "Violence: The Heart of Maternal Darkness," disturbed many by acknowledging the rage and anger of maternal experience that most mothers of Rich's generation had kept to themselves. Even Rich's supporters feared she "had given ammunition to the enemy" (xxxv). Rich relates the story of Joanne Michulski, a severely depressed mother of eight, who in June, 1974 had murdered two of her children, the two whom she had seemed to love the most. Local journalists descended on Michulski and her family in a feeding frenzy, hyping the "human interest" story (257). Researching the tragedy, Rich outlines how Joanne Michulski was mistreated by inept, counterproductive, and patronizing religious and mental health professionals. Ms. Michulski's own pastor dehumanizes her, recalling her on one hand as a "mother bear" staunchly defending her children; on the other, as a "vicious dog" (258).

Rich sets the stage for this painful discussion in her first chapter, describing a meeting of mother-poets in which they critiqued the community response to Michulski:

> Every woman in that room who had children, every poet, could identify with [Michulski]. We spoke of the wells of anger that her story cleft open in us. We spoke of our own moments of murderous anger at our children, because there was no one and nothing else on which to discharge anger. [. . .] The words are being spoken now, are being written down; the taboos are being broken, the masks of motherhood are cracking through. (24–25)

Reading this passage today raises questions, if not alarm. Can the anger that countless mothers of small children express during the "witching hour(s)" really be likened to the outburst of a mother who is mentally ill? But Rich's comparison of these two distinct conditions may itself be an effect of a literary canon that stifled a full exploration of maternal feelings, recognizing only stereotypes of "good" mothers and "bad." One can imagine that after years of saturation in such an impoverished canon, Rich's community of mother-poets regarded the Michulski tragedy as emblematic of their own, less drastic, moments of rage. At 6:00 p.m., Everymother = Medea. No one "wants" to write or read about variations of maternal anger, but Rich shows that if maternal writers do not address this topic with the authority of experience, the patriarchal institutions will circulate their own interpretations. Rich presents the existential condition: speak, or be spoken for.

Rich quotes Alta's prose poem *Momma* as "plac[ing] a finger on the raw nerve of motherhood." After screaming "OUT OUT GET OUT" at her oldest, the mother questions "[. . .] what is it like to have / a child afraid of you, your own / child, your first child, the one . . ." (279). Describing a similar scene, Marilyn Hacker's "1976" stretches the sonnet to express and contain the emotions of a mother who, after an outburst, shuts her child in a room, as much to protect her as to punish her:

> [. . .]   I picked you up, held you, lov-
> ing your cheek's curve. Yelled, shook you. I want to stop
> this day, I cringe on the warm pink tiles of
> a strange house. We cry on both sides of the door. (11–14)

These two works reflect the anger familiar to most mothers (and fathers). Children cry, whine, and misbehave. Mothers lash out, regain control, then recollect the incident in guilty tranquility. But what of the mothers like Joanne Michulski who are lost beyond control, and who cannot speak for themselves? Rich leaves her readers with the burden to imagine the unimaginable, to empathize with our society's most guarded pariahs. If we do not try, they will be spoken for anyway, and by those who likely contributed to the crisis in the first place. Toni Morrison tackles this difficult work in *Beloved*, and so does the Irish poet Nuala Ní Dhomhnaill in her poem "The Battering." The speaker of "The Battering" is a mother who seems to have heroically rescued her infant from the "fairy fort," but the more she speaks, the more her story reveals a grim truth. The poem ends with the mother preparing to battle the fairies once again. She warns of the consequences "if they try to pull another fast / one on me" (33–34):

> I'd have to bury it out the field.
> There's no way I could take it anywhere next
> or near the hospital.
> As things stand,
> I'll have more than enough trouble
> trying to convince them that it wasn't me
> who gave my little laddie this last battering. (36–42)

Ní Dhomhnaill ingeniously appropriates and exposes the tropes of Irish folk culture that would disguise maternal madness and child battering behind a "charming" veneer. Rich's chapter expands the context of Ní Dhomhnaill's poem, as Rich segues from the discussion of Joanne Michulski to one protesting women's limited access to birth control and abortion: "Motherhood without autonomy, without choice, is one of the quickest roads to a sense of having lost control." The Irish version of the "maternal institution" has long denied women reproductive choices and restricted their voices and avenues of protest, such that Rich's description of Joanne Michulski applies equally well to the maternal speaker of "The Battering." For both, "her rage and despair communicated itself in metaphors, in violence turned first inward, then upon what she loved" (264).

Of Woman Born reverses the sequence of this tragic pattern. Beginning with an admission of "anger and tenderness" toward her own children, Rich turns the raging energies of this ambivalence *outward* toward her culture, and aims to communicate, as clearly and rigorously as possible, the sources of maternal "rage and despair." We need not read every angry mother as Medea. With reference to the question raised at the beginning of this chapter, Rich's decision to write of maternal experience in prose rather than poetry may indicate an understandable wariness of the way metaphor, symbol, and myth have for centuries masked, rather than illuminated, women's experience as mothers. Certainly in the United States, the violence, threats, rhetorical wars and "false-namings" surrounding the abortion issue, and the ongoing failure of the country to regard the care of children as creative and valuable work, indicates that the "institution of motherhood" is still in place, and that maternal voices are *still* not being heard where it counts. Maternal poets and their readers need Rich's "clearing" now.

NOTES

1. See Muriel Rukeyser's book review from 1949, "A Simple Theme."

2. Many thanks to Elizabeth Butler Cullingford for suggesting this approach.

3. Nicole Ward Jouve's thoughtful chapter (inspired by Rich) names several examples of maternal poets, but she ends with "the bet that the question of the Mother and Poetry will not go away" (181).

4. Cynthia Eller challenges the "feminist matriarchal" revision of ancient history for what she considers to be its credulous use of "Goddess" figurines as archaeological evidence (180).

5. For more on H. D. and the muse, see DuPlessis, "Family, Sexes, Psyche: An Essay on H. D. and the Muse of the Woman Writer."

6. Anthropologist Wenda Trevathan theorizes that midwifery was a critical component in the development of our species (224–225).

7. Rich cites Sue Silvermarie's "The Motherbond," from *Women: A Journal of Liberation*, vol. 4., no. 1, pp. 26–27 and Robin Morgan's "The Child" from "The Network of the Imaginary Mother" in *Lady of the Beasts* (New York: Random House, 1976) in *OWB*, pp. 207–208, nn. 41 and 42.

8. For recent feminist responses to this question, see *Mothers and Sons*, special issue, *Journal of the Association for Research on Mothering* 2.1 (Spring/Summer, 2000).

WORKS CITED

Boland, Eavan. *In a Time of Violence*. Manchester: Carcanet, 1994.

Clifton, Lucille. *The Book of Light*. Port Townsend, WA: Copper Canyon, 1993.

——. *Quilting: Poems 1987–1990*. Brockport, NY: Boa, 1991.

Corea, Gena. *The Mother Machine: Reproductive Technologies from Artificial Insemination to Artificial Wombs*. New York: Harper and Row, 1985.

Derricotte, Toi. *Natural Birth*. Trumansburg, NY: Crossing, 1983.

Dolittle, Hilda (H. D.). "Tribute to the Angels." *Trilogy*. New York: New Directions, 1945.

Dove, Rita. *Mother Love*. New York: Norton, 1995.

DuPlessis, Rachel Blau. "Family, Sexes, Psyche: An Essay on H. D. and the Muse of the Woman Writer." *The Pink Guitar*. New York and London: Routledge, 1990:20–40.

Eller, Cynthia. *The Myth of the Matriarchal Prehistory: Why an Invented Past Won't Give Women a Future*. Boston: Beacon Press, 2000.

Firestone, Shulamith. *The Dialectic of Sex*. New York: Bantam, 1972.

Friedman, Susan Stanford. "Creativity and the Childbirth Metaphor: Gender Difference in Literary Discourse." *Speaking of Gender*. Ed. Elaine Showalter. New York: Routledge, 1989:73–100.

Gedo, John E. *The Artist and the Emotional World: Creativity and Personality*. New York: Columbia UP, 1996.

Gilbert, Sandra M. and Susan Gubar. *No Man's Land: Letters from the Front*, vol. 3. New Haven: Yale UP, 1994.

Hacker, Marilyn. *Selected Poems, 1965–1990*. New York: Norton, 1994.

Jouve, Nicole Ward. " 'No One's Mother': Can the Mother Write Poetry?" *Female Genesis: Creativity, Self and Gender*. New York: St. Martin's, 1998:163–182.

Levertov, Denise. *Collected Earlier Poems, 1940–1960*. New York: New Directions, 1978.

Lorde, Audre. *Chosen Poems Old and New*. New York: Norton, 1982.

Loy, Mina. *The Lost Lunar Baedeker: Poems of Mina Loy*. Ed. Roger L. Conover. New York: Farrar, 1996.

"Mothers and Sons." (special issue) *Journal of the Association for Research on Mothering* 2.1 (Spring/Summer, 2000).

Ní Dhomhnaill, Nuala. *The Astrakhan Cloak*. Trans. Paul Muldoon. Loughcrew, Oldcastle, County Meath, Ireland: Gallery, 1992.

Ostriker, Alicia. "A Wild Surmise." *Writing Like a Woman*. Ann Arbor: U of Michigan P, 1983:126–131.

Plath, Sylvia. *The Bell Jar*. New York: Harper, 1971, 1996.

————. *Collected Poems.* New York: Harper, 1981.

Pratt, Minnie Bruce. Crime Against Nature. Ithaca, NY: Firebrand, 1990.

Rich, Adrienne. "A Clearing in the Imagination." *What Is Found There: Notebooks on Poetry and Politics.* New York: Norton, 1979:107–117.

————. *Of Woman Born: Motherhood as Experience and Institution.* New York: Norton, 1976.

————. "The Transgressor Mother." *What Is Found There: Notebooks on Poetry and Politics.* New York: Norton, 1979:144–163.

————. *The Fact of a Doorframe: Poems Selected and New, 1950–84.* New York: Norton, 1984.

Rukeyser, Muriel. "A Simple Theme." *Poetry* 74 (July 1949):236–239.

Sexton, Anne. *The Complete Poems.* Boston: Houghton, 1981.

Strickland, Stephanie. *True North.* Notre Dame, IN: U of Notre Dame P, 1997.

Tamahori, Lee (director), Riwia Brown (screenplay), Robin Scholes (producer). *Once Were Warriors.* Fine Line Features, 1994.

Todd, Alexandra. *Intimate Adversaries.* Philadelphia: U of Pennsylvania P, 1989.

Trevathan, Wenda. *Human Birth: An Evolutionary Perspective.* New York: Aldine De Gruyter, 1987.

TWELVE

A "Sense of Drift"

Adrienne Rich's Emergence
from Mother to Poet

JEANNETTE E. RILEY

THE EARLY ADULT LIFE of Adrienne Rich epitomizes the cultural conflicts between pressure to perform as a wife and mother and her own desire to write in 1950s North America. Much of her younger life was governed by cultural expectations of women to marry and raise children—expectations Rich strived to fulfill. Yet, this path was not an easy one, as she explains in her groundbreaking work *Of Woman Born: Motherhood as Experience and Institution* (1976):

> I became a mother in the family-centered, consumer-oriented, Freudian-American world of the 1950s. My husband spoke eagerly of the children we would have; my parents-in-law awaited the birth of their grandchild. I had no idea of what I wanted, what I could or could not choose. I only knew that to have a child was to assume adult womanhood to the full, to prove myself, to be "like other women." (25)[1]

Even though Rich worked diligently to be "like other women," she longed to write professionally—an act in direct opposition to her identity as a wife and mother. Rich's husband, who she describes as a "sensitive, affectionate man" willing to "help" in raising their children, still came first in the household since his "was the real work of the family" (*OWB* 27). This inequality created a dilemma for Rich, and she came to understand that her "struggles as a writer were a kind of luxury, a peculiarity of mine" (*OWB* 27). Moreover, since Rich's work produced little income, she found herself having to ask her husband to pay for household help in order to find time to write for just a few hours a week. This situation caused Rich to experience "depressions, bursts of anger, sense of entrapment, as burdens my husband was forced to bear because he loved me," yet she "felt grateful to be loved in spite of bringing him those burdens" (*OWB* 27).

Such feelings of anger and depression were only increased by her responsibilities to her children. She recounts in *Of Woman Born* her 1950s and early 1960s life revolved around interruption and the need to attend to her children. Whenever she attempted to read a book or attend to her own interests, a child "would come to pull at [her] hand, ask for help, punch at the typewriter keys" (23). Rich, in turn, "would feel his wants at such moments as fraudulent, as an attempt to defraud me of living even for fifteen minutes as myself" (*OWB* 23). Believing that she was "supposed" to feel love for her children at all times, Rich's feelings of resentment at the loss of time and privacy filled her with a sense that she was a "monster of selfishness and intolerance" (*OWB* 23). Only years later, after showing a draft of *Of Woman Born* to one of her sons, did Rich realize that such feelings were not "abnormal, monstrous" (*OWB* 23). As her son remarked to her: "You seemed to feel you ought to love us all the time. But there *is* no human relationship where you love the other person every moment" (*OWB* 23). Yet for Rich, as she tried to explain, "women—above all, mothers—have been supposed to love that way" (*OWB* 23).

While the conflict between motherhood and authorship caused Rich considerable pain, it also created the breakthrough poems in her third collection, *Snapshots of a Daughter-in-Law* (1963). Rich explains that in 1958 she reached the point where she felt she "[h]ad either to consider myself a failed woman and a failed poet, or try to find some synthesis by which to understand what was happening to me. What frightened me most was the sense of drift, of being pulled along on a current which called itself my destiny, but in which I seemed to be losing touch with whoever I had been" ("WWDA" 42–43).[2] Her efforts to understand what was happening led Rich finally, after years of "reading in fierce snatches, scribbling in notebooks, writing poetry in fragments" to an emotional and literary breakthrough with *Snapshots* ("WWDA" 44). Turning away from the woman haunted by her responsibilities as mother and wife, Rich chose in *Snapshots* to reveal previously hidden parts of herself. The eight years between her second and third collections proved to be a period of artistic growth as Rich struggled to break free of the traditions confining her poetry. The time allowed a new vision in Rich's work as she composed subject matter previously avoided, resulting in a collection with new material that handles, albeit cautiously, experiences of "real" life. While not all the poems are successful, many move beyond the conventional forms that dominate her earlier collections.

Rich's first two collections of poetry, *A Change of World* (1951) and *The Diamond Cutters* (1953) illuminate the roots of *Snapshot*'s poems. Terrence

Des Pres explains in "Adrienne Rich, North America East" (1988) that "Adrienne Rich didn't start a leader. Her early work, praised by Auden and Randall Jarrell among others, shows her the dutiful daughter of the fathers, Auden and Jarrell among them" (192). However, while the poems found in *A Change of World* echo the forms of the male poets, they also reveal more than simply a dutiful repetition of those fathers. Adalaide Morris points out that, when asked about her first volume of poems, Rich stated that the craft lay not in the strict attention to detail and imitation of male formalism, but rather in the "act of covering" (137). Morris goes on to explain that Rich's language worked "more as a kind of facade than as either self-revelation or as a probe into one's own consciousness. The facade is an excellent image for these architecturally intricate and static poems, poems whose elegantly undisrupted exposition seems to conceal as much as it reveals" (137). If one attempts to discover what lies behind the facade, the poems prove to offer up many revelations, which Rich herself identifies in "When We Dead Awaken: Writing as Revision":

> poems are like dreams: in them you put what you don't know you know. Looking back at poems I wrote before I was twenty-one, I am startled because beneath the conscious craft are glimpses of the split I even then experienced between the girl who wrote poems, who defined herself in writing poems, and the girl who was to define herself by her relationships with men. (39–40)

The volume clearly indicates the beginnings of the voice we now associate with Adrienne Rich, one of our foremost contemporary American poets—the traces of confidence, concern with women's positions, and the dangers of language all exist under the seemingly "modest" surface of poems that "do not tell fibs" (Auden 125).

Furthermore, Rich understood that poetry in the 1950s in North America was "supposed" to be male, that women were not "supposed" to write poetry. As a result, Rich inevitably played by the rules set up by male literary precursors, an act she explains for us: "I took what I could use where I could find it. When the ideas or forms we need are banished, we seek their residues wherever we can trace them. But there was one major problem with this. I had been born a woman, and I was trying to think and act as if poetry—and the possibility of making poems—were a universal—a gender-neutral—realm" ("Blood, Bread, and Poetry: The Location of the Poet" 174–175). Rich found herself conditioned to use what she was most familiar with—the ideas and subject matter of "the Man, who was not a terror or a dream but a literary master and a master in other ways less easy to acknowledge" ("WWDA" 39). The poems from which she learned her craft were poems about women written by men and, for Rich, "it seemed to be a given that men wrote poems and women frequently inhabited them" ("WWDA" 39). In order to understand the conflicts this conditioning created in Rich's early voice, we only need to turn to the often anthologized and criticized poem "Storm Warnings," which opens *A Change of World.*

"Storm Warnings" opposes an encroaching storm and the emotions of an individual safely protected inside a house. The individual remains gender neutral as Rich employs the universal "I" that becomes "We" later on in the poem, thus avoiding personal subjectivity. In doing so, she adheres to T. S. Eliot's belief that the poet has "not a 'personality' to express, but a particular medium, which is only a medium and not a personality" (Kermode 42). Furthermore, Rich's avoidance of a personal "I" reflects Eliot's belief that "[p]oetry is not a turning loose of emotion, but an escape from emotion; it is not the expression of personality, but an escape from personality" (43). As the poem begins with a change in pressure embodied by the barometer, the poem's speaker realizes, unlike the inanimate instrument predictor of weather change, the approaching danger of the storm front. At the same time, the speaker acknowledges the safety that windows offer and the futility of hoping to change the weather pattern, for, as the second stanza reveals, "Weather abroad / And weather in the heart alike come on / Regardless of prediction" (13–15).³ The coming weather, like the emotions of the heart, cannot be thwarted since each force follows its own path.

The speaker questions the individual's inability to avoid the turmoil of such storms of weather and emotion in the third stanza. "Between foreseeing and averting change / lies all the mastery of elements" that no weather instruments can change since "[t]ime in the hand is not control" (15–16; 18). The word "change" stands out as the focal point of the poem, for change cannot be foreseen or averted. In the same way that a hand holding a watch cannot control time, the instruments that predict changing weather offer no defence against coming storms. The sole safety lies in the ability to "close the shutters" (21) and the speaker "draw[s] the curtains as the sky goes black" (22). At the same time, the speaker lights "candles sheathed in glass," while the storm, with an "insistent whine," pushes "against the keyhold draught" (23–24). The poem draws to a close with the speaker attempting to reconcile the storm's presence and the dangers it poses: "This is our sole defense against the season; / These are the things that we have learned to do / Who live in troubled regions" (22–28). The windows, shutters, and curtains, along with candles protected by glass and the walls of the building, provide the "sole defense" against the outer elements. The individual, forced to withdraw from the oncoming storm, believes that safety has been located through enclosure within the room.

Yet, while the poem plays upon the desire for stasis and protection from a dangerous world that can neither be predicted nor avoided, as Morris suggests "the solution, though boldly stated, seems uneasy, for the poem's imagery suggests that the protagonist has locked the door with the threat inside" (144). Morris further asserts that the room suggests a self-created "entombment" that is only avoided since the aperture in the keyhole remains unsealed (144). Here, Rich relies upon a set of oppositions to create her ideas—inside versus outside, safety versus danger, manmade structures versus nature. Each opposition enacts tensions Rich herself feels as a woman and a poet. According to Rich, such tensions occupy many women's lives, for the "twentieth-century, educated young woman, looking perhaps at her mother's life, or trying to create an autonomous self in a society which insists that she is destined primarily for reproduction, has with good reason felt that the choice was an inescapable either/or: motherhood or individuation, motherhood or creativity, motherhood or freedom" (*OWB* 160). Yet, seemingly, there is no escape at this time for Rich; while she struggles for answers and a region less stormy than the one she currently inhabits, she has yet to resolve her dueling identities.

The issues surrounding Rich's identities as a woman and a poet are reinforced by other renderings of opposing tensions in *A Change of World*. These dualisms depend upon an either/or way of thinking and move beyond male/female relationships into larger spheres that encompass nature versus society, religion/structure versus anarchy/chaos, emotion versus love, and desire versus necessity, among others. Repeatedly, Rich's early poems return to a discussion of splittings, subject matter seemingly drawn from the splitting she experienced in her own life as a wife, mother, and writer. In an attempt to cover her growing dissatisfaction with her life, Rich created a collection of poetry that, under the guise of formalism, acts as an introduction to her growing conflict between the opposing identities of woman and poet. Rich herself, in an interview with Stanley Plumly in 1971, understood the avoidance she enacted in her early work:

> I was going through a very sort of female thing—of trying to distinguish between the ego that is capable of writing poems, and then this other kind of being that you're asked to be if you're a woman, who is, in a sense, denying that ego. I had great feelings of split about that for many years actually, and there are a lot of poems I couldn't write even, because I didn't want to confess to having that much aggression, that much ego, that much sense of myself. I had always thought of my first book as being a book of very well-tooled poems of a sort of very bright student, which I was at that time, but poems in which the unconscious things never got to the surface. (31)

Unconscious or not, the splits that Rich speaks of continue to reveal themselves in her later work, revelations also found, for example, in her second collection, *The Diamond Cutters* (1955).

The Diamond Cutters continues the conflicts expressed in poems like "Storm Warnings" that Rich faces as a woman and poet. Increasingly, however, Rich found her struggle to live with her desire to express her feelings as a woman in 1950s American society in the face of expectations set by men dominating her emotions. Even reviews of her second collection added to the conflicts she faced as critics like Randall Jarrell commented that *The Diamond Cutters* showed Rich to be an "endearing and delightful poet, one who deserves Shakespeare's favorite adjective, *sweet*" (129). Rich's poetry was praised in terms of women's writing—adjectives such as "sweet," "endearing," and "delightful" obscure the seriousness of the conflicts and growing feelings of despair Rich the poet was facing. She retrospectively explains her feelings of despair in 1971:

> I went on trying to write; my second book and first child appeared in the same month. But by the time that book came out I was already dissatisfied with those poems, which seemed to me mere exercises for poems I hadn't written. The book was praised, however, for its 'gracefulness'; I had a marriage and a child. If there were doubts, if there were periods of null depression or active despairing, these could only mean that I was ungrateful, insatiable, perhaps a monster. ("WWDA" 42)

Clearly, Rich experienced the contradiction of entrapment and depression against expectations of a traditional wife and mother because of her desire to create poems expressing her thoughts as a woman. According to Rich four years later in 1975, "[i]t is an extremely painful and dangerous way to live—split between a publicly accepted persona, and a part of yourself that you perceive as the essential, the creative and powerful self, yet also as possibly unacceptable, perhaps even monstrous" ("Vesuvius at Home: The Power of Emily Dickinson" 175). Because of these ongoing tensions in her life, Rich found herself feeling "nothing but boredom and indifference" toward her work (*OWB* 26). This feeling was aggravated by Rich's desire to "deny all responsibility for and interest in that person who writes—or who wrote" (*OWB* 27). Yet, in denying her self, Rich realized the need to be responsible to her work, recognizing that if there was "going to be a real break in [her] writing life, this is as good a time for it as any" (*OWB* 27). After eight long years devoted to her domestic roles, that break appeared in the form of her third collection of poetry—*Snapshots of a Daughter-In-Law*.

Turning away from the woman haunted by her responsibilities as wife, mother, and daughter, Rich chose in *Snapshots* to bring to the surface the parts of herself that had been concealed behind the formalistic traditions she had followed. The lines of poems are looser, more experimental, and many escape conventional forms. In 1964, Rich commented that the goals of her earlier poems were control, technical mastery, and intellectual clarity. However, she also explained that with *Snapshots* she was learning to write poems based upon her growing sense of poetry as subjective rather than universal: "Perhaps a simple way of putting it would be to say that instead of poems *about* experiences I am getting poems that *are* experiences, that contribute to my knowledge and my emotional life even while they reflect and assimilate it" ("Poetry and Experience: Statement at a Poetry Reading" 89). Her experiences as a woman required revising the male canonical form to ensure accurate expression of women's lives. Increasingly, as Rich was finishing her third collection in 1963, she found herself moving back and forth between the experiences that made up her life at that point in time. The historical influences of societal beliefs regarding women and the objective, universal tone of the literary past began to meld together to form new poetry as Rich joined her art with her life.

The second poem of the collection, titled "From Morning-Glory to Petersburg," exemplifies this reconnection. Here Rich examines her new unwillingness to keep her poems and art tidy, controlled and mastered by technique. Her poem's speaker discusses how knowledge, in "all its risible untidiness" has found her out, "dragging in things I never thought about" (14, 16). The speaker questions objectivity, wondering "what facts can be / held at arm's length" (17–18). The poems also begin to question patriarchal forces other than the literary traditions that have dominated her life to this point, in particular the watchful eyes of her father, who directed her early schooling. Early on, Rich recognized the downfalls of writing for the man who made her feel special and the ways he trained her to follow the masters of the literary past: "[t]he obverse side of this [having a father who praised her], of course, was that I tried for a long time to please him, or rather, not to displease him" ("WWDA" 38–39) In "Juvenilia," Rich directly confronts her father's presence in her childhood and his demands that she master the "great" poets. Speaking out against her father's "Ibsen volumes, violet-spined, / each flaking its gold arabesque!" (1–2), Rich faces the child she was who sat "under duress," copying poems at her father's desk. Her actions imitate her growing anger as she sits "stabbing the blotting-pad, doodling loop upon loop" (6). By the mid-1970s, she recognized that the influences of her father and the masters of poetry she had studied affected her in uneasy ways. The complications presented by her past and her relationship with that past give rise to the undertones of anger in "Juvenilia" seen in words like "stabbing," "craning," and the image of "unspeakable fairy tales [that] ebb like blood."

However, as we see in another poem in *Snapshots*, "Prospective Immigrants Please Note," Rich recognized the difficult position she now occupied. The poetic persona that sought safety in *A Change of World* and *The Diamond Cutters* confronts a complicated decision as the speaker needs to decide whether or not to move through a door. For the speaker, there is a choice: "Either you will / go through this door / or you will not go through" (1–3). The choice is fraught with danger; if one goes through the door, s/he will be faced with the "risk / of remembering your name" (5–6). If the speaker chooses not to pass through the doorway, "it is possible / to live worthily / to maintain your attitudes / to hold your position" (11–14). Yet, it is also possible that "much will blind you, / much will evade you" (16–17), causing the speaker to ask "at what cost who knows?" (18). The poem concludes with a final stanza with a door that "makes no promises" for "it is only a door" (20–21). Engaging with the world, becoming an actual agent rather than remaining in the position of a neutral observer, places Rich, the woman and the poet, in a place where she is able to make choices. While risks are involved, failure to pass through the doorway would leave Rich duplicating her earlier work, lapsing back to a place where attitudes are maintained in the face of experience and emotion.

In the end, "Prospective Immigrants" calls for doing away with indecisiveness and maintenance of the either/or dichotomies that endlessly present themselves. The question "at what cost who knows?" haunts the poem and implies that failure to pass through the door will greatly harm the individual. The poet must choose whether to break the bounds of tradition and the fathers that entrap her or to remain caught by the knowledge that "[f]acts could be kept separate / by a convention" ("From Morning-Glory to Petersburg," *CEP* 136). Significantly, the person who chooses to move forward, away from safety, becomes identified as an "immigrant." The land beyond the doorway reduces both power and personal identity to that of a stranger with no claim to land or language. Rich finds herself in a similar position. Stepping through the doorway is part of Rich's attempt to understand her position as a woman in 1960s North America. As she states in the poem "Double Monologue":

> Since I was more than a child
> trying on a thousand faces
> I have wanted one thing: to know
> simply as I know my name
> at any given moment, where I stand. (6–10)

Rich's decision in *Snapshots* to date each of her poems illustrates her recognition that she was "finished with the idea of a poem as a single, encapsulated event, a work of art complete in itself" ("Blood, Bread, and Poetry: The Location of the Poet" 180). Instead, Rich felt that she "needed to indicate to readers [her] sense of being engaged in a long, continuing process," which represented for her "a rejection of the dominant critical idea that the poem's text should be read as separate from the poet's everyday life in the world. It was a declaration that placed poetry in a historical continuity, not above or outside history" ("Blood, Bread, and Poetry: The Location of the Poet" 180).

The title poem of *Snapshots*, which took Rich two years to write, sheds further light on her quest for her own identity. The poem explores representations of a number of different women—the "belle in Shreveport," the housewife "banging the coffee-pot in the sink," the woman poet in the shape of Emily Dickinson drawn away from her writing "dusting everything on the whatnot every day of life," as well as women working to preserve their fading beauty as they shave their legs "until they gleam" (*CEP* 145–146). Rich places these women in their cultural contexts as she purposefully adds quotations that reveal the expectations facing them. The poem "Snapshots" enabled her to directly express her experiences as a woman and breaks away from the traditional forms in which she had been schooled. The result was a poem written in a "longer looser mode than [she'd] ever trusted [her]self with before" ("WWDA" 44) and stands as the first solid indication of Rich's women-centered subject matter that resounds throughout her future work ("WWDA" 45).

Relying once again upon oppositions, Rich's snapshots of women call into question the expectations that have structured women's lives. For example, section four describes the actions of a housewife who is also a writer like Rich and calls upon the ghost of Emily Dickinson to reinforce its message: "[r]eading while waiting / for the iron to heat, / writing, '*My Life had stood—a Loaded Gun—*' / in that Amherst pantry . . ." (43–46). The woman imagined in the poem rarely finds time for herself and her art. Reading and writing become forbidden luxuries in the face of the endless chores expected to be performed each day. Rich purposefully opposes reading with waiting and writing with the pantry, an opposition that Betsy Erkkila believes "stresses the conflict between creative energy and destructive confinement summed up in Dickinson's lines, '*My Life had stood—a Loaded Gun—*' (549). Traditionally, women have been expected to wait within the confines of the house. While Rich sought safe enclosure in her early work, the enclosure offered here by the pantry represents a danger to women. As seen in section two, the housewife described purposefully scalds herself with hot water or holds a match to her thumbnail simply to feel something; however, "nothing hurts her anymore" and the trapped position she occupies makes her think "*Save yourself; others you cannot save*" (19). There is no solidarity or relief to be found, and confinement brought upon women by society produces the anger and tension found in Dickinson's words and Rich's own life experiences.

The poem does more than simply recount snapshots of different women's lives—it also questions women's own complicity in their locations as victims and objects of beauty and dependency. Rich's speaker accuses these women of failing to actively work against their subjugated positions. For example, section three pictures two "thinking" women arguing with one another and states that "The argument [is] *ad feminam,* all the old knives / that have rusted in my back, I drive in yours" (37–38). In section nine, Rich writes, "Our blight has been our sinecúre: / mere talent was enough for us—/ glitter in fragments and rough drafts" (92–94). Rich's lines imply women's complicity in their own oppression. Unfortunately, the women seem content to be thankful for "mere talent." In "The Friction of the Mind: The Early Poetry of Adrienne Rich" (1982), Mary Slowik accurately summarizes Rich's indictment of women's passivity in this poem:

Even more tragically, women seem to be responsible for their own repression. By quoting male literature and pointing to a larger male world to which women belong, Rich is not denying that men hold women in check. "Time is male," she says. But women acquiesce and the poem becomes stronger and stronger in its indictment of women as it goes along. . . . And the speaker herself in sections nine and ten accuses women of refusing to take responsibility for their lives because to live passively and acquiescently is far more comfortable. (154–155)

The women in the poem, "bemused by gallantry," fail to break away from the structures confining them and, in most cases argues the poem, continue to reinforce the very things that entrap them.

More importantly, as the poem presents the complexities of the women's positions, the power of patriarchy becomes even more apparent. According to Rich, again in *Of Woman Born*,

Patriarchy is the power of the fathers: a familial-social, ideological, political system in which men—by force, direct pressure, or through ritual, tradition, law, and language, customs, etiquette, education, and the division of labor, determine what part women shall or shall not play, and in which the female is everywhere subsumed under the male. It does not necessarily imply that no woman has power, or that all women in a given culture may not have certain powers. (57)

"Snapshots of a Daughter-in-Law" identifies the patriarchal forces playing upon women; more importantly, the poem reveals the ability of women to survive those forces. The poem's ending expresses this survival clearly as the speaker envisions a woman, "long about her coming, who must be / more merciless to herself than history" (109–110). More importantly, the speaker uses the personal pronoun "I" for the very first time as she firmly states: "I see her plunge / breasted and glancing through the currents" (111–112). This woman, beautiful and moving like a helicopter, brings a cargo that held "no promise then" but once delivered is now "palpable / ours" (121–122). Rich's own poetic identity takes on an active role here, and she finally finds the courage to use the pronoun "I." She also uses the word "ours"—a signal to women that they too have their own history and community that they must reclaim by breaking the confines of patriarchal expectations. In many ways, Rich's conclusion indicates her willingness to enter the public eye as a spokesperson for women's issues and rights—work she took on in the late 1960s and throughout the 1970s.

Rich, recognizing her new subject matter, explores her transition in the concluding poem of the collection, "The Roofwalker," which speaks of the risky condition in which she now finds herself. This condition has her entering new territory as she learns to record how personal experiences and a patriarchal culture have shaped and reshaped her poetic identity. Rich, again using the pronoun "I," considers the laborers repairing a roof and writes: "I feel like them up there: / exposed, larger than life, / and due to break my neck" (13–15). As if she were the one repairing the roof, Rich feels exposed and in danger of losing her footing. Breaking out of the tradition in which she was trained causes her to realize the enormity of her choice—she purposefully steps out of a secure location created by American culture into an unknown space where she has only her own self for protection.

The poem continues as Rich equates the building of a roof with the building of her own life. As she wonders whether it was worth the "infinite exertion" to build a "roof I can't live under," she questions the "blueprints / closing of gaps, / measurings / calculations" that she has built her life upon (16–21). Through this self-exploration, she realizes that "A life I didn't choose / chose me: even / my tools are the wrong ones / for what I have to do" (22–25). Although she believes she does not yet possess the proper tools for her trade, Rich remains aware that she must still choose a personal and poetic path:

> I'm naked, ignorant,
> a naked man fleeing
> across the roofs
> who could with a shade of difference
> be sitting in the lamplight
> against the cream wallpaper
> reading—not with indifference—
> about a naked man
> fleeing across the roofs. (26–34)

Rich chooses to risk asserting her creative power to write of her experiences and identities as a woman. In a 1971 interview, Rich discusses the need to take risks in order to move forward: "[y]ou know that for a long time you didn't dare yourself, that it's a slow process. It's like the end of that roof-walker poem where you know that you might have been the person who sat indoors reading the newspaper and watching somebody else risk his neck, and that's very much a part of you too. It would be really nice to be a spectator, sometimes" (Plumly 32–33). Again, Rich finds herself in a conflicted position as she is split between knowing she should actively take risks, despite having spent much of her adult life being an observer. Yet, we can understand Rich's conflicted position and her growing knowledge that she must forge her own way, knowing that "[f]or many women the stresses of this splitting have led, in a world so ready to assert our innate passivity and to deny our independence and creativity, to extreme consequences: the mental asylum, self-imposed silence, recurrent depression, suicide, and often severe loneliness" ("Vesuvius at Home" 175–176). *Snapshots of a Daughter-in-Law* portrays Rich's refusal to allow the feelings of depression, felt so often during the years she created her first two collections, and during the eight-year silence she endured as she tended to her roles as mother to three children and wife to a professor, to defeat her life and her art.

With the publication of *Snapshots*, Rich emerged as a stronger, more woman-focused poet. Only five years earlier, in 1958, Rich was angry and disillusioned about her life. In a journal entry found in *Of Woman Born*, Rich explains that for "months I've been all a tangle of irritations deepening to anger: bitterness, disillusion with society and with myself; breathing out at the world, rejecting out of hand. What, if anything, has been positive?" (*OWB* 28). Fortunately for Rich, she is able to answer her own question: "Perhaps the attempt to remake my life, to save it from mere drift and the passage of time" (*OWB* 28). In the time between her first two collections of work and *Snapshots of a Daughter-in-Law*, Rich discovered the strength to actively pursue and direct her own life. While she experienced the "primal agony" that comes from the conflict "between self-preservation and maternal feelings" (*OWB* 161), she also became "*a woman giving birth to myself*" (*OWB* 184).

NOTES

1. Subsequent references to *Of Woman Born* will be cited as *OWB*.

2. Subsequent references to "When We Dead Awaken: Writing as Re-Vision" will be cited as "WWDA."

3. All poems quoted are from *Collected Early Poems*. Numbers in parentheses refer to lines in poems.

WORKS CITED

Auden, W. H. Foreword to *A Change of World*. *Adrienne Rich's Poetry: Texts of the Poems, The Poet on Her Work, Reviews and Criticism*. Eds. Barbara Charlesworth Gelpi & Albert Gelpi. New York: Norton, 1975:125–126.

Des Pres, Terrence. *Praises and Dispraises: Poetry and Politics in the Twentieth Century*. New York: Viking, 1988.

Erkkila, Betsy. "Dickinson and Rich: Toward a Theory of Female Poetic Influence." *American Literature* 56.4 (1984):541–559.

Jarrell, Randall. "Review of *The Diamond Cutters and Other Poems*." *Adrienne Rich's Poetry: Texts of the Poems, the Poet on Her Work, Review and Criticism*. Eds. Barbara Charlesworth Gelpi and Albert Gelpi. New York: Norton, 1975:127–129.

Kermode, Frank, ed. *The Selected Prose of T. S. Eliot*. New York: Harcourt, 1975.

Morris, Adalaide. "Imitations and Identities: Adrienne Rich's *A Change of World*." *Modern Poetry Studies* 10.2 & 3 (1981):136–159.

Plumly, Stanley. "Talking With Adrienne Rich." *The Ohio Review* 13.1 (1971):28–46.

Rich, Adrienne. "Blood, Bread, and Poetry: The Location of the Poet." *Blood, Bread, and Poetry: Selected Prose 1979–1985*. New York: Norton, 1986:167–187.

——. *Collected Early Poems 1950–1970*. New York: Norton, 1993.

——. *Of Woman Born: Motherhood as Experience and Institution*. New York: Norton, 1976.

——. "Poetry and Experience: Statement at a Poetry Reading (1964)." *Adrienne Rich's Poetry: Texts of the Poems, The Poet on Her Work, Reviews and Criticism*. Eds. Barbara Charlesworth Gelpi & Albert Gelpi. New York: Norton, 1975.

——. "Vesuvius at Home: The Power of Emily Dickinson." *On Lies, Secrets, and Silence: Selected Prose 1966–1978*. New York: Norton, 1979:157–183.

——. "When We Dead Awaken: Writing as Re-Vision." *On Lies, Secrets, and Silence: Selected Prose 1966–1978*. New York: Norton, 1979:33–49.

Slowik, Mary. "The Friction of the Mind: The Early Poetry of Adrienne Rich." *Massachusetts Review: A Quarterly of Literature* 25.1 (1984):142–160.

THIRTEEN

Beginning with "I"

The Legacy of Adrienne Rich's
Of Woman Born

ANN KENISTON

Reading autobiographically is [. . .] essentially an act of giving testimony: of giving testimony to the unsuspected, unexpected "feminine resistance" in the text. [. . .] Reading autobiographically cannot, therefore, be merely a question of encroaching, with one's own
story, on the feminine resistance in the text. More demandingly
and more attentively, it is a question of *experiencing this feminine
resistance as a joint effect of interaction among literature, autobiography and theory*, insofar as all three modes *resist, precisely, one another*.
It is utilizing theory, in other words, as self-resistance. It is engaging in a paradoxical attempt of reading literature and one's own life
with the tools—and through the resources—of theory but, at the
same time, reading literature and one's own life as, precisely, a *resistance to theory:* using one's autobiography as a resistance to theory
but, at the same time, just as crucially, using theory and literature
as, precisely, a *resistance to autobiography*.
—Shoshana Felman, *What Does a Woman Want?*
(emphases in original)

FELMAN'S FORMULATION ABOUT the way that women's writing should be
read, deriving partly from an examination of Adrienne Rich's poems and prose
writings, is both oppositional and generous. Autobiographical reading, she

claims, sets usually distinct genres into relation and tension with one another. It requires the reader to unearth the contradictions in texts and examine how, exactly, they exert force over one another. As such, Felman's notion functions at once as invitation and warning: Reading autobiographically requires, in the case of *Of Woman Born*, a consciousness both of the temptation and the danger of identifying with its protagonist and plot. It demands, in other words, that the reader, like Rich herself, be part autobiographer, part researcher, part analyst of her own process of identification.

"It seemed to me impossible from the first to write a book of this kind without being often autobiographical, without often saying 'I'" (15), Rich writes in the foreword to *Of Woman Born*. The same is true of me, although I know that in beginning with identification, in "encroaching, with [my] own story" on *Of Woman Born*, I am risking the kind of simplistic reading against which Felman cautions. Yet my impulse toward autobiography feels necessary, if dangerous, an homage to what I will argue in this chapter is most significant in *Of Woman Born*, what Rich later called its "odd-fangled approach: personal testimony mingled with research, and theory derived from both" (x). I am adopting a similar approach: This chapter begins with autobiography, then moves to analysis. While this choice may emphasize rather than eradicate the difference between my "confessional" and "scholarly" voices, it also provides, I hope, a way of commenting on the difficulty of achieving an integration of memoir and critique as profound as Rich's, even as I elaborate a critique of *Of Woman Born* that begins with the dividedness of Rich's depiction of "I."

I first read *Of Woman Born* five weeks into my first semester of a doctoral program in English. Exposed for the first time to literary theory, I was miserable. In my essay of application to graduate school, I had described a paper "of urgent personal importance" I had written in an earlier class that, I claimed, "opened up the idea of scholarship for me: essay writing felt for the first time like a way of self-exploration and speech as crucial and fully engaging to me as writing poems is." Yet now, that notion seemed hugely naïve. Even in a class on feminist theory, my predilections, my past experiences, my identity as a poet seemed less a help with than a hindrance to "good reading." The paper my essay had described focused on my sense of kinship with the struggles of earlier women poets. Yet this kind of identification, my recent readings were teaching me, was overly emotional and reductionistic, eradicating differences between women while embracing essentializing notions of femininity. My first reading of *Of Woman Born* was thus both formalist and greedy: I came to it in the middle of trying to find a way to integrate my poems with my scholarship, and to figure out whether it was possible to write impassioned literary criticism at all.

Three years later, when I returned to Rich, I was trying to conceive a child and failing. I had become sensitive, then hypersensitive, to the ways that maternity is foregrounded in our culture. Once I had to get off a subway car on which a mother was murmuring tenderly to her newborn. Much feminist criticism, I noticed, used maternity as the touchstone, the master signifier for femininity.[1] If earlier I had realized that I had been essentializing femininity, I now felt betrayed by the essentialism of much feminist writing, including Rich's: I felt excluded by her book, which focused on maternity as a crucial, even necessary, part of women's experience.[2] Although feminism helped me explain the cultural sources of my feelings of inadequacy at failing to conceive, it did not give me tools to mitigate those feelings. My first reading had focused on Rich's tone and method, but I was compelled back to *Of Woman Born* to notice what had before seemed irrelevant: both her subject matter and her differences from me.

I have come back to *Of Woman Born* most recently as a mother, a mother moreover of twin boys (as Rich is the mother of three boys). My reading of Rich has changed again, in at least two ways. Being a mother, I often joke to my academic friends, is the great test of the feminist notion that gender is socially constructed. On the playground, apologetically, helplessly, I wonder why my sons, like the other boys, are drawn to trucks, cars, and trains; boys, I have noticed, tend to speak later than girls and are less willing to sit still. (There are, of course, exceptions: my sons like to push their trucks on the playground swings and "feed" them.) More moving and frightening is my gratitude for Rich's insistence on articulating her ambivalence about mothering.[3] Although other mothers regularly comment on my "refreshing" cynicism about being a mother, my ambivalence is so concealed from me, so hard to speak of, even to myself, that I am only now beginning to sense its influence on my recent life. Yet Rich did speak of this, over twenty-eight years ago.

What I have given is perhaps less autobiography than a chronicle of shifting readings. Yet I leave the mode with which I began, with its hesitant, inscribed "I," for the analytic center of this chapter, from which "I" as narrator will be largely absent, reluctantly. As I do so, I want to emphasize that my responses have been not only changeable but inconsistent, as well as to note how this essay's recurrent themes—the relation between form and subject, the dangers and temptations of essentialism, and most centrally the difficulty of conveying "I" with candor, directness, consistency—derive from my own experiences. At the same time, my three readings, forming a narrative in which identification gives way to disillusionment, then approaches a different, perhaps more negative, kind of identification, elaborates, at a personal level, how resistance can function in texts: It can approach, in the end, a kind of mercy.

Of Woman Born's fusion of personal recollection with social critique, or in its subtitle's terms "experience" with "institution," remains strikingly successful even now, when personally inflected theory has become commonplace. Yet the book's importance is revealed most dramatically through what might at first seem to be its limitations. Rich's text, as I will argue below, presents two opposed narratives, which profoundly divide the book and in particular its representation of "I." But *Of Woman Born* also locates common elements of loss and recuperation in the apparently opposed genres of autobiography and polemic, even as it anticipates and helps make sense of divisions in subsequent feminist theory. Beginning with "I," *Of Woman Born* contradicts—or perhaps, to adapt Felman's term, resists—its depiction of self, while never abandoning the first person entirely.

Rich's wish to "mingle"—not merely juxtapose but interweave—personal recollections with information derived from "research" is ambitious: it connects two antithetical entities, conventionally defined by feminism as the "personal" and the "political" and recurrently termed by Rich as the "out there" and the "in here."[4] Yet Rich's aim is also modest. Personal experience is meant primarily to provide one of many sources of information on which Rich as author can draw: Her account, as she writes in the new introduction to the book's reissue in 1986, focuses on "concrete and particular experiences of women, *including my own*, and also of some men" (ix, my emphasis). In many places throughout the book, Rich's "I" does function in this way. Personal examples both lead into general discussions and provide illustrations of them; Rich's association of "I" with "we" and "they" underscores her more general argument about the position of women as victims of patriarchy. Fairly typical is her description of her experience giving birth under anesthesia. Rich recounts her own experience, then moves to the pronoun "we," returning parenthetically to herself before generalizing her discussion first to American women, then women all over the world:

> *We were*, above all, in the hands of male medical technology. [. . .] The only female presences were nurses, whose training and schedules precluded much female tenderness. (*I remember* the gratitude and amazement I felt waking in the "recovery room" after my third delivery to find a young student nurse holding my hand.) The experience of lying half-awake in a barred crib, in a labor room with other women moaning in a drugged condition, where "no one comes" except to do a pelvic examination or give an injection, is *a classic experience of alienated childbirth*. The loneliness, the sense of abandonment, of being imprisoned, powerless, and depersonalized is the chief collective memory of *women who have given birth in American hospitals*.
> But not just American hospitals. (176, my emphasis)

Yet, despite at least one critic's claim that this equivalence of personal and general narratives prevails throughout *Of Woman Born*, Rich's attempt to present her "I" as exemplary is often confounded: The book tends to divide into two distinct and contradictory narratives.[5] The personal account foregrounds Rich's coming into power or what she calls in one of her essays "awakening [from] dead or sleeping consciousness" ("When" 34–35). But the public, historical narrative foregrounds female victimization under patriarchy and in particular various scenes in which female power and autonomy have been lost or stolen by men. Rich never refers directly to this conflict, but her 1986 introduction comes close to articulating her awareness of this dividedness, or at least of the dangers of insisting too vehemently on a narrative of female victimization and loss: "like much radical-feminist writing of its period, this book relies heavily on the concept of patriarchy as a backstop in which all the foul balls of history end up" (xxiii), a tendency which she notes often leads to "the idealization of women" (xxiv).[6]

Paradoxically, early reviews of *Of Woman Born* acknowledge its doubleness of narrative far more accurately than more recent academic readers, who generally accept uncritically Rich's assertion that "I" is equivalent to "we."[7] Yet these reviews are most striking now for the vehemence of their discomfort with what several readers identify as Rich's anger and hatred of men; they generally attack its division into what one critic called "almost two books, one moving, one maddening" (Gray 3).[8] Rich's 1986 suggestion that early readers were disconcerted by the book's straddling or fusing of genres (x) is only partly correct. Rather, Rich's effort to present her "I" as a typical member of a collective "we" leads to strains and contradictions that many theorists of autobiography would find unsurprising.[9]

"I did not then understand" (27), "when I try to return to the body of the young woman of twenty-six [. . .] I realize" (39), "slowly I came to understand" (40): In extended autobiographical sections at the beginning and ending of *Of Woman Born*, Rich foregrounds the process by which she learned to see what was formerly invisible. Even when memory fails or when Rich is hesitant or reluctant to proceed, she emphasizes the importance of attempting to make sense of the past:

> *I don't remember* when it was that my mother's feminine sensuousness [. . .] began to give way for me to the charisma of my father's assertive mind and temperament; *perhaps* when my sister was just born, and he began teaching me to read (219, my emphasis).

Writing about the past, Rich suggests, allows her access to what would otherwise remain unreliable. Rich's account is in this way a fairly typical memoir, especially by recent standards: It chronicles its author's movement from silence to speech, from ignorance to knowledge and thus empowerment.[10]

Several times in the course of *Of Woman Born*, Rich asserts her desire to focus on something distinct from, if not antithetical to, scholarly research:

> For many months I *buried my head* in historical research and analysis in order to *delay* or prepare the way for the plunge into areas of my own life, which were painful and problematical, *yet from the heart of which this book has come.* (15–16, my emphasis)

A folder lies open beside me as I start to write, spilling out references and quotations, all relevant probably, but *none of which can help me begin.* (218, my emphasis)

Yet this valorization of the personal realm is belied by the book's central chapters. In many extended passages, a scholarly, objective voice conveying information gained from research and reading overwhelms the first person narrator altogether. In others, "I" appears merely as a placeholder or a persona with no relation to Rich herself. For example, Rich's discussion of lesbian sex, marshalled as a counterexample to Freudian notions of sexuality, is anatomically explicit and emphasizes the erasure of the boundary between self and other. Yet the shifting pronouns, seemingly autonomous body parts, and formal language also dissociate the description from the Rich's personal recollections:

> *I do not perceive myself* as a walled city into which certain emissaries are received and from which others are excluded. [. . .] The identification with another woman's orgasm as if it were *one's* own is one of the most intense interpersonal experiences: nothing is either "inside" *me* or "outside" at such moments. Even in autoeroticism, *the clitoris* which is more or less external delivers its throbbing signals to *the vagina* and all the way into *the uterus* which cannot be seen or touched. (63, my emphasis)

The submersion of Rich's autobiographical "I" reflects a deeper shift in these sections of the book. Their narrative, in direct opposition to the personal account of awakening and self-reclamation, focuses on decline and loss, and looks back with longing at what no longer exists. In the book's central historical accounts—most strikingly in chronicles of patriarchy's triumph over prehistorical matriarchies and the male medical establishment's appropriation of obstetrics—Rich posits an earlier era in which women controlled their lives and bodies. The narrative of patriarchal domination thus blots out the personal narrative of coming to consciousness: The "I" too is lost.

I do not mean to imply that there is no connection between the narratives of personal empowerment and sociohistorical loss. Clearly Rich's awareness of a larger historical and political framework, full of loss though it may be, enables her to understand her individual suffering and so begin to be free of it. Yet the two narratives often collide. One of the most striking examples seems at first to contain little conflict. In the midst of a universalizing, impersonal description of the prehistoric Great Mother, complete with a diagram, Rich shifts parenthetically to the scene of herself in her writing room: "(As I was writing this, one of my sons showed me the cover of the current *National Geographic* [. . .])" (116). The illustration, she claims, exemplifies the points she has been making: As the Great Mother merges "dark" and "life-giving" forces, this photo links violence with the "bringing of life."

Yet her son's appearance profoundly complicates the general point Rich is making about the necessary mix of positive and negative attributes in the Great Mother. Just before her son's entry, Rich has been describing "the potentially 'evil' half of the Mother's profile," which patriarchy would later "completely split off, [. . .] personif[ying it] as the fanged blood-goddess Kali, the killer mother Medea, the lewd and malign witch, the 'castrating' wife or mother" (116). These terms strongly evoke those she has earlier used to describe her experiences as a mother, although Rich does not here acknowledge the connection, and the earlier reference is somewhat insulated from Rich as narrator by the use of the past tense:

> I do know that for years I believed I should never have been anyone's mother, that [. . .] I was Kali, Medea, the sow that devours her farrow, the unwomanly woman in flight from womanhood, a Nietzschean monster. (32)

Her son's entry offers her a way to deny the analogy her own language suggests; his presence allows her to affirm her role as a "good mother." Although Rich earlier describes her anger that, whenever she began to write, her children interrupted her (23), here she not only accepts her son's interruption, she integrates it into her writing. In this case, then, the personal narrative not only contradicts the emphasis of the general narrative; it also suggests, like her disembodied account of lesbian sex, that some things are too shameful to speak of directly. The depths of Rich's anxiety about being judged a bad mother are revealed only indirectly, through the discrepancy between her account's two narratives.[11]

It is tempting to join many earlier readers and Rich herself in explaining *Of Woman Born*'s flaws, including its dividedness, as a product of its time: Like many other early feminist works, Rich's lacks sophistication, cultural sensitivity, and theoretical fluency that come more naturally to later feminism.[12] Certainly, Rich's extended eulogy for prehistorical matriarchies now seems almost embarrassingly dated. Yet to excuse *Of Woman Born* in this way is ultimately to undermine its importance by relegating the book to the category of mere period piece, whose interest is purely historical. Such a dismissal is also inaccurate. The book's double narrative, its inconsistent depiction of "I," and in particular its repeated recourse to terms of loss and recuperation link political writing with autobiography as they suggest the importance of genre and form in feminist writing.

I have been emphasizing until now the contrasts between the book's personal and political narratives, yet these two narratives are at a more fundamental level alike. Both foreground change through time; both connect loss with recovery and juxtapose nostalgia for what is irretrievable with a more pragmatic effort to regain what somewhere persists. Both Rich's historical and personal narratives emphasize the multiple ways that the past infuses and defines the present, yet both do so in terms that emphasize the persistence of loss into the realm of celebration and recovery. As *Of Woman Born*'s historical account of loss is performed through and intensified by the loss of the "I" as empowered subject, Rich's coming into self-knowledge is also tinged by an awareness that what is recalled is incomplete, even inaccurate.

This underlying similarity of theme foregrounds the connection between the book's seemingly opposed genres: Both autobiography and polemic rely on a similar narrative structure. Autobiography derives from the assumption that a chronicle of the past is interesting, even dramatic, as well as restorative, without being written, the details of an individual life would be lost. Memoir thus by definition affirms the importance of remembering. Polemic, especially feminist polemic, is similar. It articulates its dissatisfaction with present ills through juxtaposition with a lost past or a longed-for future.[13] Here too, then, memory recurs, along with both loss and recuperation.

Idealization also recurs. Rich's idealizations of the feminine have been routinely, if somewhat inaccurately, noted by subsequent readers, who routinely chastise her for essentialism.[14] Yet, as I have suggested, Rich seems in 1986 somewhat baffled by the book's essentialism, or its tendency to be read in terms of essentialism; she repeatedly claims that she did not intend to idealize women. I am suggesting that Rich's confusion can be at least partly explained by defining the book's essentialism in generic rather than ideological terms. Like the other tendencies I have been describing, Rich's idealization is a generic byproduct, an inevitable effect of her account's narrative and theme. Thus the book's essentialism does not amount to an assertion that women are more nurturing than men, or more long-suffering, or more or less powerful. Instead, Rich's idealization of women derives from subjects—motherhood and female identity—and her focus on losses of different kinds.[15] That the book's personal account more radically and directly undermines whatever elements of essentialism are contained in its historical account only affirms the importance of genre in *Of Woman Born*. The book's mixing of autobiography with history continuously undermines reductive readings.

My aim in making these general, schematic claims is not to set down absolute principles, but rather to suggest ways that *Of Woman Born* elucidates issues relevant to both literary study and feminism. In the final section of this chapter, as I consider more directly *Of Woman Born*'s relation to subsequent feminist theory, I will become more speculative still, partly because it is impossible, given the dearth of references to *Of Woman Born* by subsequent authors, to speak definitively of influence. Yet the issues I have been considering in relation to Rich's work—the connection between apparently conflicting narratives of loss and recovery, and the function and dangers of essentialism—remain central to and divisive in recent feminist thought. Reading contemporary theory through Rich's text suggests ways that this theory's divisions can be, if not unmade, at least brought into contact.

Subjectivity is arguably the central concern of late twentieth-century theory; much of feminist theory's current dividedness originates in the difficulty of defining the female "I."[16] This dividedness can be variously derived and defined: as a split between Anglo-American and French feminism; or a split between deconstructive and historicist readings of femininity; or a split between those who define femininity as essential or socially constructed.[17] Many recent feminists agree that these alternatives are equally untenable. In broad terms, the absence of any coherent "I" seems too extreme, as well as untrue to women's documented struggles for visibility, but the notion of "woman" as defined by a fixed series of attributes ends up constricting and limiting femaleness. Recent characterizations of women's writing have attempted to evade or chart a middle ground between these extremes, emphasizing resistance of different kinds, self-consciousness, and the collapse of traditional boundaries.[18] Yet these revisionary definitions of women's writing often reinforce the theoretical splits they are attempting to unmake. Focusing on defining female "difference," however loosely or negatively, they inadvertently glorify certain elements of women's writing or experience. Contemporary feminist theory thus reveals strikingly, even devastatingly, the pervasiveness of self-division in writing about women; in the process, it recalls the importance and difficulty of Rich's undertaking. *Of Woman Born* was among the first feminist works to foreground the issue, but more than twenty-five years later, theorists have not overcome their dividedness about the female "I."[19]

Yet Rich's self-contradicting, double narrative of loss and recovery also helps illuminate the common aims of apparently opposing feminist views. Poststructuralist-influenced theory tends to embrace a narrative in which an earlier or male-dominated textual coherence is lost; its most important maneuver is to imagine this loss in positive terms, as disruptive or subversive. Theorists emphasizing the possibility of social and political change, in contrast, subscribe to a narrative of recompense, in which absence gives way to abundance or, perhaps, reveals a buried canon of women's texts. Yet not only do both theories rely on narratives of loss and recovery, both also celebrate the characteristics they claim are distinctive to women's writing. *Of Woman Born* in this context suggests a kind of model of rapprochement. The similarities underlying its oppositions as well as the openness of its form suggest a model expansive enough to contain without undermining opposing points of view.

I suggested above that *Of Woman Born*'s essentialism was a product of its genre, narrative, and structure. But reading *Of Woman Born* in relation to contemporary feminism also suggests several more radical ways of reevaluating essentialism. First, the historical argument that has often been marshalled as a rationale for not taking Rich's work seriously can be more broadly applied: *Of Woman Born*'s treatment by later feminist critics provides a powerful, because extreme, reminder that antiessentialism is itself historically contingent.[20] The

recent tendency of many feminist critics to hunt down and denounce essentialism in feminist texts including Rich's, marks this historical moment just as
surely as Rich's essentialism itself marks its time. *Of Woman Born*'s reception
thus invites us to question antiessentialism that is too hastily embraced.

In this way, Rich's book anticipates Diana Fuss's more recent reconsider-
ation of the essentialist/constructionist binarism. Essentialism, Fuss claims, is
inherent to feminism, even feminist attempts to evade essentialism. It

> emerges [. . .] within the very discourse of feminism, a discourse which pre-
> sumes upon the unity of its object of inquiry (women) *even* when it is at
> pains to demonstrate the differences within this admittedly generalizing and
> imprecise category (2).

Fuss is not arguing that the critical tendency to denounce essentialism
should be entirely or unthinkingly reversed, nor am I. Yet her comment
implies that feminism would do well to acknowledge, if not wholeheartedly
embrace, its own essentializing tendencies. *Of Woman Born* ultimately does
something similar: It suggests that essentialism may not be such a bad thing
after all. I mentioned earlier my exultation and relief at finding that my own
feelings—often of rage—had already been articulated both by earlier women
poets and by Rich's memoir, as well as my more recent startled conviction as
a mother that more is biological than I had thought. Such admissions do
more, I hope, than define me as a closet essentialist. They evoke the power
and plausibility of notions of gender difference, in which, as Fuss points out,
essentialism always lurks. Even at its most essentializing, Rich's account is
powerful. Or perhaps its essentialism is a source of the book's power. Certainly, I am not alone in sensing that feminism may need to overcome its
aversion to necessarily reductionistic generalizations in order to garner con-
stituents and build consensus.[21]

Rich's work is not merely feminist theory: It is among other things a
memoir challenged and complicated by its attempt to situate in and explain
through a larger context the experiences of its protagonist. Read this way—as
personally informed criticism, as memoir, as chronicle of motherhood—the
book remains a model of candor, authenticity, integrity. Much autobiographical criticism by women since Rich has tended toward coy self-deprecation, as
if the authors, in Rich's own terms, were "almost in touch with their anger
[but . . .] determined not to appear angry" ["When" 37].[22] Rich is unusual in
her ability to articulate her anger and self-doubt directly, with little embar-
rassment or dissimulation. It is striking that Rich's account of mothering
articulates the ambivalence of motherhood far more candidly and unapolo-
getically than many more recent accounts.[23]

So far, despite my preoccupation with questions of genre, I have scarcely
alluded to the fact that Rich is also, and preeminently, a lyric poet. But per-

haps the most plausible way of explaining Rich's conflicted depiction of self-hood is as the prose articulation of a lyric impulse. That its flaws are so visible reveals the awkwardness of Rich's translation. The gaps between self and other, self and reader, self and world are easy for lyric to accommodate and articulate, yet in a work of prose they seem jarring, awkward, like flaws.[24]

At the same time, this notion of translation allows me to address, by reference to the passage from Felman with which I began, a question that has underlain my discussion: whether what I have been calling a contradiction between Rich's two narratives can instead be explained in more positive terms, as a necessary and productive resistance. Felman's model converts or translates the self-contradictions of women's writing into a method of reading, shifting onto the reader what might more usually be attributed to the text. It remains convincing as a way of reading Rich because, like any good translation, it remains true to the oppositions in Rich's text without balking at recasting them. Felman's model honors Rich's concern with generic manipulation and her ability to transform and shape what seems contradictory through patient, prolonged scrutiny. At the same time, it offers an ingenious way out of the dividedness I have argued has beset much feminist theory. While embracing the negative, inconsistent features of texts, Felman also imposes on the reader the onus of response and, perhaps by implication, political action and in this way rescues women's writing from non or self-referentiality. My own somewhat halting impulse has been similar: If my critique of Rich's inconsistencies derives from the pragmatic strand of American feminism, my compulsion to convert the darker sources—loss, nostalgia—of Rich's narrative into signifying entities and my emphasis on the demands imposed by form derive, if indirectly, from poststructuralism.[25] That I have tried to juxtapose, even combine, these two theoretical impulses to articulate my aversion along with my admiration, my personal response along with my scholarly one is possible because of Rich's example. And so I set the parts of what I have written side by side, since they will not fully cohere: maybe it is enough that they will, like magnets, sometimes resist, sometimes attract one another.[26]

NOTES

1. Although they tend to define women's writing in radically different ways—as nurturing, celebrative of the body, conflicted about it, or subversively fragmented—many feminists assume that what is distinctive about women is their ability to have children. Even in discussions of childless authors—Virginia Woolf seems to be the most common example—the underlying implication is often that women have an impulse, even an obligation, toward maternity. The suppression of this impulse, many suggest, causes psychological and literary problems: Actual engendering, that is, can never be adequately replaced with mere literary offspring.

2. Rich acknowledges her lack of sensitivity to the negative connotations of the term "barrenness" in a 1986 footnote and perhaps in the process acknowledges that she has in fact made too easy an equivalence between "women" and "mother": "The term 'barren woman' was easy for me to use, unexamined, fifteen years ago. [. . .] It seems to me now a term both tendentious and meaningless, based on a view of women which sees motherhood as our only positive definition" (21–22).

3. Carolyn Heilbrun summarizes some of the "hidden truths" articulated by *Of Woman Born:*

> That only when visibly pregnant did [Rich] feel, in her whole adult life, not-guilty. That, like so many women with "male" dreams in childhood, she had set her heart on a son, and had felt triumphant over her mother, who had brough forth only daughters, at the birth of her "perfect, golden, male child." That her husband's "helping" was unusual in the 1950s, but there was no question that the major career was his, all the initiative for domestic responsibilities hers (68).

4. See, for example, "When" 44; "Husband-Right" 216; and "Blood" 181.

5. Jeanne Perreault notes that in *Of Woman Born* "Rich's autobiographical material [is . . .] often used as illustration or example." Perreault finds for this reason that the book is "conventional in that [Rich] seems to treat the present summations as the 'true' story" (36). Perreault offers this description to justify her exclusion of *Of Woman Born* from her discussion of Rich's autobiographical prose.

6. Rich also asserts, seemingly in contradiction to this claim, that "I didn't, and most certainly today don't, want to let 'patriarchy' become a catchall" (xxiii) and that "I never wished this book to lend itself to the sentimentalization of women" (xxxiv). The implication of these claims, though, is that that book has been read in exactly these terms and that Rich herself is at least partly responsible for this outcome.

7. While nearly all scholars writing on Rich have ignored *Of Woman Born*, or mentioned it only in passing, critics of Rich have generally affirmed the success of what Perreault calls Rich's ability to shift from "personal speaking [. . .] to communal speech" (43). Perreault's claim that Rich's "written 'I' [is] an element of the 'we' of communities" (2) is echoed by Helen Dennis, who argues that Rich uses "consciousness raising as [a] poetic method": "her prose uses the strategies of confessional poetry to make connections between the autobiographical or personal and the public, cultural arena" (178). Alice Templeton's characterization of Rich's poetry also emphasizes the interconnectedness of the personal and political: "the subjective experience of poetry [is] inseparable from the social and political considerations that inform it" (2). While several readers have noted in Rich's writings tensions and contradictions—in Templeton's terms between poetry, feminist theory, and literary theory (7)—such comments have not been directly applied to *Of Woman Born*.

8. Similarly, Vendler claims that the book is marred by "mixed motives": the intensity of Rich's anger at her father, she claims, explains her rage at patriarchy (263–264). The more positive reviews of *Of Woman Born* affirm the dividedness of Rich's account in another way: They focus exclusively on the book's autobiographical passages while ignoring the more polemical passages. Typical is Heilbrun, who has

called Rich the writer "who has done more than anyone else to revolutionize women's autobiography" (66) and says nothing of *Of Woman Born*'s importance as historical analysis or social critique.

9. Most critics concerned with personal narratives that include social critique acknowledge tensions between these two forms of writing. For example, Joan Scott argues that accounts deriving their authority from personal experience, like Rich's, fail as social critique because they often "reproduce [. . .] rather than contest [. . .] given ideological systems. The project of making experience visible precludes critical examination of the ideological system itself" (59). Sidonie Smith makes a similar claim, but from the opposite vantage point: Polemical narrative tends to subordinate experientially based or traditionally autobiographical writing. Smith has noted, in what she calls the feminist autobiographical manifesto, the tendency to redefine the personal so that it articulates communal rather than individual values: "group identification rather than radical individuality is the rhetorical ground of appeal" (437). Anne E. Goldman is troubled by a similar tendency among readers of autobiographies by members of oppressed or disenfranchised groups. "In privileging the 'we' over the 'I,'" such readers "run the risk of oversimplifying the relationship between distinction and affiliation" (288). It is necessary, she claims, to recall and affirm the importance of the individual "I" in autobiographical writings.

10. Many recent memoirs recount an early loss or trauma and the process by which the author overcame it, or at least made progress in overcoming it. See, for example, Mary Karr on her conflicted relationship with her mother; Michael Ryan on sexual addiction; Kathryn Harrison on incest. Television talk shows tend to stress a similar movement from ignorance to knowledge, suffering to relief, a tendency that may derive in part from the testimonials of recovery central to twelve-step programs. See Smith and Watson's *Getting a Life* for essays on these and other nontraditional forms of recent autobiography.

11. This example also complicates the distinction I have been making in general terms between Rich's "personal" and "academic" accounts. While Rich's personal narrative often allows her to interrogate her own motives and impulses far more directly than her general narrative does, here the opposite is true: The personal voice normalizes by denying what the impersonal narrative seems to imply.

12. Rich's 1986 assertion that her work resembles other radical feminist accounts of its era in some ways invites such a response, as does her decision to insert in the ten-year anniversary edition a series of footnotes that comment on and often amend earlier claims, a choice that affirms her book's historical particularity and limitations. Many critics have similarly dismissed *Of Woman Born* as an example of early feminism and more particularly of Rich's early writings. Perreault justifies her exclusion of *Of Woman Born* from her study of Rich's prose by opposing this earlier, "conventional" work to Rich's later prose, which she claims "inscribes a textual self that is unstable, provisional, urgently self-disclosing, attentive to its processes, and explicit in displaying them" (46–47). Alcoff makes a similar distinction between *Of Woman Born* and Rich's more interesting later writings (408n.). Templeton's assertion that Rich's poems from the same era as *Of Woman Born* embrace a similar prepatriarchal ideal and "eulogistic [. . .] recover[y of] a displaced past" (176) generalizes this trait across generic

boundaries. Yet my claim is that *Of Woman Born* also embodies at least partly the attributes that Perreault and others locate exclusively in Rich's later writings.

13. Smith's characterization of feminist "autobiographical manifesto," a hybrid genre that in many ways resembles that of *Of Woman Born*, emphasizes a similar opposition of terms: It embraces "hope . . . [and] attempts to actively position the subject in a potentially liberated future distanced from the constraining and oppressive identifications inherent in the everyday practices of the *ancien regime*" (438). Smith's characterization is in some ways opposed to my view of Rich, whose gaze tends to be directed backward more than forward and whose emphasis is on "the constraining and oppressive" more than on the "liberated future." Yet Smith's terms are nonetheless similar to my own.

14. Domna Stanton, for example, notes its "undeniable traces of essentialism," including "pre-oedipal unboundedness, relatedness, plurality, fluidity, tenderness, and nurturance" (176), while Alcoff argues that Rich "identifies a female essence, defines patriarchy as the subjugation and colonization of this essence out of male envy and need, and then promotes a solution that revolves around rediscovering our essence and bonding with other women" (410). Yet it is not always clear that Rich's account does in fact contain pure or unqualified, much less deliberate, essentialism. As Alcoff points out, Rich's account focuses on historical change and development, yet such a focus is, to Diana Fuss, antithetical to essentialism, which "assum[es . . .] a totalizing symbolic system which subjugates all women everywhere, throughout history and across cultures" (2). Furthermore, even when focusing on issues that now seem dubious or naïve (the passages drawn from Joseph Campbell and others affirming a prehistoric era of goddess worship), Rich remains skeptical, noting that the beliefs of many early archeologists reflected the dominant beliefs of the time and culture in which they wrote.

15. As several critics have in different ways argued, all writing about motherhood is to some extent essentializing; it emphasizes maternity as a central, even definitive, attribute of womanhood. Thus, Ann Rosalind Jones finds in French feminist Helene Cixous's apparent celebration of maternity "echoes of the coercive glorification of motherhood that has plagued women for centuries." To write about motherhood at all, she claims, is to risk trapping women in limiting, constraining notions of femininity: "If we define female subjectivity through universal biological/libidinal givens, what happens to the project of changing the world in feminist directions?" (369). Linda Alcoff's more extreme terms locate the danger not merely in the equivalence of "woman" with "mother" but in attempts to define gender differences more generally: "a subjectivity that is fundamentally shaped by gender appears to lead irrevocably to essentialism" (424).

16. I am here adapting and generalizing several similar claims, especially Jeanne Costello's 1991 review of several critical studies of women's autobiography. Her assertion that "autobiography as a genre foregrounds the question of subjectivity" (125) itself revises that of one of the books under review: "autobiography localizes the program of much feminist theory" (Brodzki 1).

17. Anglo-American feminism tends to emphasize identity politics, pragmatic political action, and the affirmation of an "I," however hesitant, while French feminism foregrounds instead female dissolution and absence. Poststructuralist or deconstructive

feminism tends to emphasize female invisibility, fragmentation and self-erasure, while more historically based feminists have emphasized women's historical struggles for visibility and voice. These disputes in some ways underlie the intense debate about the extent to which "identity" or "selfhood" is essential—whether, that is, certain attributes are, in Diana Fuss's terms, based on "transhistorical, eternal, immutable essences"—or socially constructed, the products of extrinsic forces. Many of these disputes are enacted through disagreements about the possibility of definition. While some critics, that is, are working to identify and define the attributes of women's (or lesbian or African-American) writing, others, often in response, stress the inaccuracy of such generalizations along with the dangers of generalizing more generally. These categories, while interconnected, are not equivalent: Neither American nor French feminism can be unequivocally associated with either essentialism or constructionism.

18. These widely held and often overlapping views are laid out, in some cases in relation to Rich, by Perreault (3–4), Goldman (passim), and Templeton (180) respectively. The passage from Felman with which I began combines these notions of women's writing.

19. It is worth noting, however, that *Of Woman Born* does take sides. Perhaps unsurprisingly, given its status as one of the founding texts of American feminism, it opposes notions of an evanescent or nonexistent self. Inconsistent though it may be, Rich's "I" never dissipates or multiplies into something with which we as readers cease to identify.

20. My argument here relies on Mary Poovey's assertion that recent deconstructionist feminism must "deploy [deconstruction] upon itself," acknowledging that deconstruction is the product of a particular historical moment in order to avoid being "trap[ped . . .] in a practice that once more glorifies the 'feminine'" (267).

21. Susan Gubar and others have recently argued that feminism has become divided into subgroups, each with its own agenda; in its attempt to be sensitive to the diversity of women's experiences, feminism has lost sight both of the possibility of political action and of a wide base of support among women. See Appian for a discussion of Gubar's book and her relation to the contemporary feminist debates.

22. Rich makes this comment about Woolf's *A Room of One's Own*, a book which is a sometimes explicit prototype or model for later feminist critics in its combination of potentially disturbing subject matter and witty personal anecdote. Yet many recent works also tend to apologize in exaggerated terms for what may seem shrill or unorthodox. Sandra Gilbert's "What Do Feminist Critics Want?" for example, contains several passages of extreme but humorous self-deprecation: "let me take a moment to explain my odd self-division, for so bizarre a rhetorical strategy does require some justification" (29); "Lest I seem entirely solipsistic [. . .]" (43). Carolyn Heilbrun's "Women, Men, Theories, and Literature" and Domna Stanton's "Autogynography" adopt similar tones.

23. The autobiographical sections of Julia Kristeva's "Stabat Mater," whose double-columned text makes more extreme the division in Rich's work between "academic" and "personal," tend to glorify, even sentimentalize the experience of mothering; Anne Lamott's more popular writings on motherhood, as well as the writings in the

recent *Mothers Who Think* anthology and on-line column, anatomize the ambivalence, sacrifices, and resentment that are part of the daily life of a mother with a candor that may derive from Rich, but they tend to affirm in the end the joys and rewards of motherhood. It is worth noting that a number of contemporary poets are more directly concerned with interrogating stereotypes of maternity through accounts of specific experiences. Preeminent among them is Sharon Olds.

24. Such a reading affirms by extending Felman's claim that multiple genres interact in Rich's writing. Felman does not discuss Rich's poetry in her general formulation, though most of the citations in her discussion are from Rich's poems.

25. In particular, my study, like much work on autobiography, has been affected by Paul de Man's link between autobiography, epitaph, and "de-facement" and his claim that autobiographies both "openly declare their cognitive and tropological constitution [and . . .] are equally eager to escape from the coercions of this system (71).

26. I am grateful to Susan Mizruchi, for encouraging and supporting my early ideas about Rich; to Louise Harrison Lepera, for help with particular problems in the writing process; and to Julia Lisella, who patiently read and thoughtfully commented on several versions of this piece.

WORKS CITED

Alcoff, Linda. "Cultural Feminism versus Post-Structuralism: The Identity Crisis in Feminist Theory." *Signs: Journal of Women in Culture and Society* 13.3 (1988):405–436.

Appian, K. Anthony. "Battle of the Bien-Pensant." *New York Review of Books* 27 April 2000:42–44. (Review of Susan Gubar, *Critical Condition: Feminism at the Turn of the Century.* New York: Columbia UP, 2000.)

Brodzki, Bella and Celeste Schenck, eds. *Life/Lines: Theorizing Women's Autobiography.* Ithaca: Cornell UP, 1988.

Costello, Jeanne. "Taking the 'Woman' Out of Women's Autobiography: The Perils and Potentials of Theorizing Female Subjectivities." *Diacritics: A Feminist Miscellany* 21.2–3 (1991):123–134.

de Man, Paul. *The Rhetoric of Romanticism.* New York: Columbia UP, 1984.

Dennis, Helen. "Adrienne Rich: Consciousness Raising as Poetic Method." *Contemporary Poetry Meets Modern Theory.* Eds. Antony Easthope and John O. Thompson. Toronto: U of Toronto P, 1991:177–194.

Felman, Shoshana. *What Does a Woman Want? Reading and Sexual Difference.* Baltimore: Johns Hopkins UP, 1993.

Fuss, Diana. *Essentially Speaking: Feminism, Nature and Difference.* New York: Routledge, 1989.

Gilbert, Sandra. "What Do Feminist Critics Want? A Postcard from the Volcano." Showalter 29–45.

Goldman, Anne E. "Autobiography, Ethnography, and History: A Model for Reading." Smith and Watson, *Women*, 288–298.

Gray, Francine du Plessix. "Amazonian Prescriptions and Proscriptions." *New York Times* 10 October 1976:3–12.

Harrison, Kathryn. *The Kiss*. New York: Random House, 1997.

Heilbrun, Carolyn. "Women, Men, Theories, and Literature." *Hamlet's Mother and Other Women*. New York: Ballantine, 1990:216–228.

——— . *Writing a Woman's Life*. New York: Ballantine, 1988.

Jones, Ann Rosalind. "Writing the Body: Toward an Understanding of *l'Écriture féminine*." Showalter 361–377.

Karr, Mary. *The Liar's Club: A Memoir*. New York: Penguin, 1996.

Kristeva, Julia. "Stabat Mater." Trans. Arthur Goldhammer. *Poetics Today* 6.1–2 (1985):133–152.

Lamott, Anne. *Operating Instructions: A Journal of My Son's First Year*. New York: Ballantine, 1993.

"Mothers Who Think." *Salon Magazine*. <*http:\\www.salon.com.mwt*>

Olds, Sharon. *The Dead and the Living*. New York: Knopf, 1984.

——— . *The Gold Cell*. New York: Knopf, 1987.

——— . *The Unswept Room*. New York: Knopf, 2002.

——— . *The Wellspring*. New York: Knopf, 1996.

Peri, Camille and Kate Moses. *Mothers Who Think: Tales of Real-Life Parenthood*. New York: Washington Square, 1999.

Perreault, Jeanne. *Writing Selves: Contemporary Feminist Autography*. Minneapolis: U of Minnesota P, 1995.

Poovey, Mary. "Feminism and Deconstruction." *Feminist Literary Theory: A Reader*. Second ed. Ed. Mary Eagleton. Cambridge, MA: Blackwell, 1996:262–266.

Rich, Adrienne. "Blood, Bread, and Poetry: The Location of the Poet." *Blood, Bread, and Poetry: Selected Prose 1979–1985*. New York: Norton, 1986:167–187.

——— . "Husband-Right and Father-Right" (1977). *On Lies* 215–222.

——— . *On Lies, Secrets, and Silence: Selected Prose 1966–78*. New York: Norton, 1979.

——— . *Of Woman Born: Motherhood as Experience and Institution*. New York: Norton, 1986.

——— . "When We Dead Awaken: Writing as Re-Vision" (1971). *On Lies* 33–50.

Ryan, Michael. *Secret Life: An Autobiography*. New York: Pantheon, 1995.

Scott, Joan. "Experience." Smith and Watson, *Women* 57–71.

Showalter, Elaine, ed. *The New Feminist Criticism: Essays on Women, Literature, and Theory*. New York: Pantheon, 1985.

Smith, Sidonie. "Autobiographical Manifestos." Smith and Watson, *Women* 433–440.

Smith, Sidonie and Julia Watson, eds. *Women, Autobiography, Theory: A Reader*. Madison: U of Wisconsin P, 1998.

———, eds. *Getting a Life: Everyday Uses of Autobiography*. Minneapolis: U of Minnesota P 1996.

Stanton, Domna C. "Autogynography: Is the Subject Different?" Smith and Watson, *Women* 131–144.

———. "Difference on Trial: A Critique of the Maternal Metaphor in Cixous, Irigaray, and Kristeva." *The Poetics of Gender*. Ed. Nancy K. Miller. New York: Columbia UP, 1986:157–182.

Templeton, Alice. *The Dream and the Dialogue: Adrienne Rich's Feminist Poetics*. Knoxville: U of Tennessee P, 1994.

Vendler, Helen. "Of Woman Born." *Part of Nature, Part of Us*. Cambridge: Harvard UP, 1980:263–270. (Originally published in *New York Review of Books*, 30 September 1976.)

Contributors

Diana Ginn is an associate professor with the Faculty of Law, Dalhousie University. She lives in Halifax, Nova Scotia with her husband and three children. Her research interests include gender issues relating to health law, violence against women, mothering, aboriginal title, and administrative law.

Fiona Joy Green, PhD, the mother of a teenaged son, is in an assistant professor and coordinator of the Women's Studies Program at the University of Winnipeg. She teaches courses addressing gender and the sciences, feminist research methodologies, and feminist praxis. Fiona is a long-standing member and active participant in the Association for the Research on Mothering and her work can be found in *The Journal of the Association for Research on Mothering, BirthIssues,* and *The Madwoman in the Academy.* Her research interests include feminist/maternal pedagogy, gendered performance, and more recently, gendered uses of bathroom space.

Margaret Morganroth Gullette is a cultural critic and prize-winning writer of nonfiction, an internationally known age critic, an essayist, feminist, and activist. Her book, *Declining to Decline: Cultural Combat and the Politics of the Midlife,* won the national Emily Toth award in 1998 as the best feminist book on American popular fiction. Her next book is entitled *Aged by Culture* (University of Chicago Press, 2004). She is also the author of *Safe at Last in the Middle Years.* Her work has received NEH, ACLS, and Bunting fellowships. She has written for the *New York Times Magazine, Nation, Ms., Boston Globe, Miami Herald;* appeared on "The Connection," RadioNation, WBAI, "To the Best of Our Knowledge"; and contributed to many literary quarterlies, including *Kenyon Review* and *Yale Review;* scholarly journals like *Feminist Studies, Representations, Journal of the History of Sexuality,* and many encyclopedias. Her essays have been cited as notable in *Best American Essays.* She is a member of PEN-America and a Scholar at the Women's Studies Research Center, Brandeis University. She is the theorist of the term "postmaternal."

Karin Voth Harman lives and works in London. She has taught courses on mothering and literature in many different adult education contexts and at the University of Sussex. She has published on birth poetry and wrote the entry on "Motherhood" in the *Encyclopedia of Life Writing* (Fitzroy Dearborn). She is currently teaching at South Hampstead High School.

Emily Jeremiah gained a PhD in German Studies from the University of Wales Swansea in 2001. She subsequently spent two years researching and teaching German and Women's Studies at the University of Helsinki, Finland. She now lives in London where she is a teacher and translator.

Ann Keniston is completing a book on address and subjectivity in post-World War II American poetry. Her articles have appeared in *Contemporary Literature* and *Threepenny Review,* and her poems have appeared in various journals and quarterlies.

Dannabang Kuwabong is an assistant professor of English at the University of Puerto Rico. His main areas of interest include Literature by Women of the Caribbean, Africa, and North and South Americas. He is a founding member of ARM. Presently, he is working on a full-length book study of the role of the grandmothers and African-derived spiritualities in the organization of the family in Caribbean women's texts. Dr. Kuwabong has published in various journals, including *ARM Journal, Canadian Feminist Studies, Ariel, Sargasso, Journal of Dagaare Studies, Caribbean 2000,* and other internationally refereed journals.

Kate McCullough specializes in nineteenth- and twentieth-century U.S. fiction as well as gender studies. She is the author of *Regions of Identity: The Construction of America in Women's Fiction, 1885–1914* (Stanford UP, 1999). Her article, "'Marked by Genetics and Exile': Narrativizing Transcultural Sexualities in Memory Mambo," appeared in *GLQ* 6.4 (Autumn 2000). She is currently at work on two projects, one on nineteenth-century U.S. women's writing and imperialism and one on twentieth-century lesbian narrative. She is also busily at work putting feminist theory into practice in the raising of her daughter.

Andrea O'Reilly, PhD, is an associate professor in the School of Women's Studies at York University where she teaches a course on motherhood (the first course on Motherhood in Canada; now taught to more than two hundred students a year as a Distance Education course) and the Introduction to Women's Studies course. She has published six books on motherhood: *Redefining Motherhood: Changing Identities and Patterns* (Second Story Press, 1998), *Mothers and Daughters: Connection, Empowerment and Transformation*

(Rowman and Littlefield, 2000), *Mothers and Sons: Feminism, Masculinity and the Struggle to Raise Our Sons* (Routledge Press, 2001), *Mother Outlaws: Theories and Practices of Empowered Mothering* (Women's Press, 2004), *Mother Matters: Motherhood as Discourse and Practice* (ARM Press, 2004), and *Toni Morrison and Motherhood: A Politics of the Heart* (SUNY Press, 2004). She is currently working on three edited books: *Motherhood: Power and Oppression, Feminist Mothering*, and, with her daughter, *Voices Across the Third Wave*. O'Reilly is founding president of the Association for Research on Mothering (ARM), the first feminist association on the topic of mothering-motherhood with more than five hundred members worldwide, and is founding president and editor-in-chief of the *Journal of the Association for Research on Mothering*. In 1998 she was the recipient of the university-wide "Teacher of the Year" award at York University. She has given many talks and conducted numerous workshops on motherhood and mothering. She has been interviewed widely on the subject. Andrea and her spouse of twenty-two years are the parents of a twenty-year-old son and two daughters, ages fourteen and seventeen.

D'Arcy Randall is a visiting professor of English at the University of Texas, Austin. She is a founder of the journal *Borderlands: Texas Poetry Review*, and has published articles, essays, and poetry in a variety of journals in Australia, Canada, and the United States. Her awards include an AWP *Intro* award, the *Malahat Review* Long Poem Prize, and two Michener Fellowships in Creative Writing.

Jeannette E. Riley is an assistant professor of English and the director of the Women's Studies program at UMass Dartmouth. Riley's areas of interest focus on post-1945 women's literature and feminist theory, and she has published articles most recently on Eavan Boland and Terry Tempest Williams.

Sarah E. Stevens currently teaches women's studies at Southern Oregon University, where she is the Acting Associate Director of International Programs. She received her PhD from Indiana University, Bloomington (2001) in Chinese, with a minor in gender studies. Her research focuses on female sexuality and body culture in twentieth-century China.

Maria-Barbara Watson-Franke, PhD, is professor of Women's Studies at San Diego State University, and has conducted fieldwork in South America and Europe. She has published extensively on the matrilineal Guajiro of Venezuela and Colombia with special emphases on gender, ethnic identity, migration, and urbanization. Together with L. C. Watson she is coauthor of *Interpreting Life Histories. An Anthropological Inquiry* (Rutgers University Press 1985). Recent publications include: "Changing Views of Women-Centered Families: An Example from South America," *Antropologica* 1998–99, 90 (with

L. C. Watson) and "'A World in Which Women Move Freely Without Fear of Men': An Anthropological Perspective on Rape," *Women's Studies International Forum* 2002, 25/6. Current research centers on matrilineal societies with a focus on male roles and fatherhood, women-centered philosophies and mothers, and matriliny and nationhood.

INDEX